The Political Economy of
European Monetary Unification

The Political Economy of
Global Interdependence

Thomas D. Willett, Series Editor

The Political Economy of European Monetary Unification

SECOND EDITION

EDITED BY

Barry Eichengreen
University of California at Berkeley

AND

Jeffry A. Frieden
Harvard University

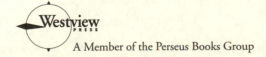

A Member of the Perseus Books Group

The Political Economy of Global Interdependence

Copyright © 2001 by Westview Press, A Member of the Perseus Books Group

Published in 2001 in the United States of America by Westview Press, 5500 Central Avenue, Boulder, Colorado 80301-2877, and in the United Kingdom by Westview Press, 12 Hid's Copse Road, Cumnor Hill, Oxford OX2 9JJ

Visit us on the World Wide Web at www.westviewpress.com

Library of Congress Cataloging-in-Publication Data
    The political economy of European monetary unification / edited by Barry Eichengreen and Jeffry A. Frieden—2nd ed.
        p. cm.—(The political economy of global interdependence)
    Rev. ed. of: The political economy of European monetary unification. c1994.
    Includes bibliographical references and index.
    ISBN 0-8133-9761-8
    1. European Monetary System (Organization).   2. Monetary policy—European Economic Community countries.   3. European Economic Community countries—Economic conditions.   4. Monetary policy—European Union countries.   5. European Union countries—Economic conditions.   I. Frieden, Jeffry A.   II. Eichengreen, Barry J.   III. Political economy of European monetary unification.   IV. Series.

HG930.5 .P65   2000
332.4'94—dc21   00-043702

The paper used in this publication meets the requirements of the American National Standard for Permanence of Paper for Printed Library Materials Z39.48-1984.

10   9   8   7   6   5   4   3   2   1

Contents

Preface

This book is the outgrowth of a research group on the Political Economy of European Integration convened jointly by the Institute for European Studies at the University of California, Berkeley, and the Weatherhead Center for International Affairs at Harvard University. The group met, typically twice a year, from 1991 until 1999.

The first edition of this book was published in 1994, when the future of monetary unification in Europe was very much in doubt. With Economic and Monetary Union in place, it is appropriate to bring the scholarship in the volume up to date. To this effect, four of the original chapters have been revised substantially to reflect new conditions, and the editors have completely rewritten their introductory essay. Three of the original chapters have been replaced with new chapters (by Gabel, Engel, and De Grauwe et al.) that deal with issues of great relevance to the current European situation. The result is a volume that is almost entirely different from the first edition in content, although its purpose—to bring the latest in scholarship in economics and political science to bear on the topic—remains the same.

Our first debt is to the German government and the Center for Excellence Grant it provided the University of California, which allowed for the initial formation of the research group. At Berkeley, we owe debts of thanks to Gerry Feldman (director of the Institute for European Studies), Mindy Ruzicka, Kira Reoutt, and Gia White. At Harvard, those to whom we are indebted include Jorge Domínguez (director of the Weatherhead Center for International Affairs), Ros deButts, and Matthew Johnson. Above all, we thank the dozens of dedicated research group members from universities throughout the United States and around the world.

Barry Eichengreen
Jeffry A. Frieden

1

The Political Economy of European Monetary Unification

An Analytical Introduction

BARRY EICHENGREEN AND JEFFRY A. FRIEDEN

European monetary unification (EMU)—the process that led to the creation of a single European currency (the euro) and a European Central Bank (the ECB)—is both an economic and a political phenomenon. It is economic in that monetary unification has far-reaching consequences for economic policy and performance Europe-wide. Transactions costs have been reduced by the advent of the single currency, stimulating intra-European trade and capital flows. Interest-rate differentials have narrowed now that the separate monetary policies of the founding member states have been replaced by the single policy of the ECB.[1] European finance is being transformed by the explosive growth of euro-denominated bond issues, strategic alliances among national stock exchanges, and a continent-wide wave of bank mergers as the advent of the euro creates for the first time a truly continental financial market.

But European monetary unification is also a political phenomenon. The decision to create the monetary union, the decision of whom to admit, and the decision of whom to appoint to run the ECB are political decisions, taken by political leaders, subject to political constraints, not the social-welfare-maximizing decisions of some mythical social planner. They result from a political process of treaty negotiation, parliamentary ratification, and popular referendum. Individuals and interest groups support or oppose monetary unification—not just in European Union (EU) member states that have not yet joined the euro area, but even now in the founding members—on the basis of how they perceive it as affecting their individual welfare, not the welfare of the nation as a whole, much less the welfare of the entire European Union.[2]

Despite the outpouring of research prompted by EMU, few accounts have systematically analyzed both its political and its economic aspects. That is the goal of this book. The contributors describe both the political and economic dimensions of the process. They demonstrate how political constraints have shaped the design and operation of Europe's monetary union at the same time that the changes in economic structure brought about by monetary integration continue to transform European politics.

A Short History of European Monetary Unification

Monetary unification has always been at the center of the larger process of European integration. Economically, the creation of a single currency was long seen as necessary for forging a truly integrated European market. Politically, monetary unification has been seen as a practical and symbolic step toward the development of a capacity to formulate social and foreign policies at the European level. Both advocates and opponents of further European political integration have long regarded monetary integration as the thin end of the wedge. For all these reasons, the desirability of European monetary unification has been contested since the idea was first mooted.

Serious discussion of monetary unification goes back to the 1960s.[3] In 1969 the Werner Report set forth an ambitious plan for a three-step transition to monetary union to be completed within a decade. In the event, its blueprint was rendered obsolete within weeks by the slow-motion collapse of the Bretton Woods international monetary system. When the Bretton Woods system of par values, which had provided a framework for holding European exchange rates within fluctuation bands of plus or minus 2 percent, finally collapsed in 1971, the European Community's six founding member states had to focus their energies on limiting the volatility of their exchange rates, lest complaints of arbitrary and capricious changes in competitiveness undermine European solidarity. They resolved to hold their currencies within 2.25 percent bands (only slightly wider than those they had operated under Bretton Woods). They were joined in the "snake," as this arrangement was prosaically known, by the United Kingdom, Ireland, and Denmark as those three countries prepared to become members of the European Union.[4]

Soon, however, divergent economic conditions and policies, reflecting the impact of the first oil shock in 1973/74, rendered the snake unworkable. The least committed members suffered repeated balance-of-payments crises, forcing them to alter or abandon their currency bands. By 1975 only Germany, the Benelux countries, and Denmark remained in the snake. The European countries whose policies diverged most from Germany's—the United Kingdom, Ireland, France, and Italy—simply left, and the Danes were able to remain only by virtue of serial devaluations.

Discussions of monetary unification resumed once this turbulence had passed. The outcome was the establishment of the European Monetary System (EMS) and its Exchange Rate Mechanism (ERM) in March 1979. All EU member states except the U.K. participated in the ERM, linking their currencies via a multilateral parity grid that again allowed for fluctuations of plus or minus 2.25 percent.[5] Provision was made for realignments, although these were expected to be rare. Financing facilities were provided for countries attempting to stabilize their exchange rates in the face of balance-of-payments shocks, and capital controls were relied upon to limit speculative pressures.

Conventional wisdom at the time was that the EMS was unlikely to succeed. The inflation rates of the participating countries differed widely. High-inflation countries had demonstrated an inability to put in place the measures needed to stabilize their currencies against the deutsche mark. Faith meant believing that the creation of the EMS itself would strengthen the willingness of high-inflation countries to pursue painful policies of austerity.

Initially, skepticism seemed more than justified. In the first four years of the EMS, balance-of-payments pressures were intense. Exchange rates were realigned seven times, and there were few signs of monetary convergence. Then, however, the outlook began to brighten. Rates of price increase in the high-inflation countries began to decline. From April 1983 to January 1987 there were only four realignments, generally smaller than those that had come before. And from January 1987 to September 1992 there were no major realignments within the ERM. Attracted by its improved performance, Spain, Portugal, and the U.K. all joined the mechanism in this period.

This transformation was stimulated by, and stimulated in turn, progress on the larger project of European integration. The Single European Act of 1986 called for the removal of controls on the movement of goods, capital, and persons within the Union. A true common market, in which only countries with well-behaved exchange rates would be permitted to participate, created the prospect of additional rewards for ERM participation. And by mandating the removal of capital controls, the Single European Act pointed up the need for further policy convergence in order for the stability of exchange rates to be maintained.

In this context, and specifically in response to calls by the French and German foreign ministries, the European Council appointed a committee in 1988 headed by European Commission president Jacques Delors to investigate the prospects for further monetary integration. The Delors

Committee recommended that the EU begin moving immediately toward the creation of a single currency. The next step in this process came at Maastricht in the Netherlands in December 1991, when the member states agreed to a sweeping treaty on economic union, giving diplomatic content to the recommendations of the Delors Report.

The Maastricht Treaty, echoing the Delors Report and the Werner Report before it, sketched a transition in three stages. Stage I involved the elimination of Europe's remaining capital controls, the accession of all EU members to the ERM, and hardening of the exchange rate commitment. In Stage II, with the EMS credible and encompassing, member states would reinforce the independence of their national central banks and strive to satisfy a set of "convergence criteria" designed to facilitate the harmonization of their economic policies and to distinguish member states prepared to live with the consequences of a single monetary policy from those lacking the requisite commitment. A European Monetary Institute would be created to lay the groundwork for the establishment of the ECB. Finally, in Stage III, to commence no later than the beginning of 1999, the European Central Bank would begin operations, to be followed in three years by the issuance of euro banknotes and coins.

With a plan in place and all EU members but Greece participating in the ERM, it appeared that the single currency was only a matter of time. But while Europe's political leaders had had their say, the markets and voters were still to be heard from. The backdrop for their intervention was German reunification, underway since 1990. The costs of reunifying the two Germanys gave rise to huge budget deficits for the Federal Republic, which excited fears of inflation in the corridors of the Bundesbank. The response of the latter was to raise interest rates. But high interest rates were uncomfortable for Italy, whose debt and deficits were large. They were uncomfortable for the U.K., where mortgage interest rates were indexed, whose business cycle was not synchronized with that of the rest of Europe, and where the commitment to European integration was less than firm. More generally, chronically high unemployment rates, which by the early 1990s had become a fact of Europe's economic and political life, made it difficult for governments to stomach high, German-style interest rates. The result was pressure on sterling, the lira, and other weak European currencies in the summer of 1992.

In the midst of this gathering storm, public opposition to the Maastricht Treaty materialized. The failure of Danish voters to ratify the treaty in that country's June 1992 referendum and fears that a subsequent referendum in France might also fail raised the possibility that the entire Maastricht process might be derailed. An indefinite postponement of EMU would have rendered it all the more unlikely that high-unemployment countries would be prepared to stay the austerity course. Knowing this, the markets pounced. Despite committing billions of dollars to their battle with currency-market speculators, the Bank of England and Bank of Italy were forced to surrender to the markets. On September 16, 1992, their respective governments withdrew from the ERM and allowed their currencies to depreciate.

Having toppled two of Europe's larger currencies, speculators turned their attention to the smaller ones. Yet more crises and realignments then drove the currencies of Spain, Portugal, and Ireland downward.

Unsettled conditions persisted into 1993. In the summer, with unemployment continuing to rise continent-wide, the pressure intensified for interest rate reductions. None of this deterred the Bundesbank, still preoccupied by inflation, from maintaining a tight monetary stance that prevented other EMS members from reducing their interest rates. The resulting dilemma was most serious in France, where a new government took office amidst the recession. The Bank of France attempted to lead by example, reducing interest rates in the hope that the Bundesbank would follow. In this they were disappointed. Inferring that the French authorities were unprepared to hold the line, currency speculators turned their fire on the franc. Massive intervention by the Bank of France failed to repel them. With pressure continuing to mount, European leaders were forced to acknowledge that the old narrow-band ERM had been rendered unworkable by the removal of capital controls, the liquidity of the markets, and the existence of other political and economic imperatives. But rather than abandoning the mechanism, they adopted the stopgap of widening its currency fluctuation bands from 2.25 to 15 per cent.[6] This removed the one-way bets that speculators had found irresistible (since currencies could now appreciate rather than depreciate if speculators turned out to be wrong) and gave governments more room for maneuver. At the same time, however, it raised questions about the capacity of EU member states to keep their exchange rates stable and, more fundamentally, their willingness to subordinate other social goals to a single monetary policy.

In this, Europe's darkest hour, fears were widespread that the Maastricht process was doomed. With only a weakened exchange rate commitment to bind them, member states might fail to make progress on convergence. And if other EU member states failed to solve their inflation, debt, and deficit problems, Germany would be unwilling to embrace them as partners in a monetary union. Most alarmingly of all, if exchange rates grew more volatile as policies diverged, the Single Market might be placed at risk.

This pessimism turned out to be exaggerated. Economic developments help explain why the convergence of policies and institutions between 1994 and 1998 turned out to be more successful than anticipated. By 1994 the shock of German unification had begun to recede, allowing the Bundesbank to reduce rates. The 1993 recession passed, and with the resumption of economic growth, fiscal consolidation and policy harmonization became easier to undertake.

Politically, the transition to EMU was eased by the strong demonstrations of support that plans for a single currency elicited following the 1992/93 crisis. Even governments that had been forced to devalue reiterated their commitment to the completion of the monetary union, and despite the widening of the currency bands, most were indeed able to keep their currencies close to their central rates. Powerful business groups were vocal in support of EMU, arguing that the 1992/93 devaluations had disrupted progress toward the Single Market and deeper integration. And electoral support for anti-European parties and candidates waned as economic difficulties receded.

Institutionally, interstate negotiations allayed some of the fears of those who remained wary of EMU. A Growth and Stability Pact committed EMU members to avoid large budget deficits, thus extending the commitment to fiscal retrenchment beyond the creation of the single currency. This helped to pacify fiscal conservatives concerned about the profligacy of Southern European (and other) governments. At the same time, member states exhibited some flexibility in interpreting the fiscal criteria, which reassured those who worried that EMU would be too rigid a policy straitjacket. All in all, negotiations signaled that the architects of the monetary union were aware of the political constraints and willing to work within them.

Together, then, favorable economic conditions, political momentum, and institutional flexibility combined to make it possible for most EU member states to complete the fiscal retrenchment necessary to qualify for monetary union. While the letter of the convergence criteria was not always strictly met, European policymakers concluded that the aspirants had satisfied their spirit, and each of the eleven member states wishing to participate was deemed worthy when the decision was taken in 1998. Right on schedule, on January 1, 1999, Europe's monetary union came into being.

The Economics of Monetary Unification

Most analyses of the economics of European monetary unification build on the theory of optimum currency areas, one of the contributions for which Robert Mundell was awarded the Nobel Prize in Economics in 1999. In Mundell's model, the benefits of monetary unification, which take the form of the reduction in transactions costs consequent on replacing distinct national currencies with a single (common) currency, are balanced against the costs of sacrificing monetary and fiscal autonomy. One might think that the savings in transactions costs are considerable. Tourists changing money at airports pay commissions amounting to anywhere from 2 to 5 percent of the cash they exchange. But banks and firms doing larger volumes of business in wholesale markets pay much smaller commissions. And such costs, as a share of GNP, depend on the openness of the economy. European Commission estimates suggest that conversion costs absorbed about 1 percent of national income for the EU's small, low-income countries but as little as one-tenth of 1 percent of national income for the large member states for which international transactions are less important. Overall, currency conversion costs averaged less than one-half of 1 percent of EU national income in the late 1980s. This, it would seem, is a modest return on a process riddled with risks and uncertainties.

It can be argued that the real efficiency advantages come not from the single currency but from the Single Market and that the two initiatives are linked. The Single Market allows European producers to exploit economies of scale and scope. By creating a Europe-wide financial market, it promises to stimulate efficiency-enhancing mergers of banks and securities exchanges. By heightening cross-border competition, it forces European producers to shape up or ship out. By intensifying regulatory competition, it compels European governments to remake their policies in market-friendly ways. This is only one vision of the intentions of architects of the Single Market, to be sure, but it is a compelling one.

And the single currency is indispensable, the argument continues, if Europe is to reap the benefits of the Single Market. It enhances transparency. It makes it that much harder for automobile producers to charge different prices in different countries when a single unit of account allows consumers to more readily compare those prices across countries. It makes it harder for banks steeped in traditional ways to survive in sleepy national backwaters, insofar as the elimination of currency risk encourages savers to seek out higher deposit rates and investors to seek out lower loan rates abroad. It makes it harder for unions to insist on restrictive work rules, insofar as a single currency makes it easier for employers to compare labor costs and the elimination of currency risk facilitates the establishment of branch plants in member states where labor is less expensive and workers are more productive.[7]

At the same time, the efficiency advantages of a single currency must be balanced against the disadvantages of a single monetary policy. Those disadvantages take the form of the sacrifice of policy autonomy that comes with moving from ten or more separate monetary policies to a single level of interest rates across the euro-zone. Recall how in 1992/93, when some European countries feared inflation but others were preoccupied by unemployment, the group as a whole found it hard to agree on a one-size-fits-all monetary policy. Asymmetric disturbances, such as the German reunification shock that was the source of the tension in 1992/93, can still occur under monetary union, but the member states now have no choice but to grin and bear them.[8] A single monetary policy may then mean uncomfortably high inflation for some but uncomfortably high unemployment for others. The question for those seeking to gauge the costs of monetary unification is how frequently such asymmetric disturbances will occur.

The standard way of gauging whether a given correlation of shocks to different national economies is high or low is to compare it with the correlation of the same variables across the various regions within a functioning monetary union, typically the United States.[9] By this measure, while the core members of the European Union (Germany, France, the Benelux countries, and Denmark) are good candidates for monetary union, the same is less true of the EU periphery. The problem with this approach is that the shocks in question are likely to change with the advent of monetary union, rendering history a poor guide to the future. Demand shocks result from erratic changes in demand-management policy, whose formulation will be transformed by EMU. Asymmetric monetary shocks will disappear with the advent of a single monetary policy (although differences in the monetary transmission mechanism will remain). Asymmetric fiscal shocks will be limited by the Growth and Stability Pact. Supply shocks will be transformed as Europe reorganizes itself to capitalize on the single currency and the Single Market.[10]

Other optimum currency area criteria are less likely to be endogenous with respect to the policy regime. Mundell observed that the costs of subjecting several separate economies experiencing asymmetric shocks to a symmetric monetary policy will be less when labor flows freely from depressed to booming regions. His intellectual descendants pointed out that a single monetary policy is similarly less problematic when wages adjust downward in high unemployment regions, obviating the need to relax monetary policy to fight unemployment. So far, there is little sign that the hardening of the EMS constraint and the transition to EMU have transformed these aspects of labor-market performance. The mobility of labor between EU member states remains low, reflecting deeply entrenched cultural and linguistic barriers. Wages remain rigid, reflecting the inheritance of strong unions and generous social programs. Where economic arrangements are embedded in social institutions, as in the case of labor markets, they are slow to change.

The implication for Europe is not a happy one. Insofar as these rigidities are both serious and slow to change, the costs of monetary unification may be considerable. A shock that raises unemployment in one EMU member state but does not elicit a reduction in interest rates by the ECB, because it does not produce comparable unemployment elsewhere in the monetary union, may give rise to a problem of a chronically depressed region. This suggests that the politics of EMU may be more compelling than the economics, or at least that the decision to go ahead needs to be understood on political as well as economic grounds.

The Politics of Monetary Unification

A number of political factors are commonly adduced to help explain the course of European monetary integration. As a point of departure we distinguish interstate bargaining and domestic distribution.

Interstate Bargaining

Even if monetary union does not enhance the welfare of all countries, it still may be in the interest of some, which then cajole, coerce, or bribe others into participating. This approach, generally associated with what political scientists refer to as "intergovernmentalism," interprets observed outcomes as the result of strategic interaction among national governments.[11]

Most of those who utilize this approach have in mind a process in which governments trade off objectives—that is, they have in mind a form of "linkage politics." By linkage is meant the tying together of two (or more) otherwise unconnected issue areas, permitting the parties to an agreement to make concessions on one in return for concessions on the other(s). Thus, one country might "give" monetary union (which it does not favor inherently) in return for "getting" political union (which it does) if the perceived benefits of the latter exceed the costs of the former.[12]

This approach, while appealing, is not unproblematic. For one thing, it is easy to fall into a vague invocation of a link among policy areas without paying careful attention to governments' preferences; for years, journalists and others invoked unspecified "geopolitical" motives to explain bargains among EU members. Any analysis that relies on implicit links must explain how it is we know that these links exist. While many commentators have argued that full participation in the Single Market might be hampered by nonparticipation in the EMS, for example, there is no provision in the Single European Act or any other EU document explicitly establishing this tie.

Moreover, there is scope for the trade-offs on which linkage arguments rely only when different nations place different values on different issues. If all EU members placed similar weight (positive or negative) on

EMU, there would have been little room for trading off concessions in different areas, and no room for linked bargaining that might improve the likelihood of agreement.

Finally, effective interstate bargaining requires that governments be able to make credible threats or promises. Otherwise they will fear that their foreign partners will renege on the commitment or refuse to enter into it in the first place. This is more problematic when issues are linked than when bargaining over each issue occurs in isolation, for not only must commitments on each dimension be credible, but the commitment to link dimensions must be credible as well.

Thus, while interstate bargaining can be important and may involve linkage politics, its use in analysis requires caution and detail. The parties' goals must be specified and analyzed. And given the importance of credibility, particular attention must be paid to how the parties bind themselves to the linkages they create.

Domestic Distributional Issues

Just as countries attracted to EMU may bargain with other member states over participation, interest groups that stand to benefit or lose may play an analogous role domestically. While not benefiting a country as a whole, EMU may still enhance the welfare of particular groups, which prevail on their government to support it. EMU, in this view, is just one example of the special-interest politics common to virtually every economic policy arena.

Serious analysis of the distributional implications of EMU is scarce, although there is some suggestive work (such as Giovannini 1993 and Hefeker 1997). A few observations are probably uncontroversial. Those for whom currency volatility is most costly stand to gain the most from EMU. They include banks and corporations with pan-EU investment or trade interests: for them forgoing national macroeconomic policy is a price worth paying for the elimination of currency risk. For those for whom cross-border transactions are inconsequential, on the other hand, predictable exchange rates are of little value, while national autonomy in the formulation of macroeconomic policies may be extremely important.

Many of the distributional concerns raised by EMU have had to do not so much with the desirability of a single currency per se as with the more immediate problems of adjusting macroeconomic policy to the requisites of a fixed exchange rate. In a high-inflation country, fixing the exchange rate typically leads to real appreciation, which puts pressure on producers of import-competing goods. This can cause a broad constituency to develop reservations about both fixed exchange rates and monetary union. In the context of EMU, because qualifying for participation required meeting the Maastricht fiscal criteria, those who worried about the impact of budget cuts or tax increases on them tended to resist making these sacrifices.

One implication of many distributional arguments is that support for EMU will be shaped by the rise of intra-EU capital mobility and trade. As the EU becomes more financially integrated, the choice between monetary policy autonomy and exchange rate stability becomes increasingly stark. Meanwhile, higher levels of intra-EU trade heighten the importance of exchange rate fluctuations for producers and consumers alike. Meanwhile, increased cross-border investment expands the ranks of those for whom exchange rate fluctuations created problems. Inasmuch as the increased openness of EU economies has involved more economic agents in cross-border economic activity, and these firms and individuals care about reducing exchange rate volatility, the drive toward the free movement of goods and capital might be expected to have strengthened support for EMU.

Problems with the distributional approach are not so much theoretical as practical. There is almost no empirical work that successfully measures the distributional effects of different international monetary regimes. Even if such work did exist, it would tell us little about outcomes, because interests are mediated by political institutions. Since institutions can magnify the political influence of some groups while diminishing that of others, similar interests may be expressed differently when, for example, parliaments are chosen by proportional representation than when members come from single districts in a first-past-the-post system.[13] Thus, any rounded account of EMU must pay close attention to domestic political factors, specifically to the role of interest groups with strong views on EMU and how they operate within national political institutions.

While additional variables can undoubtedly be brought to bear, the two we have described would appear to be central. We need a clear picture of the interests at stake and the institutional setting within which they are situated. We then need to understand how national governments with divergent goals interact at the EU level, including an exploration of the ways in which EMU is linked to other EU policy areas.

The Political Economy of Monetary Unification in Practice

The domestic distributional effects of international monetary policies have been crucial for European monetary developments. Support for EMU has come from international banks and corporations with an interest in reducing currency volatility and deepening the integration of the European market, and from those in high-inflation countries who saw

EMU as a way to achieve German-style monetary conditions. Opposition has come from domestically oriented economic actors and those who expected to bear the brunt of macroeconomic austerity measures. This includes those in high-inflation countries where a fixed exchange rate and subsequent real appreciation undermined domestic producers' international competitiveness.

In France and Italy in the early 1980s, for example, opposition to policies aimed at sustaining the commitment to a fixed exchange rate came from workers in import-competing industries such as steel and transportation equipment. In the early years of the Mitterrand government, France's commitment to the EMS was weakened by the resistance of Communists and left Socialists—whose constituencies were in declining manufacturing sectors hard hit by imports—to the austerity measures needed to bring French inflation down to German levels. A similar dynamic was evident in Italy, where the Communist party and its supporters in the labor movement—again concentrated in import-competing industries like steel—were reluctant to agree to real wage reductions needed to keep the lira in line with its ERM partners.

The 1992/93 EMS crisis provides another example of how domestic political factors affected monetary integration, in this case by impeding the coordination of member states' macroeconomic policies. The British government might have raised interest rates to defend sterling except that the higher rates would have been passed on by mortgage lenders, and many within the ruling Conservative party worried about the objections of property owners. The Italian government might have enacted drastic fiscal measures to solidify its commitment to low inflation, but this was difficult to achieve over the objections of public employees and others who felt threatened by the prospect of cuts. The French government might have raised interest rates to defend the franc but was reluctant to pursue a policy that ran the risk of raising the country's already high unemployment. The German authorities might have loosened monetary policy in order to reduce pressure on their EMS partners but for the Bundesbank's preoccupation with inflation, which was reinforced by strong domestic anti-inflationary constituencies.

Distributional considerations also help to explain the breadth of the euro-zone as it was ultimately established. Once the 1992/93 crisis was history, a new round of domestic debates began over the desirability of monetary union. It was argued that the single currency was indispensable for maintaining domestic political support for the Single Market. This logic went as follows: The more integrated European economies became, the more pronounced were the distributional consequences of intra-EU currency swings.[14] With the completion of the Single Market, countries that depreciated their currencies would be able to flood other member states with exports—as happened after the southern European devaluations in 1992/93. Import-competing producers' complaints about opportunistic exchange rates grew more intense as European integration proceeded. Countries that fail to hold their exchange rates stable, aggrieved import-competing producers insisted, were not good Europeans. They needed to choose, it was said, between getting into the monetary union or getting out of the Single Market. And the Single Market was too significant an economic achievement to be placed at risk. Note that the argument here was that the single currency was a necessary concomitant of the Single Market for political economy, not narrowly economic, reasons.

Yet the timing and character of the milestones in European monetary integration remain difficult to explain on the basis of interest-group politics alone. They were almost certainly heavily influenced by interstate bargaining. For example, it is observed that the Italian government in 1979 was not enthusiastic about the EMS but was presented with a fait accompli by the French and Germans. It is similarly argued that the French government in the 1990s was eager to use EMU to reduce German influence over European monetary policy, while Germany was less ardent in its pursuit of EMU.

The core of the complex bargaining process that has characterized European monetary integration has been the threat or fear that a country refusing to go along with EMU might bear costs on other dimensions of EU policy. In other words, the bargaining relationship involved explicit or implicit links between EMU and other issue areas. Linkages are indeed central to what Garrett (see Chapter 5, this volume) has in mind when he argues that the German government went along with EMU—which it found unattractive on the merits—in return for assurances that the EU would move forward on political matters, especially a common foreign policy. Martin (see Chapter 6, this volume) also emphasizes institutionalized linkages. The explanation of French and Italian commitments to the EMS in the early 1980s presented by Frieden (see Chapter 2, this volume) explores the domestic political impact of such linkage effects. And many analysts have pointed to the connection between the EU's search for exchange rate stability and its Common Agricultural Policy (CAP), the operation of which was severely complicated by fluctuations in EU currency values.[15]

Thus, both domestic politics and interstate bargaining help us understand why the momentum for EMU was sustained, and why it was not initially sufficient to bring Denmark, Sweden, and the United Kingdom into the fold. Domestic support for monetary unification grew over the course of the 1980s and early 1990s, as continued economic integration created heightened and widened the interest in European-wide markets and policymaking institutions. Some of the effects of the 1992/93 crisis, such as the impact of "competitive devaluations" on Northern European producers, strengthened the resolve to work for as rapid and encompassing an EMU as possible. Meanwhile, the growing importance of EU-wide decisions on trade, regulation, social policy, and even foreign policy made governments loath to risk being second-class European citizens. By the same token, it is not surprising that the three countries that are least enthusiastic about European federalism—the United Kingdom, Denmark, and Sweden—balked at the single currency. Domestic political considerations and interstate bargaining thus worked together to bring Europe's monetary union into being in 1999.

The Future of EMU

What picture do these perspectives paint of the future of EMU? From a narrowly economic viewpoint, high capital mobility, which will undoubtedly be a fact of economic life in the twenty-first century, effectively leaves most countries only the choice between adopting a flexible exchange rate or pegging it once and for all. The growth and articulation of international financial markets, which is ongoing, suggests that countries that cannot live comfortably with a flexible exchange rate—small countries with open economies highly dependent on international trade and financial flows in particular—will prefer policies that promise to stabilize the currency. Some countries, in Eastern Europe for example, may solve this problem by joining the EU and its monetary union. The implication is that Europe's monetary union will gain a constituency of faithful members who see EMU as a zone of monetary and financial stability and their only viable alternative to the unpalatable option of floating rates.

What of countries like the United Kingdom, residents of which are apparently happy to participate in the Single Market, but among whom there remains deep and abiding skepticism about the single currency? A political-economy perspective suggests that this skepticism reflects the low level of British commitment to European political integration. For many in the U.K., there is a fear that the EU's much-vaunted spillovers and linkages suggest that "one damn thing leads to another"—in this case, that monetary integration will reinforce the movement toward political integration. The decision for the U.K. may therefore be whether to join Europe's monetary union, and thereby to sign on to the larger project of creating a politically as well as economically integrated Europe, or else to withdraw from the European Union. Given that neither of these options is particularly appealing, one appreciates why the British see themselves as facing a dilemma.

All this assumes that EMU is here to stay. What of the scenario where it falls apart? Feldstein (1997) observes that EU member states with very different preferences are shackled together by a single monetary policy. There is no political union at the outset. National leaders will continue to plump for policies that reflect the differing preferences of their constituencies. Inevitably, some will be disappointed. And since Europeans are unlikely to agree to the extension of large-scale cross-border transfers prior to the creation of a true political union, there is no way of compensating the losers. Disagreement over the stance of monetary policy could then mean serious dispute. Exit, not just voice and loyalty, is one conceivable way for the disaffected to respond.

Technically, exiting the monetary union is straightforward: the government of the participating member state needs only to restart the printing press and reissue the national currency.[16] If a country left the monetary union because it felt that the ECB was following excessively inflationary policies, its "good" domestic currency would drive out the "bad" European currency. If the country instead left because it felt that the ECB's overly restrictive policies were aggravating unemployment, it would in addition have to declare that the euro would no longer be accepted as legal tender within its borders.

But the decision to continue to support or choose to abandon the monetary union will, like its predecessors, be made on political economy, not economic, grounds. The principal interstate bargaining consideration is that a country that withdraws from the monetary union could face considerable costs in the form of its standing in the EU on other fronts. Just as issue linkage contributed to the establishment of Europe's monetary union, issue linkage stands in the way of its demise. The principal domestic distributional consideration is that support for EMU is in fact substantial in its member countries, and likely to grow over time. Creating a common currency leads to the formation of groups and lobbies with an interest in its persistence. Investments are planned and made, contracts are signed, firms expand and merge, all with the Single Market and the single currency in mind. The economic realities thereby created generate political pressure to maintain the economic policies upon which they were built. As European banks and firms become more European, their stake in the single currency becomes greater, in turn lessening the likelihood that monetary unification will be reversed subsequently.

About This Volume

The contributors to this volume analyze European monetary integration from both the political and economic points of view. The second chapter, by Jeffry Frieden, considers the experiences of France and Italy in the early years of the EMS. Frieden argues that two factors were central to the politics of exchange rate policy in these countries. First were the distributional effects expected to result from binding the franc and the lira to the EMS. Import-competing manufacturing sectors opposed fixing exchange rates in ways that would erode their ability to compete with foreign producers, while internationally oriented sectors favored currency stability. Second was the linkage constructed between the EMS and the other aspects of European integration. This forced interest groups in both countries that were ambivalent or hostile to the EMS to weigh these concerns against their general attitude toward the EU, and in many cases to go along with monetary policies that they otherwise might have tried to block.

Chapter 3, by Matthew Gabel, investigates the domestic political bases of support for EMU in more detail. Gabel considers how socioeconomic status affects sentiment toward monetary union. He confirms that members of socioeconomic groups that expected to gain most from the reduction in currency volatility and the removal of barriers to cross-border trade and finance tended to be most enthusiastic.

Even if special interests are important, it would still be puzzling that domestic political support for EMU was so strong if, as much economic analysis has insisted, monetary union has few economic benefits in and of itself. In Chapter 4, Charles Engel presents evidence that monetary unification might not entail the economic sacrifices many expect. He shows that local prices have not responded quickly to exchange rate movements, which means that the exchange rate has not been an effective tool of macroeconomic policy. To the extent that local-currency pricing mitigates the ability of currency policy to affect national economies, giving up an independent currency may involve fewer costs than is usually anticipated.

Chapters 5 and 6, by Geoffrey Garrett and Lisa Martin, examine how interstate bargaining made EMU possible and affects its future. Garrett analyzes the Maastricht Treaty as a bargain between Germany, a country standing to gain little from monetary union per se, and the rest of Europe. EMU must be understood, he argues, as a trade across issue areas. Germany made significant concessions on matters monetary, according to Garrett, in return for general European support for German unification, as well as for a deepening of trade and investment ties with the rest of the EC.

Martin insists that the EMU debate be viewed as embedded in an institutionalized pattern of interstate cooperation. The same set of countries is engaged in negotiations over defense, social policy, competition policy, and, of course, monetary policy, and the way those negotiations are structured and institutionalized means that failure to reach agreement on one issue places agreement on the others at risk. The fact that countries stand to lose all the gains they have made from cooperation on a variety of issues has thus tended to lock in agreement on monetary matters.

The role of these institutional arrangements is key, Martin argues, to understanding the outcomes thereby achieved. For example, the disproportionate influence of small states in the governance of the monetary union must be understood as a function of formal decisionmaking procedures such as unanimity requirements used to solidify cross-issue links.

In Chapter 7, Paul De Grauwe, Hans Dewachter, and Yunus Aksoy provide a detailed analysis of one such arrangement: the decisionmaking structure of the European Central Bank. They show how the monetary policy of the ECB will depend on the structure of EMU institutions and on whether the members of the ECB board remain primarily national in orientation or develop a more pan-European perspective. Only if a more European view prevails, they argue, will EMU improve conditions in the Euro area.

Their analysis, like most of the literature, takes for granted that monetary union is irreversible. Chapter 8, by Benjamin Cohen, challenges this assumption. Contrasting the experience of three surviving monetary unions (the CFA Franc Zone, the East Caribbean Currency Area, and the Common Monetary Area) with three that failed (the East African Community, the Latin Union, and the Scandinavian Union), Cohen asks whether economic, political, or organizational factors explain success or failure. He concludes that appropriate economic conditions (high factor mobility, symmetric shocks) and organizational structures (an independent central bank, legal provisions for currency issue) have not always been sufficient to hold a monetary union together; rather, political factors broadly defined are key. The presence or absence of a dominant power or sufficient political cohesion are needed to sustain monetary union over time.

Conclusions

The essays in this volume testify to the complexity of economic and monetary union in Europe and to the need for an integrated political economy approach to understanding it. Macroeconomic analyses help clarify the economic costs and benefits of monetary integration. The benefits include reductions in transactions costs and in the uncertainty associated with cross-border trade and payments. The costs are principally due to the loss of a policy instrument with which to respond to unexpected shocks. Political analyses point to the role of domestic interests and to institutionalized relationships among EU member states. The distributional concerns of interest groups have powerful effects on the political constraints facing national governments and monetary policymakers. But these effects operate within an environment of ongoing negotiation among the European governments engaged in the search for mutually acceptable agreements on the road to broader and deeper integration.

These economic and political factors will continue to be central to the evolution of Europe's economic and monetary union. They will determine its membership—whether any current members leave the Union, which of the EU member states that are not in EMU join it, and whether candidate members in Central and Eastern Europe abandon their currencies for the euro. They will have a powerful impact on the policy of the European Central Bank as it establishes itself as the monetary authority for Europe and as one of the world's three principal central banks. For all these reasons, the political economy perspectives presented here help explain the past and understand the future of European monetary integration.

Notes

1. While "Euroland," as the area comprised of the founding members is fondly known, is made up of eleven countries, they had only ten monetary policies, Belgium and Luxembourg having long since formed a monetary union.

2. Throughout this chapter, we use the term "European Union" even where the organization was at the time going by another, earlier, name.

3. Even at this early date, plans for monetary union were linked to broader political problems associated with French ambivalence about the European Community in the aftermath of the franc crisis of 1969. On early monetary plans, see Tsoukalis (1977) and Ypersele (1985). For surveys of the process of monetary integration more generally, see Fratianni and von Hagen (1992), and Gros and Thygesen (1998).

4. Norway and Sweden also tied their currencies to the mechanism. On the snake, see Tsoukalis (1977), Ludlow (1982), and Coffey (1987).

5. Six percent for the Italian lira.

6. The bilateral band for the deutsche mark and the Dutch guilder, a currency whose stability was never in question, was kept at 2.25 percent.

7. The benefits are likely to be considerable insofar as barriers to full price convergence appear to have persisted well into the 1990s. Indeed, the existence of different currencies appears to have been one of the principal obstacles to the emergence of a truly integrated market. This is demonstrated by Engel (see Chapter 4, this volume), whose results imply that a common currency could make a major contribution to the development of more fully integrated, and thus more efficient, goods markets in the European Union.

8. The divergence between the euro "core" and "periphery" (Ireland and Iberia on the one hand, Germany on the other) in the opening quarters of Stage III was one indication that this dilemma was real.

9. A prototypical study of the incidence of aggregate supply and demand disturbances affecting different candidates for EMU, with comparisons to the United States, is Bayoumi and Eichengreen (1993).

10. Whether this last development makes supply shocks more or less asymmetric, and therefore raises or reduces the costs of monetary unification, is, unfortunately, uncertain. This is the "Krugman versus Krugman" debate, Krugman (1993) having argued both positions.

11. For summaries and applications of "intergovernmentalism" in the EU context, see Moravcsik (1991), Moravcsik (1998), and Sandholtz (1993). Moravcsik (1998) uses a blend of the first and second approaches to analyze monetary integration (pages 238–313). Andrews and Willett (1997) discuss the analysis of international monetary relations both in general and with regard to Europe.

12. Early variants of this analysis spoke of the "spillover" from one area of European integration to another. This was one of the arguments associated with the "neofunctionalist" approach to regional integration, although the approach tended to focus even more on how integration would create or reinforce bureaucratic or social interests in further integration. Moravcsik (1998), Webb (1983), and Keohane and Hoffman (1991) discuss this and other perspectives; an early statement of the approach is Haas (1958).

13. For a summary of such arguments and their application to the area of trade policy, see Rogowski (1987).

14. This argument is elaborated in Eichengreen and Ghironi (1996).

15. The CAP is far too complex to explore in detail here. Suffice it to point out that in the context of major agricultural subsidies, the EC sets Community-wide food prices. When a currency is devalued, the EC reference price would normally be raised in the devaluing country to counterbalance the devaluation—thus "passing through" the exchange rate change in full to food prices. The inflationary impact of this pass-through would mitigate the devaluation's attempt to restore price competitiveness in nonagricultural sectors. For this reason, the Community devised a series of compensatory arrangements and accounting exchange rates. For our purposes, what is important is only that exchange rate fluctuations complicate Community agricultural policy by changing compensatory farm payments in ways that could disrupt the delicate balance within the EC on farm policy. For more details see McNamara (1998).

16. Our discussion of the exit question follows Eichengreen (1998).

References

Andrews, David, and Thomas Willett, 1997, Financial interdependence and the state: International monetary relations at century's end. *International Organization* 51:3, 479–511.

Bayoumi, Tamim, and Barry Eichengreen, 1993, Shocking aspects of European monetary unification, in: Francisco Torres and Francesco Giavazzi, eds., *The transition to economic and monetary union in Europe* (Cambridge: Cambridge University Press).

Coffey, Peter, 1987, *The European monetary system—past, present and future* (Amsterdam: Kluwer).

Eichengreen, Barry, 1992, Should the Maastricht Treaty be saved? Princeton Studies in International Finance 74 (Princeton: International Finance Section).

_____, 1993, Thinking about migration: Notes on European migration pressures at the dawn of the next millenium, in: Horst Siebert, ed., *Migration, a challenge for Europe* (Ann Arbor, Mich.: University of Michigan Press).

_____, 1998, European monetary unification: A tour d'horizon. *Oxford Review of Economic Policy* 14, 24–40.

Eichengreen, Barry, and Fabio Ghironi, 1996, European monetary unification: The challenges ahead, in: Francisco Torres, ed., *Monetary reform in Europe* (Lisbon: Catholic University Press), 83–120.

Eichengreen, Barry, and Charles Wyplosz, 1993, The unstable EMS. *Brookings Papers on Economic Activity* 1, 51–143.

Feldstein, Martin, 1997, EMU and international conflict. *Foreign Affairs* 76, 60–73.

Fratianni, Michele, and Jürgen von Hagen, 1992, *The European monetary system and European monetary union* (Boulder, Colo.: Westview).

Garrett, Geoffrey, 1992, International cooperation and institutional choice: The European Community's internal market. *International Organization* 46, 533–560.

Giovannini, Alberto, 1993, EMU: What happened? Exploring the political dimension of optimum currency areas, in: Guillermo de la Dehesa, Alberto Giovannini, Manuel Guitián, and Richard Portes, eds., *The monetary future of Europe* (London: Centre for Economic Policy Research).

Goodman, John, 1992, *Monetary sovereignty: The politics of central banking in Western Europe* (Ithaca, N.Y.: Cornell University Press).

Gros, Daniel, and Niels Thygesen, 1998, *European Monetary Integration,* 2d ed. (London: Longman).

Haas, Ernst, 1958, *The uniting of Europe* (Stanford, Calif.: Stanford University Press).

Hefeker, Carsten, 1997, *Interest groups and monetary integration: The political economy of exchange regime choice* (Boulder, Colo.: Westview).

Keohane, Robert, and Stanley Hoffman, 1991, Institutional change in Europe in the 1980s, in: Stanley Hoffman and Robert Keohane, eds., *The new European Community* (Boulder, Colo.: Westview).

Krugman, Paul, 1993, Lessons from Massachusetts for EMU, in: Francisco Torres and Francesco Giavazzi, eds., *Adjustment and growth in the European Monetary Union* (Cambridge: Cambridge University Press), 241–261.

Ludlow, Peter, 1982, *The making of the European monetary system* (London: Butterworth).

McKinnon, Ronald, 1963, Optimum currency areas. *American Economic Review* 53, 717–725.

McNamara, Kathleen, 1998, *The currency of ideas: monetary politics in the European Union* (Ithaca, N.Y.: Cornell University Press).

Moravcsik, Andrew, 1991, Negotiating the Single European Act: National interests and conventional statecraft in the European Community. *International Organization* 45, 19–56.

_____, 1998, *The choice for Europe* (Ithaca, N.Y.: Cornell University Press).

Mundell, Robert, 1961, A theory of optimum currency areas. *American Economic Review* 51, 657–665.

Rogowski, Ronald, 1987, Trade and the variety of democratic institutions. *International Organization* 41, 203–224.

Sandholtz, Wayne, 1993, Choosing union: Monetary politics and Maastricht. *International Organization* 47, 1–39.

Tsoukalis, Loukas, 1977, *The politics and economics of European monetary integration* (London: George Allen and Unwin).

Webb, Carole, 1983, Theoretical perspectives and problems, in: Helen Wallace, William Wallace, and Carole Webb, eds., *Policymaking in the European Community,* 2nd ed. (Chichester, England: John Wiley and Sons), 1–42.

Ypersele, Jacques van, 1985, *The European monetary system: Origins, operation and outlook* (Cambridge: Woodhead-Faulkner).

2

Making Commitments

France and Italy in the European Monetary System, 1979–1985

JEFFRY A. FRIEDEN

Abstract

European monetary integration has depended on commitments by member states of the European Union (EU) to sustain monetary policies consistent with stable exchange rates. These commitments in turn have depended on the domestic political support that governments can muster for such policies. Two domestic political dimensions were central to the development of the European Monetary System (EMS): the role of economic interest groups with preferences toward the policies associated with EMS membership, and the domestic implications of linking EMS commitments with the broader process of European integration. This chapter[1] analyzes the domestic politics of French and Italian policy toward the EMS from 1979 through the mid-1980s, during which the two countries' commitments to monetary integration gradually hardened.

European monetary integration (MI) has experienced dramatic twists and turns over the past thirty years. The "snake" of the 1970s was a general failure, and in the early 1980s the new European Monetary System (EMS) seemed little better.[2] In the late 1980s the EMS appeared to settle into something approaching a currency union, but appearances of stability were shattered by the currency crisis that began in September 1992. In the aftermath of the crisis, many doubts were raised about the prospects of Economic and Monetary Union (EMU). But the euro was introduced on schedule in 1999, and the monetary union seems firmly in place. At the center of the process were national governments' commitments to maintain fixed exchange rates with their European Union (EU) partners. The manifest weakness of such commitments on the part of several important EC members—especially France and Italy—in the 1970s and early 1980s led to great skepticism about the EMS. It is widely recognized that a crucial turning point came in the early 1980s, as policy in France and Italy evolved in ways that seemed to presage a much brighter future for monetary integration than had previously appeared likely.

This chapter elucidates the ways in which the French and Italian governments' commitments to a fixed exchange rate became increasingly credible between 1979 and 1985. In this context, I argue for the central role of two factors within the domestic political arena. The first was the confluence of economic interests expected to favor or oppose a system of fixed exchange rates within the European Union. The second was the linkage between monetary integration (MI) and other EU policies, which led actors otherwise indifferent about currency developments per se, or even hostile to the EMS on its merits, to support MI in the interest of broader EU goals.

The first section evaluates a series of common explanations of EU members' decisions to commit to fixed exchange rates over the years, concluding that linkage politics is crucial to the process. The next section discusses both the political implications of the distributional impact of currency arrangements and the logic of a linkage-based argument. The third section analyzes the domestic politics of French and Italian monetary policies between 1979 and 1985, tracing the operation of the distributional and linkage-related factors that helped the two countries' currency commitments acquire credibility. The final section explores the implications of these experiences for the subsequent development of European monetary integration, and for its future.

Credible Commitments and European Monetary Integration

Monetary integration depends on commitments by EU member governments to particular exchange rates. This implies committing to similar national monetary policies, as currency values depend first and foremost on underlying national monetary conditions. These commitments were, on average, quite lacking in credibility in the 1970s, but gained increasing credibility over the 1980s.

The snake of the 1970s did hold together for Germany, Denmark, and the Benelux countries, but it was widely regarded as a failure. In the late

1980s the EMS and its exchange rate mechanism (ERM) had these countries as members, along with France, Italy, and Ireland, and it was widely regarded as a success. The crucial difference between the failed snake and the relatively successful mature EMS, then, was the adherence of France, Italy, and Ireland. For reasons of size, the French and Italian cases are central.

But this raises a major puzzle. The French and Italian governments had not been able to sustain fixed exchange rates during the 1970s. Nor had either government been able to commit itself to serious inflation reduction over this period. Indeed, bringing them into a German-dominated monetary union was a special challenge: both had run inflation substantially higher than German levels since the late 1960s. There was, therefore, little reason to believe that they would be able to implement the domestic policies necessary to sustain their EMS commitments in the 1980s—and yet they did.

Various solutions to this puzzle have been proposed.[3] The first is that the formal institutions of the EMS were more effective at sustaining cooperation among member states than those of the less formal snake because an exchange rate agreement requires a number of explicit provisions for consultation about parity changes and the financing of payments deficits.

It is true that the EMS was a somewhat more developed institutional mechanism than the snake, and that the EMS made more money available to members than did the snake. Much of the difference, at least at the outset, was undoubtedly due to the fact that the snake was planned while the Bretton Woods system was still (barely) alive, which made more formal arrangements redundant. In any event, very short-term financing arrangements were extended from thirty to forty-five days, and their capacity expanded from 6 billion to 14 billion European Currency Units (ecus). Medium-term financing ceilings were raised from 5.45 billion to 14.1 billion ecus, and 5 billion ecus in concessionary loans over a five-year period were made available to Ireland and Italy (van Ypersele 1985, pp. 61–64). Certainly the greater resources committed to the EMS made affiliation more attractive.

However, there is little evidence that these organizational factors were particularly important to the process. In fact, many of the new mechanisms were not part of the original EMS but evolved as (or after) it became credible. From the financial side, the money involved was not really substantial, and Italy did not even use its concessionary finance. Certainly there is no evidence that the evolution of French policy was at all related to the formal institutions of the EMS.[4]

A second explanation is that the exchange rate targets chosen in the EMS were more transparent than the monetary targets announced, and not met, by the French and Italian governments in their prior attempts to fight inflation. The idea here is that economic agents are more likely to be convinced by a government's commitment to a specific exchange rate, which the markets can observe, than by a general commitment to reduce inflation or even a specific commitment to a monetary target, which the markets cannot directly observe.

This, however, does not explain why the French and Italian governments were better able to commit to a fixed exchange rate in the late 1980s than in the 1970s. If transparency in and of itself increased a government's credibility, a government serious about reducing inflation would *always* use the exchange rate as such a signal. The fact that the signal sent by the French and Italian governments in the 1970s turned out to be untrustworthy, while it was far more reliable in the late 1980s, simply pushes the question back a step.

A third potential explanation of the greater success of monetary integration in the 1980s than in the 1970s is that national preferences had converged.[5] Certainly if countries' desired inflation levels had been more similar in 1979 than in 1973, they would have been better able to sustain fixed exchange rates. However, to judge from inflation levels, there is little evidence for such preference convergence. French and Italian inflation rates were higher in the first three years of the EMS than in the first three years of the snake, and differed more from that of Germany. Perhaps politicians and voters *wanted* lower inflation, but they appeared unable to achieve it outside the EMS—which again pushes us back to the need to explain the success of the mechanism as it evolved between 1979 and 1985.

A fourth reason often given for the relative accomplishments of the 1980s is that the international economic environment was easier than in the 1970s, especially in the absence of oil price shocks. This confuses overall *levels* of inflation with *divergences* from German levels. If all EMS members had had lower inflation rates in the 1980s than in the 1970s, this would not necessarily have made fixed exchange rates easier to sustain, so long as national inflation rates differed substantially. For external economic conditions to explain the differential successes of the two decades, these conditions would have to have been asymmetric in such a way that the shocks to Germany were more inflationary than shocks to other EMS countries. Only if this had come to pass—and there is very little evidence that it did—would international conditions have made it easier for other EMS countries to sustain fixed rates against the deutsche mark (DM).[6]

A fifth explanation for EMS success is that structural economic characteristics of member countries had changed over the course of the 1970s. The principal point here is that the welfare benefits of currency union rise as economies become more financially and commercially integrated, and the members of the EC became more integrated over the course of the 1970s.

There is much truth to this argument, and I have presented the case for it elsewhere (Frieden 1996). Levels of economic integration within the EC grew after the late 1960s, and as they grew, so did interest in monetary union. By the same token, those countries most strongly integrated into other EC economies (especially that of Germany) have been most enthusiastic about MI. However, the change in levels of economic integration between 1973–75, when France and Italy fell out of the snake, and 1983–85, when they acquired credibility within the EMS, was small. Indeed, a more relevant comparison might be the last years of the snake (1976–78) and the first years of the EMS (1979–83), over which time the economies in question changed hardly at all. It is, in any case, hard to believe that marginal changes in structural economic conditions could have such striking effects on national commitments to currency policies.

The final argument made for the success of the EMS in the 1980s rests on linkage politics. Many analysts believe that monetary integration succeeded to the extent that it was tied to other goals at the European level. Countries went along with MI because cooperation on the monetary front was essential to cooperation on other fronts that they valued highly.[7]

In the remainder of this chapter, I develop the argument that linkage between monetary integration and European integration more generally was central to the success of MI in the 1980s, and specifically to French and Italian exchange rate commitments between 1979 and 1985. However, the invocation of linkage politics is not without problems. As Alt and Eichengreen (1989) point out, such linkage effects hold only under certain conditions, having especially to do with different national valuations of the policies in question.[8] Such valuations can best be understood as a function of domestic political factors; I analyze the domestic circumstances in France and Italy that made linkage politics feasible.[9]

Distributional Preferences and Linkage Politics in European Monetary Integration

Linkage politics raises the benefits of initial and continuing cooperation because tying two issue areas together enables gains from political trades. A group that has a strong preference for a policy in one arena and a weak preference against a policy in another arena can compromise with another group that has a weak preference against the first policy and a strong preference for the second policy. In this way, each group gets what it cares about more in return for giving up what it cares about less. Without the linkage process, the two groups would oppose each other in the two arenas; with the arenas linked, exchange is possible.[10]

French and Italian commitments to fixed exchange rates, I argue, were made more credible by the link between MI and broader European integration. This redefined the domestic politics of monetary policy and the choices available to domestic groups in ways that made a previously unattainable outcome possible. To clarify this argument, I discuss the constellation of interests on both dimensions—monetary integration and broader European integration—and show how trade-offs along the two dimensions made domestic political agreement possible.

The first step is to specify preferences in the first issue area, monetary integration.[11] Tying the franc and the lira to the ERM implied a fixed and relatively appreciated exchange rate against the deutsche mark. The real appreciation was a function of the fact that France and Italy had inflation substantially above that of Germany, and in any foreseeable circumstances inertial inflation would lead to a transitional real appreciation of their currencies after they were fixed in nominal terms.

Moving from floating to fixed exchange rates provides greater predictability in foreign trade and exchange. However, it makes it impossible for the government to alter exchange rates to affect domestic macroeconomic conditions and relative prices. The level of the exchange rate has straightforward relative price implications: An appreciated ("strong") currency raises the domestic price of nontradable goods and services relative to the domestic price of tradables.

On this basis we can project the positions of economic groups toward fixing the franc and the lira. A fixed exchange rate is favorable to those heavily involved in international trade and payments, especially major international banks and corporations. Exporters of goods or services for which nonprice dimensions (quality, reputation) are very important will also tend to favor exchange rate stability even if the currency's level imposes some cost disadvantage (within limits, of course). Nontradables producers, such as those in the public sector, are pulled both ways: A strong currency is good for them, but forgoing national monetary independence is undesirable inasmuch as they depend upon national economic conditions (and exchange rate stability is irrelevant to them).

Producers of tradable goods that compete primarily on price, on the other hand, are hostile to both the strong currency and its being fixed. The principal groups in question are producers of standardized manufactures, for whom a real currency appreciation causes substantial difficulties in competing with imports and, where relevant, in maintaining export markets. The fixed exchange rate is of little value, especially inasmuch as these producers are oriented toward maintaining their domestic markets.[12] In the EU, farmers are essentially indifferent, as they are protected against EU exchange rate movements by complex arrangements that are part of the EU's Common Agricultural Policy.

Thus traditional import-competing manufacturing sectors are hostile to a strong fixed currency, internationally oriented firms are favorable, and nontradables producers are ambivalent. Translating this interest group perspective into partisan politics is difficult, as many of the economic sectors in question cut across traditional party lines. It is, however, possible to present a highly simplified picture of French and Italian party positions on the EMS. Generally speaking, in both countries, the Right was oriented toward a mix of international business and nontradables, the center (especially the Socialists) reflected nontradables and manufacturing, and the Left (especially the Communists) represented workers in traditional manufacturing.

· In France, the Right was weakly favorable to a strong franc, the Socialists (PS) were weakly opposed, and the Communists (PCF) were strongly opposed.[13] In Italy, the Christian Democrats (DC) were ambivalent about a strong lira, the Socialists (PSI) were moderately opposed, and the Communists (PCI) were a bit more strongly opposed.

These positions on the exchange rate issue made movement toward MI difficult. In France neither Right nor Socialist governments were enthusiastic about a strong franc, while in Italy, neither Right-center nor broad national governments were so inclined. Indeed, only a fraction of the French Right (the Union pour la Démocratie Française) and Left (the Rocard faction of the PS) strongly favored MI, and in Italy only one tiny member of the center-Left coalition (the Republican party) was a strong supporter of monetary integration. This made MI on its own merits unattainable in both countries.

The second step is to specify preferences along the second policy dimension, that is, toward European integration more generally. The relative placement of partisan camps on this dimension is amenable to analysis, but for the sake of brevity, here I simply assert such preferences.[14] In France, the PCF was hostile to the EC, while the PS and the Right were moderately favorable.[15] In Italy, all three major parties were strongly favorable to the EC; if anything, the DC was somewhat more ambivalent than the others.

This implies that in both countries there was broad agreement on European integration, despite the disagreement on MI. Both Right and Socialist governments in France were generally pro-EU, as were all conceivable Italian governments. Linking the exchange rate issue to European integration more generally, then, created a new political reality, for a country's inability to join MI implied moving away from the EU.[16]

For political actors, the choice had been on two dimensions: pro- or anti-EU, pro- or anti-strong currency. Linkage collapsed these two dimensions into one: either pro-EU and pro-strong currency, or anti-EU and anti-strong currency. The result was to change the set of likely outcomes. In Italy all major parties were more intensely pro-EU than they were anti-EMS. In France, most of the PS and most of the Right were similarly positioned, while the PCF and a portion of the PS were both anti-EMS and anti-EU (or were more strongly anti-EMS than they were pro-EU).

This stylized discussion is meant simply to illustrate the operation of linkage politics, and its potential application to the French and Italian experiences. I have no illusions that this treatment represents the nuanced nature of the two countries' political debates over the issue between 1979 and 1985. However, I hope that it does help provide a framework in which these debates can be examined.

From Skepticism to Success: France and Italy, 1978–1985

Despite the general failure of the snake in the 1970s, discussion of European monetary union began to gather new momentum in October 1977, when Roy Jenkins, the president of the European Commission, made a prominent public appeal for MI. In April 1978, the French president, Valéry Giscard d'Estaing, and the German chancellor, Helmut Schmidt, proposed a new European Monetary System, which was approved by the European Council in December 1978 and went into effect in March 1979. At that time all EU members except the United Kingdom affiliated with the exchange rate mechanism of the EMS, which allowed a 2.25 percent band among currencies (6 percent for the lira).[17]

The prevailing opinion at the time was that French and Italian inflation rates were too high and intractable to allow the ERM to operate as planned. Indeed, in the first four years of its operation, there were seven realignments of EMS currency values. During this period, deutsche mark revaluations and lira and franc devaluations reduced the nominal DM value of the two problem currencies by 27 and 25 percent, respectively—hardly a sign of commitment to fixed rates. But over the following four years, between April 1983 and January 1987, there were only four more realignments, and the lira and franc were brought down only 13 and 9 percent against the deutsche mark, respectively. Indeed, after 1983, exchange rate variability within the EMS declined substantially, while monetary policies converged on virtually every dimension.[18] It is generally agreed that the decisive turning point in the evolution of the EMS came between 1981 and 1985, when the French and Italian governments changed course to bring their inflation rates in line with the EU average.[19]

This turning point was in large part made possible by the linkage of the EMS to European integration more generally. The system was launched personally by the French president and German chancellor, and its founding documents explicitly tied monetary stability to broader European integration. There had not been any sense that the snake was essential to the EU, to which in fact two non-EU members (Norway and Sweden) affiliated. Neither national politicians nor Community leaders had staked much political capital on the snake. The EMS was different, and its success was publicly related to other aspects of European integration, in ways that implied that a country not in the ERM would become a second-tier member of the Community.

Linking MI with EU integration affected the domestic political lineup in many member nations. This was especially the case during the early 1980s when, beset by stagnation and unemployment, many Europeans began to look upon an intensification of economic integration as the last best hope for the region.[20] As the pace of European integration quickened, MI came to be seen as a near essential component of a broader trend. The process was particularly striking in France and Italy.

France, 1981–1983

François Mitterrand and the PS took power in May–June 1981.[21] In the two years since the EMS had begun operation, with French inflation still well above German levels, the franc had appreciated about 12 percent against the deutsche mark in real terms, putting serious competitive pressure on French manufacturers.[22] As French prices continued to rise and the trade balance to deteriorate, the government (represented at Brussels by the finance and economy minister, Jacques Delors) negotiated an October 1981 EMS realignment in which the franc and lira were devalued by 3 percent and the deutsche mark and Dutch florin were revalued by 5.5 percent. The devaluation proved inadequate in the face of continued French inflation, and in June 1982 another realignment raised the deutsche mark and florin by 4.25 percent and lowered the franc by 5.75 percent (the lira was devalued by 2.75 percent). This second realignment gave rise to serious disputes within the French government.

President Mitterrand's government was headed by Prime Minister Pierre Mauroy, and included four ministers from the Communist party. The Communists were unenthusiastic about European integration and hostile to austerity (*rigueur* in French economic policy parlance). The Socialist–Communist differences were especially important because they implicated the trade unions. The largely pro-Communist Confédération Générale du Travail (CGT) was most adamant in its resistance to austerity, even at the expense of French membership in the EU (toward which it had been indifferent or opposed). Inasmuch as the economic policies necessary to control inflation affected real wages, the CGT and the PCF were recalcitrant at best, obstructionist at worst (Kesselman 1980, 1985).

The PS was divided in several factions, running roughly from right to left as follows. The group led by Michel Rocard was economically liberal and strongly pro-European. Mitterrand's faction was more tied to his personality than to any particular policy stance. The group around Mauroy tended toward standard social democracy—friendly to economic liberalism but committed to traditional socialist goals; Mauroy generally had the support of the Marseilles-based federation led by Gaston Deferre. Finally, the CERES (Centre d'Etudes, de Recherches, et d'Education socialiste) faction led by Jean-Pierre Chevènement was a stronghold of nationalistic and economic policy views similar to those of the Communists (Bell and Criddle 1988; Hanley 1986). Mitterrand and his followers dominated the PS, largely by means of a series of tactical alliances with other factions.

In the labor movement, the Socialists' principal allies were the Confédération Française Démocratique du Travail (CFDT) and the Fédération de l'Education Nationale (FEN). The former was a general labor federation that explicitly competed with the CGT; the latter was a teachers' association. There was a Socialist presence in the CGT, but it was a minority of the confederation. A third major labor federation, Force Ouvrière (FO), was not partisan, although it tended to combine hostility toward the organized Left with general militancy over wage issues (Adam 1983; Mouriaux 1985).

There were important sociological differences among these parties and labor unions. The Communist party was, as elsewhere in Europe, heavily oriented toward blue-collar workers in traditional industries. The Socialist party was essentially middle class, dominated by managers, professionals, and white-collar workers. The PS membership relative to the population at large in 1973, for example, had a heavy overrepresentation of upper managers (11 percent of the party and 6 percent of the labor force), and of teachers (17 percent of the party and 3 percent of the labor force); workers were underrepresented (19 percent of the PS and 37 percent of the labor force) (Hardouin 1978). Of the 169 PS deputies elected in 1981, to take another example, fully 47 percent were teachers; another 22 percent were professionals; and 20 percent were upper managers and senior civil servants.[23]

The trade unions differed quite a bit in their composition. The CGT was especially strong in traditional manufacturing industries. Table 2.1 shows how much heavier was the industrial bent of the CGT than that of the CFDT and FO: three-fifths of those who voted for CGT in 1979 were in industry, compared to less than half of those who voted for CFDT or FO.

The CGT's industrial orientation is indicated by other measures as well. CGT votes in union elections in 1981 were 32 percent of total votes. In such industries as metalworking, pulp and paper, and chemicals, the CGT vote was between 45 and 51 percent of the total, while in finance and services, the CGT vote was between 10 and 22 percent of the total.[24] Within the public sector, the CGT dominated the steel, chemical, and auto firms, but had little strength in high-technology and financial firms (Mouriaux

TABLE 2.1 France: Sectoral Composition of Votes for Three Major Labor Federations and for All Federations, 1979 (percent)

	CGT	CFDT	FO	All Federations
Industry	59.7	49.1	45.3	50.5
Trade	23.8	24.1	26.9	23.8
Agriculture	2.6	5.2	4.7	3.5
Various	9.7	13.6	14.7	11.7
Management	4.2	8.0	8.4	10.4

SOURCE: Adam (1983, p. 164).
NOTES: N = 3.3 million for CGT, 1.8 million for CFDT, 1.36 million for FO, and 7.79 million for All Federations. All Federations includes a number of smaller labor unions; percentages do not total 100 because of roundings.

1985, pp. 201–202). In the 1979 union elections, the CGT received 50 percent of the votes of industrial workers, 30 percent of the votes of agricultural workers, and 33 percent of the votes of other workers.[25]

The CFDT, like the PS, tended to be more oriented toward services and high-technology firms than the CGT. Table 2.2 shows how some of these differences played out in union elections in several important French firms. While the CGT overwhelmed the CFDT within Renault and led in Michelin, for example, the CFDT dominated such financial firms as the Banque National de Paris and the insurance company Assurances Générales de France. The CFDT and an autonomous union swamped the CGT in IBM-France.

The general pattern within the labor movement, then, was that the CFDT was concentrated in nontradables (service) sectors and competitive high-technology firms, while the CGT was prominent among producers of tradables, especially those most affected by competition from imports. This division was mirrored to some extent by that between the Socialist and Communist parties. In this context, recall the expected policy differences among uncompetitive tradables sectors, competitive internationally oriented firms, and nontradables producers. The first are expected to be especially hostile to a strong currency, the second favorable, and the third ambivalent.

These sectoral divisions were exacerbated by the economic trends of the early 1980s. As the franc appreciated in real terms against other EMS currencies, domestic relative prices moved against tradables and in favor of the nontradables (and cross-border investing) segments of the French economy. In 1981/82 the prices of industrial products rose 19.5 percent, while prices of private services rose 28.3 percent and those of public services rose 34.8 percent. This put serious pressure on tradables producers (Fonteneau and Muet 1985, p. 319). Indeed, between 1980 and 1983, em-

TABLE 2.2   France: CGT and CFDT Strength in Selected Firms, 1979–1981 (percent of voters)

Firm and Date of Vote	Votes for CGT	Votes for CFDT
Renault, 1981	61.2	16.6
Michelin, 1980	46.1	43.8
Banque Nationale de Paris, 1980	25.1	30.0
Assurances Générales de France, 1980	22.4	50.1
IBM-France, 1979	12.4	56.2

SOURCE: Hervé Hamon and Patrick Rotman, 1982, *La deuxième gauche* (Ramsay, Paris), 423–427.
NOTES: The elections in question were for enterprise commissions. In the case of IBM-France, votes for the CFDT include votes for an autonomous union.

ployment in tradable sectors declined 7 percent. Meanwhile, employment in construction, trade, and services held steady, while that in energy, transport, telecommunications, and finance rose 5 percent.[26] It is not surprising that manufacturers demanded further devaluations.

This cleavage was an important component of French debates over the EMS, which largely became couched in terms of austerity and commitment to a fixed exchange rate within the EMS, versus reflation, devaluation, and abandoning the EMS.[27] The Communists and the CGT, along with the CERES faction within the PS, opposed austerity and advocated devaluing the franc and leaving the EMS. The CFDT and the Rocard and Mauroy factions of the PS were pro-European and thus in favor of maintaining EMS commitments, even at the expense of austerity. Mitterrand and his supporters within the PS were in the middle, and they were crucial to the ultimate disposition of the issue.

After the June 1982 realignment, it was clear that the government faced a distinct choice. The franc continued to appreciate in real terms, and after October 1982, it came under constant attack on foreign exchange markets. Battle lines were drawn between EMS partisans and opponents. In March 1983 the issue came to a head in a period that has been called "ten days that shook Mitterrand" (Bauchard 1986, p. 139). France had to devalue to avoid running out of reserves in a matter of days, and this devaluation had either to take place within the ambit of the EMS or to represent a definitive break with the monetary union.

At the political level, the Socialists were in trouble. The Left did poorly in the March 6 first round of the municipal elections. Concerned that austerity had alienated the government's constituents, Mitterrand leaned toward taking France out of the EMS.[28] However, the message of the second round of municipal elections held on March 13 was conflicting. The

Left did badly, but the losses were less severe than anticipated and, per-haps more important, the PCF suffered a major setback.

Mitterrand apparently read the election results as an indication that the economic nationalism espoused by the PCF would not succeed in shoring up the Socialists' political base. The municipal elections, in other words, led Mitterrand to conclude that while popular discontent with austerity was widespread, anti-EU sentiment was limited.[29] This appar-ently pushed him toward keeping France inside the EMS and reconfirm-ing Mauroy in office. At the same time, he increased the hold of the Mit-terrand and Mauroy factions on the cabinet, removed several leftist Socialists from office, and appointed Jacques Delors as a super minister in charge of Economics, Finance, and Budget. A series of new economic policy measures were announced, from tax increases and budget cuts to a tightening of exchange controls.

Austerity was the order of the day. Inflation was more than halved, from 12.6 to 6 percent, between 1982 and 1985, and the current account was in surplus by the latter year; but meanwhile unemployment rose from 8.1 to 10.1 percent, and GDP growth stagnated. Nevertheless, the new ERM parities held for more than three years, until the readjustment of April 1986. By then, French commitment to the EMS was credible, and Jacques Delors, as president of the European Commission, was leading the charge to accelerate the process of monetary integration.

Two features of the French experience are worth highlighting. First, there were clear differences, as expected, in the EMS preferences of vari-ous sectors of the economy. Import-competing tradables producers, rep-resented especially in the labor movement by the CGT and the PCF, were the strongest opponents of a strong franc. Internationally integrated firms and nontradables sectors, represented especially by the CFDT and segments of the PS, were more enthusiastic about monetary union de-spite its association with austerity.

Second, the link between the exchange rate and France's relations with its EU and EMS partners was explicit. It was clear by mid-1982 that com-mitment to the EMS required major changes in policy so that French macroeconomic conditions would converge with those of Germany; it was also clear that the EMS commitment was of paramount importance to broadening French participation in the EU. The linkage between MI and European integration was crucial in leading the Socialist govern-ment to abandon its economic policies and commit itself to austerity.

Italy, 1980–1985

The decisions that bound monetary policy to the EMS were less striking in Italy than in France. Italian credibility on this score developed gradually between 1981 and 1986, but several important turning points can be identified. In most instances we observe the sorts of divisions familiar from the French case, and a link between these debates and general attitudes to the EU.

There were two defining characteristics of Italian macroeconomic problems after 1973. The first was a high level of budget deficits, a substantial portion of which was monetized. In fact, in 1975 the central bank committed itself to buy all unsold Treasury securities, thereby ensuring that budget deficits would translate automatically into money creation.

The second feature of Italian macroeconomic conditions was that inflation had taken on something of an inertial character. In 1975 the unions and businesses had negotiated a tight wage indexation scheme, the *scala mobile*, and defense of this arrangement had become a rallying cry for labor. Both the explicit commitment of the central bank to monetize a portion of the budget deficit and extensive wage indexation led to a strong inflationary tendency, which made a fixed exchange rate nearly impossible. Both would have to be altered for Italy to abide by its EMS commitments.

The first major step in reorienting monetary policy was taken in 1981, when the governor of the Banca d'Italia indicated that he would no longer be guided by the 1975 commitment to purchase unsold Treasury securities.[30] This shift in policy, known as the "divorce" of the central bank from the Treasury, was strengthened in 1982 by the implementation of a new, compulsory commercial bank reserve system, and strengthened further in 1983 when administrative controls on credit were eliminated.

Almost immediately after the "divorce" Italian real interest rates shot up from well below German levels to well above them. Real interest rates in Italy went from an average of –1.5 percent between 1977 and 1981 to an average of 3.8 percent between 1982 and 1986. Meanwhile, the share of the public debt held by the central bank declined from 23.7 percent in 1981 to 16.6 percent in 1984 (Tabellini 1988).

Restrictive monetary policy was not enough: inflation's inertial component had to be reduced, which required an assault on the *scala mobile*. Attempts to renegotiate the index were frustrated by the opposition of the Communists, and the Communist-oriented labor federation, Confederazione Generale Italiana del Lavoro (CGIL). The Socialists and the Christian Democrats, along with the labor federations associated with them, the Confederazione Italiana di Sindicati Liberi (CISL) and Unione Italiana del Lavoro (UIL), were willing to reduce indexation. Finally, in February 1984, Socialist Bettino Craxi, the new prime minister, simply decreed a reduction in the *scala mobile*. The CGIL and the PCI were outraged, and collected signatures for a national vote on the *scala mobile* (Lange 1986).

The campaign leading up to the June 9, 1985, referendum was divisive. The costs of austerity were counterposed to the benefits of being in step with Italy's partners in the EMS and the EC. In the event, the no votes prevailed (with 54.3 percent of the total), and the decree loosening the *scala mobile* stood. This was the second crucial set of changes necessary to bring Italian inflation down and make it possible for the country to keep the lira within the ERM.

Domestic political divisions over the EMS and EMS-related issues, such as the *scala mobile,* date back to the original debate over Italian entry into the agreement. Bargaining over these issues took place against the backdrop of important political changes in the country. In 1976, the PCI gave its tacit support to the coalition government led by the Christian Democrats. In early 1978 the CGIL announced a significant moderation of its overall strategy.[31]

Nonetheless, both the PCI and the CGIL were ambivalent about the EMS. In 1978 the Communists voted against the law authorizing Italian accession to the exchange rate agreement, arguing that a delay of at least six months was advisable to avoid too severe a shock to employment and wages. The Socialists abstained, and the bill passed.[32] As discussed above, the PCI and the CGIL similarly fought against the reform of the *scala mobile.*

Some insight into the reason for these divisions is provided by a look at the socioeconomic differences among the major labor federations. The membership breakdown in Table 2.3 indicates that the Communist-dominated CGIL was more heavily represented in traditional industries, while the Socialist-oriented CISL and the more independent UIL had larger shares of their memberships in services. Expressed differently, in 1983, CGIL members constituted 55 percent of Italy's unionized industrial workers, with CISL members accounting for 29 percent and UIL members for 16 percent; 48 percent of the country's organized workers in private services, with CISL members accounting for 31 percent and UIL members for 21 percent; and 36 percent of union members in public services, with CISL members accounting for 43 percent and UIL members for 21 percent.[33]

Although quantitative data are not available, impressionistic evidence indicates that the Communist-Socialist social composition mirrored that of their unions, and was therefore similar to that of France. In both instances, the French generalization held for Italy: the Socialists were more representative of those in services and high-technology industries, while the Communists were concentrated in traditional import-competing manufacturing. This, again, helps explain why the PCI was more inclined toward devaluations, with the PSI more favorable to the EMS.

The link between European issues and the EMS was rarely drawn as explicitly in Italy as in France, perhaps because no single decision ever became the focus of popular attention. However, the presence of the link

TABLE 2.3   Italy: Nonagricultural Membership in the CGIL, CISL, and UIL by Sectors, 1983 (percent of members)

	CGIL	CISL	UIL
Industry	59.4	45.6	44.8
Services	40.6	54.4	55.2
Private	18.4	16.8	21.8
Public	22.2	37.6	33.4

SOURCE: Calculated from Baglioni, Santi, and Squarzon (1985, p. 196).

is evident from the beginning of the story. Indeed, when the arrangement was being negotiated in 1978, Prime Minister Giulio Andreotti originally announced that Italy would not participate. Only after substantial pressure was brought to bear on Andreotti by the French and Germans did the government change its position. On the stick side, both Giscard and Schmidt made it clear that they would regard Italy's nonadhesion as a blow to Italy's Europeanist credentials. On the carrot side, they permitted the lira a much wider (12 percent) band of fluctuation and incorporated financial assistance to Italy into the EMS agreement.

Andreotti swung toward EMS entry as the implications for Italian relations with its EU partners became clear. The issue was also tied up with DC–PCI relations at a time when many of Italy's allies were uneasy about the role of the Communists in the government. Extracts from Andreotti's diary for December 1978 are instructive. While still undecided, he noted in frustration: "If we do not adhere immediately it will be said that the Communists are not 'Europeans' and that the government is their slave." Once Andreotti decided to enter the EMS, he named as the most important considerations "the guarantees of Schmidt and Giscard and the need to safeguard our European prestige" (Andreotti 1981, pp. 287–288).

Indeed, the tie between the EMS and other European policy issues served to mitigate the Communists' opposition. Unlike their French counterparts, the PCI and the CGIL were generally Europeanist. The PCI regarded its relations with Chancellor Schmidt, and the German Social Democrats more generally, as crucial to their future as a serious political force, and Schmidt regarded the EMS as a major personal achievement on his part. According to one major PCI leader, "Chancellor Schmidt put a great deal of pressure on both the Italian government and the PCI. In fact, Schmidt called [PCI leader Enrico] Berlinguer to try to get a reassurance that the PCI would not cause a government crisis over the EMS, and Berlinguer gave him that reassurance."[34] In other words, general Communist commitment to the EU, and the specific importance of the EMS for European integration, softened the PCI and CGIL concern about the exchange rate agreement.

There is little doubt among informed observers that the "foreign link" (*vincolo estero*) was crucial to the ability of the government to achieve austerity measures in the early and mid-1980s. A former central bank president put it succinctly: "With a weak government, the external link is a crucial anchor. In this context, a fixed exchange rate is the firmest guarantee of monetary stability when the authorities do not have the ability to impose a responsible monetary policy for *political* reasons."[35] Another Bank of Italy official was even more explicit:

In the absence of specific *government* commitments to *macroeconomic* policy, we took the EMS as the foundation stone of our policy. The central element responsible for the changes was the desire of the political system and of public opinion for European integration. This is a reflection of the lack of confidence on the part of public opinion in the quality of our own political leaders. This has been exploited by the Bank of Italy. The external constraint was not enough to induce discipline on a full range of policies—fiscal policy is a clear exception—but on monetary issues it did have an effect.[36]

As this last informant indicated, one interesting aspect of the Italian case is the relationship between monetary and fiscal policy. During the 1980s, monetary policy conformed increasingly to the requirements of Italy's EMS commitments. This imposed severe costs on the manufacturing sector, and especially on labor within it. However, although many manufacturing jobs were lost because of the real appreciation of the lira, the government picked up a great deal of the slack by running an expansionary fiscal policy. Put somewhat differently, the costs borne by manufacturing were counterbalanced by benefits that accrued to the nontradables sectors, especially those connected to public spending. In fact, over the course of the 1980s, employment in manufacturing declined more than 10 percent, and manufacturing investment was stagnant in real terms. Meanwhile, employment in services rose 27 percent, while investment in nonresidential services grew 5 percent a year in real terms (Confindustria 1992; Rey 1992, p. 52). Eventually, of course, the government's fiscal deficits became large enough to pose economic and political problems for it.

In this light, it is not surprising that adjustment to the EMS was most painful to the PCI's constituencies among industrial workers, while supporters of the DC and the PSI in the public sector were sheltered from the impact of the country's tight monetary policy. It is with this in mind that the man principally responsible for the PCI's economic policies at the time is somewhat bitter about the experience:

Sectors tied to international competition hoped that the EMS and the single market would serve as a whip against the less competitive, more inefficient sectors, which they saw as a ball and chain around their legs. The most international sectors had to restructure, and had to demand a change in Italian policies.

There is a broad national consensus in favor of European integration, and waving this flag one can ask for sacrifices. In 1984 the reduction of labor costs seemed key. We had indexation that other countries did not have. The inflation issue was crucial, and certainly there was a link to the exchange rate.

The principal costs of this policy were paid by industrial workers. The public sector did well; management did well. But traditional industrial workers were sacrificed.[37]

The Italian experience, then, is one in which the redefinition of austerity and wage restraint as interconnected with the country's European commitments led to the adoption of policies that would probably not otherwise have been accepted. The PCI and the CGIL were forced to support a set of monetary initiatives about which they were very wary, largely because more ardent opposition would have called into question their long-standing commitment to European integration. The linkage drawn between the EMS-based austerity measures and Italy's role in Europe allowed the government to change course in a way that had been impossible for over a decade.

Implications and Conclusions

This discussion of the early years of the EMS leads to several conclusions about the reasons for the course of European monetary integration after 1978. Three features of the process deserve to be highlighted. First, the ERM required credible national commitments to austerity measures needed to bring high-inflation countries in line with German macroeconomic conditions. Second, these national commitments depended in large part on the response of various groups to the expected economic effects of the transitional real appreciation that would occur if the EMS commitment were honored. Third, a major component of the domestic political support for the EMS commitment was the linkage of European monetary union with other aspects of European integration: inasmuch as a nation's inability to conform to EMS constraints compromised its ability to be a full participant in other aspects of the EU, more domestic actors were drawn toward support for the measures required to fix the exchange rate.

It is reasonable to believe that the factors that affected the development of the EMS in the early 1980s have continued to influence the course of European monetary integration. In the aftermath of the currency crisis of 1992/93, the future of monetary integration depended on the trade-offs countries that had fallen out of the ERM were willing to make between national policy autonomy and full membership in the Economic and Monetary Union. The forces that operated in the domestic politics of European monetary integration in France and Italy in the early 1980s almost certainly continued to operate there and elsewhere in the 1990s, as the EU moved toward EMU.

The consolidation and enlargement of the Economic and Monetary Union will also depend on the factors important to the development of the EMS. Domestic support for the EMU in place, and for its potential expansion to other European countries, is essential, and this chapter has emphasized the importance of the link between currency union and other EU agenda items to cement this domestic support. The analysis presented tends to indicate the importance of the linkage among various EU policies to smooth the passage to their adoption.[38]

Even within the functioning currency union, monetary integration is still closely tied to other aspects of European integration. This is doubly true in the case of current and future EU members who are not now members of EMU. Whether this linkage is sufficient to bring about the change in national monetary politics necessary to incorporate the entire present (and future) Union, or whether domestic political lineups force consideration of alternatives to an EU coterminous with EMU, will be largely a function of developments in the domestic politics of monetary policy within EC member states.

Notes

1. The author acknowledges support for this research from the Social Science Research Council's Program in Foreign Policy Studies, the German Marshall Fund, the UCLA Institute for Industrial Relations, and the UCLA Center for International Business Education and Research, and comments from Benjamin J. Cohen, Barry Eichengreen, John Goodman, Jürgen von Hagen, Peter Lange, Lisa Martin, and John Woolley.

2. It is actually more accurate to speak of the Exchange Rate Mechanism (ERM) of the EMS, which is the agreement to bind currency values. The United Kingdom, for example, was a founding member of the EMS but only tied sterling to the ERM in October 1990. However, inasmuch as the two are closely linked in popular and scholarly discussion, I use the terms more or less interchangeably.

3. For a summary of some of these analytical perspectives, see Eichengreen and Frieden (Chapter 1, this volume). Other good surveys are Giavazzi and Giovannini (1989) and Fratianni and von Hagen (1992).

4. This conclusion is analogous to that drawn from a broader historical survey by Cohen (see Chapter 8, this volume). If one defines institutions more broadly as does Martin (see Chapter 6, this volume), then the linkage argument developed below might be regarded as a special case of a broader institutional expla-

nation. However, most of the literature that relies on institutional changes to explain the success of the EMS is referring, as is Cohen (Chapter 8, this volume), to the formal organizational mechanisms by which the system itself was governed.

5. Collins and Giavazzi (1993) present a strong case for this argument, purporting to show a change in national attitudes toward inflation. However, their study does not in fact look at public *policy* preferences, but rather at the weight that household respondents accord inflation (as opposed to unemployment) in formulating their forecasts of general economic outcomes. This is several steps removed from public willingness to support the political measures necessary to reduce inflation, which is the actual shift asserted in the literature. See also Moravcsik (1998).

6. Fratianni and von Hagen (1992) present one of the more systematic arguments for a combination of the third and fourth explanations (in other words, that national preferences and the international environment changed). They focus more on alleged changes in national preferences, as seen in changes in inflation rates in EMS and non-EMS countries, arguing that there is little evidence that the EMS itself had a significant inflation-reducing impact.

However, questions can be raised about the data they use. Fratianni and von Hagen include successful members of the snake (Benelux) in the EMS sample, but the inflation rates of these countries had already converged with that of Germany by the start of the EMS. Similarly, they include Austria and Switzerland in the non-EMS control group, although the Austrian and Swiss currencies formally or informally tracked the deutsche mark for most of the period. Finally, they use average inflation rates weighted by GNP, even though each country is an equally valid observation.

Reworking the data accordingly, in 1977/78 the average unweighted inflation rate for the eventual new EMS members (France, Italy, Ireland, and Denmark—including this last as it was only a nominal member of the snake) was 11.3 percent, 8.1 percent higher than in Germany. By 1987/88 the average inflation rate for these four countries was 3.7 percent, just 2.9 percent higher than Germany's. In contrast, the non-EMS group (Australia, Canada, Finland, Greece, Japan, the United Kingdom, and the United States) had an average inflation rate of 9.5 percent in 1977/78, which came down to 5.8 percent in 1987/88, 5 percent higher than Germany's. This would appear an appreciable difference in convergence of inflation rates between the two groups.

Perhaps more significant is that for my purposes it is not particularly important to show that the EMS was necessarily the only reason for inflation reduction; it is sufficient to show that the EMS required convergence with Germany monetary conditions. This was also the case with the snake, and raises once more the same question: Why were these countries willing and able to reduce inflation sufficiently to stay in the EMS when they had been unwilling or unable to do so for the snake?

7. Garrett (Chapter 5, this volume), makes a variant of this argument. Martin (Chapter 6, this volume), presents an explicit linkage-based explanation of EMU in the Maastricht process that is analogous to mine but focuses on the ways in which linkages are made binding by institutional characteristics of the EU itself.

8. In addition, as pointed out in Eichengreen and Frieden (Chapter 1, this volume), the invocation of linkage politics simply pushes the credibility problem

back one step: If linking two policy arenas raises the costs of defection in each, as it may under certain carefully specified conditions, what makes the link itself credible? I do not address this issue here, but take the tie between the EMS and European integration as given.

9. A parallel argument is presented in Woolley (1992).

10. This is simply a somewhat special case of the common observation that while a median voter result is possible when policy is on one dimension, increasing the number of dimensions makes all outcomes unstable. Linkage politics can, in this sense, be regarded as a process by which a two-dimensional policy space is reduced to one dimension.

11. I have written at some length about this general analytical problem in Frieden (1991). Here I summarize the implications for the French and Italian cases.

12. These categories are merely first approximations. Clearly the policy preferences of any firm or individual depend on a wide variety of considerations, and firms' preferences on exchange rates are far more nuanced than is allowed for here. Nonetheless, these divisions are good enough to serve as a starting point for analysis.

It should also be clarified that this abstract discussion ignores the obvious fact that what really matters to such groups is not international trade and payments generally, but trade and payments within the prospective monetary union. This refinement is, of course, crucial to the European case: A British firm, say, whose market was primarily in the United States would be far less enthusiastic about European monetary unification than a British firm whose market was primarily in the EU. The discussion also glosses over many important details, such as the relative importance of competition on nonprice dimensions.

13. In reality one portion of the Right (the UDF) was favorable to a strong franc, while another portion (the neo-Gaullist RDR) was ambivalent; meanwhile, the Socialists were similarly divided between those mildly favorable and those quite opposed. Here I ignore intragroup differences and simply take averages of the two parties.

14. Such preferences could be derived more systematically with reference to particular groups' or parties' positions relative to national and EU median voters. If, for example, the national median voter is to the right of the EU median voter, the national Left will be favorable to European integration, which will push the country toward its preferred policies. On the other hand, if the national median voter is to the left of the EU median voter, the national Left will be hostile to European integration. I believe that this—rather than political culture or other ideological considerations—explains why in the early 1980s Italian Communists were pro-EU while French Communists and leftist Socialists were anti-EU. However to avoid introducing another controversial set of assertions I restrain myself to observing this partisan placement.

15. Again, I ignore intraparty divisions (the leftist Socialists and the Gaullists were more hostile to the EU) and take party means.

16. In this sense, I assume that the linkage was credible, that is, that nonparticipation in MI implied less than full membership in the EU. I do not explore how or why this linkage was made credible, which, of course, is an important question.

17. Ludlow (1982) is especially detailed on the negotiations and early opera-tion of the EMS; see also van Ypersele (1985, pp. 71–95) and Ungerer (1983). Out-standing surveys of the EMS experience more generally are Fratianni and von Hagen (1992) and Giavazzi and Giovannini (1989).

18. Relative parity changes are calculated from exchange rate data in Interna-tional Monetary Fund (1988, pp. 20–34).

19. See, e.g., International Monetary Fund (1988, p. 48).

20. For one among many possible interpretations of this trend, see Katseli (1989, pp. 186–195).

21. The literature on these years is enormous. Most of the discussion below is drawn from detailed journalistic accounts of the experience, which will be cited as used. More general analyses of the period can be found in Sachs and Wyplosz (1986), McCarthy (1990), Cameron (1992), and Friend (1989). Macroeconomic data are taken, except where otherwise noted, from Sachs and Wyplosz (1986). Among the many edited volumes on the experience, the following contain partic-ularly useful discussions of economic policy: Ambler (1985); Machin and Wright (1985); and Ross, Hoffmann, and Malzacher (1987).

22. Real bilateral exchange rate calculated from Wood (1988).

23. Bell and Criddle (1988, p. 203). Hanley (1986, pp. 177–197), has a useful compilation of his own survey of the PS and that of Cayrol, which address both the party's social composition and the differences among the factions.

24. Groux and Mouriaux (1992, p. 103).

25. Adam (1983, p. 164). The elections in question were the *élections prud'homales*.

26. These are the figures given, and the aggregations (tradable, nontradable, and "sheltered") used, in Sachs and Wyplosz (1986, p. 275).

27. For the account that follows, in addition to the general works cited already, I have relied primarily on a series of detailed narratives, by well-informed jour-nalists, of the early Mitterrand years: Favier and Martin-Roland (1990); Bauchard (1986); July (1986); and Nay (1988).

28. On this period, see Favier and Martin-Roland (1990, pp. 465–493) and Bauchard (1986, pp. 139–154). Both books, especially the former, are based on ex-tensive interviews with participants both at the time and after the fact.

29. In the meantime, there is some evidence that many in the business commu-nity—including the largely Socialist executives of many newly nationalized French multinational banks and corporations—were pressing strongly for a deepening of French commitment to the EC, which implied staying in the ERM. On this point, see Green (1993). Another argument advanced (Goodman 1992, p. 136) is that an internal French government report indicated that the costs of a de-valuation would be greater than the costs of conforming to the fixed rate. Without being able to evaluate the evidence fully, I find the report's alleged conclusions, and the likelihood that its arguments were crucial in influencing Mitterrand, quite questionable.

30. The "divorce" is one of the few aspects of Italian economic policy in this pe-riod on which there is a substantial literature. See, e.g., Goodman (1992); Tabellini (1987); Salvemini (1983); Addis (1987); and Epstein and Schor (1989).

31. On this so-called EUR line see Lange, Ross, and Vannicelli (1982, pp. 165–180).

32. For two informed discussions of Italian accession see Spaventa (1980) and Andreotti (1981, pp. 284–289).

33. Baglioni, Santi, and Squarzon (1985, pp. 194–196). Figures exclude retirees.

34. Interview, Giorgio Napolitano, Rome, July 21, 1992.

35. Interview, Guido Carli, Rome, July 21, 1992.

36. Interview, Fabrizio Saccomanni, Rome, July 16, 1992.

37. Interview, Giorgio Napolitano, Rome, July 21, 1992.

38. This is also the conclusion drawn by Martin (Chapter 6, this volume).

References

Adam, Gérard, 1983, *Le pouvoir syndical* (Paris: Dunod).

Addis, Elisabetta, 1987, Banca d'Italia e politica monetaria: La riallocazione del potere fra stato, mercato, e banca centrale. *Stato e Mercato* 19 (April), 73–95.

Alt, James, and Barry Eichengreen, 1989, Parallel and overlapping games: Theory and an application to the European gas trade. *Economics and Politics* 1:2, 119–144.

Ambler, John, ed., 1985, *The French socialist experiment* (Philadelphia: ISHI).

Andreotti, Giulio, 1981, *Diari 1976–1979: Gli anni della solidarietà* (Milan: Rizzoli).

Baglioni, Guido, Ettore Santi, and Corrado Squarzon, 1985, *Le relazioni sindicali in Italia: Rapporto 1983–1984* (Rome: Edizioni Lavoro).

Bauchard, Philippe, 1986, *La guerre des deux roses: Du rêve à la réalité, 1981–1985* (Paris: Bernard Grasset).

Bell, D. S., and Byron Criddle, 1988, *The French Socialist Party*, 2d ed. (Oxford: Clarendon Press).

Cameron, David, 1992, The franc, the EMS, *rigueur*, and "l'autre politique": The regime-defining choices of the Mitterrand presidency (New Haven: mimeo).

Collins, Susan, and Francesco Giavazzi, 1993, Attitudes toward inflation and the viability of fixed exchange rates: Evidence from the EMS, in: Michael Bordo and Barry Eichengreen, eds., *A retrospective on the Bretton Woods system* (Chicago: University of Chicago Press), 547–577.

Confindustria, 1992, *Previsioni dell'economia italiana* 6:1 (Rome: Confindustria).

Epstein, Gerald, and Juliet Schor, 1989, The divorce of the Banca d'Italia and the Italian treasury: A case study of central bank independence, in: Peter Lange and Marino Regini, eds., *State, market, and social regulation* (Cambridge: Cambridge University Press), 147–164.

Favier, Pierre, and Michel Martin-Roland, 1990, *La décennie Mitterrand*. Vol. 1. *Les ruptures (1981–1984)* (Paris: Seuil).

Fonteneau, Alain, and Pierre-Alain Muet, 1985, *La gauche face à la crise* (Paris: Presses de la Fondation Nationale des Sciences Politiques).

Fratianni, Michele, and Jürgen von Hagen, 1992, *The European Monetary System and European monetary union* (Boulder, Colo.: Westview).

Frieden, Jeffry A., 1991, Invested interests: The politics of national economic policies in a world of global finance. *International Organization* 45, 425–451.

_____, The impact of goods and capital market integration on European monetary politics. *Comparative Political Studies* 29, 193–222.

Friend, Julius, 1989, *Seven years in France: François Mitterrand and the unintended revolution, 1981–1988* (Boulder, Colo.: Westview).

Giavazzi, Francesco, and Alberto Giovannini, 1989, *Limiting exchange rate flexibility: The European Monetary System* (Cambridge, Mass.: MIT Press).

Goodman, John, 1992, *Monetary sovereignty: The politics of central banking in Western Europe* (Ithaca, N.Y.: Cornell University Press).

Green, Maria, 1993, Setting the agenda for a new Europe: The politics of big business in EC 1992 (Cambridge, Mass.: mimeo).

Groux, Guy, and René Mouriaux, 1992, *La CGT* (Paris: Economica).

Hanley, David, 1986, *Keeping left? Ceres and the French Socialist party* (Manchester, England: Manchester University Press).

Hardouin, Patrick, 1978, Les caractéristiques sociologiques du Parti Socialiste. *Revue Française de Science Politique* 28:2 (April), 220–256.

International Monetary Fund, 1988, *Policy Coordination in the European Monetary System.* IMF Occasional Paper, no. 61 (Washington, D.C.: IMF).

July, Serge, 1986, *Les années Mitterrand* (Paris: Bernard Grasset).

Katseli, Louka, 1989, The political economy of European integration: From Euro-sclerosis to Euro-pessimism. *International Spectator* 24:3/4, 186–195.

Kesselman, Mark, 1980, The economic analysis and program of the French Communist party, in: Philip Cerny and Martin Schain, eds., *French politics and public policy* (New York: St. Martin's Press), 177–190.

———, 1985, The French Communist Party: Historic retard, historic compromise, historic decline—or new departure? in: Philip Cerny and Martin Schain, eds., *Socialism, the state and public policy in France* (London: Frances Pinter), 42–59.

Lange, Peter, 1986, The end of an era: The wage indexation referendum of 1985, in: R. Leonardi and R. Nanetti, eds., *Italian politics* vol. 1 (London: Pinter), 29–46.

Lange, Peter, George Ross, and Maurizio Vannicelli, 1982, *Unions, change and crisis: French and Italian union strategy and the political economy, 1945–1980* (London: Allen and Unwin).

Ludlow, Peter, 1982, *The making of the European Monetary System* (London: Butterworth).

Machin, Howard, and Vincent Wright, eds., 1985, *Economic policy and policy-making under the Mitterrand presidency, 1981–1984* (New York: St. Martin's Press).

McCarthy, Patrick, 1990, France faces reality: *Rigueur* and the Germans, in: David Calleo and Claudia Morgenstern, eds., *Recasting Europe's economies* (Lanham, Md.: University Press of America), 25–78.

Moravcsik, Andrew, 1998, *The Choice for Europe* (Ithaca, N.Y.: Cornell University Press).

Mouriaux, René, 1985, *Syndicalisme et politique* (Paris: Editions Ouvrières).

Nay, Catherine, 1988, *Les sept Mitterrand ou les métamorphoses d'un septennat* (Paris: Bernard Grasset).

Rey, Guido, 1992, I mutamenti della struttura economica: Fattori produttivi, distribuzione del reddito, domanda, in: Confindustria Centro Studi, ed., *L'Italia verso il 2000: Le istituzioni, la società, l'economia* 2 (Rome: SIPI,) 3–55.

Ross, George, Stanley Hoffmann, and Sylvia Malzacher, eds. 1987. *The Mitterrand experiment* (Cambridge, Mass.: Polity Press).

Sachs, Jeffrey, and Charles Wyplosz, 1986, The economic consequences of President Mitterrand. *Economic Policy* 2 (April), 262–322.

Salvemini, Maria Teresa, 1983, The Treasury and the money market: The new responsibilities after the divorce. *Review of Economic Conditions in Italy* 1 (February), 33–54.

Spaventa, Luigi, 1980, Italy joins the EMS: A political history. Occasional Paper, no. 32, Johns Hopkins University Bologna Center (June).

Tabellini, Guido, 1987, Central bank reputation and the monetization of deficits: The 1981 Italian monetary reform. *Economic Inquiry* 25 (April), 185–200.

_____, 1988, Monetary and fiscal policy coordination with a high public debt, in: Francesco Giavazzi and Luigi Spaventa, eds., *High public debt: The Italian experience* (Cambridge: Cambridge University Press) 90–134.

Tsoukalis, Loukas, 1977, *The politics and economics of European monetary integration* (London: Allen and Unwin).

Ungerer, Horst, 1983, *The European Monetary System: The experience, 1979–82.* IMF Occasional Paper, no. 19 (Washington, D.C.: IMF).

Wood, Adrian, 1988, *Global trends in real exchange rates, 1960 to 1984,* World Bank Discussion Paper, no.35 (Washington, D.C.: World Bank).

Woolley, John, 1992, Policy credibility and European monetary institutions, in: Alberta Sbragia, ed., *Europolitics: Institutions and policymaking in the "new" European Community* (Washington, D.C.: Brookings Institution).

Ypersele, Jacques van, 1985, *The European Monetary System: origins, operation and outlook* (Brussels: Commission of the European Communities).

3

Divided Opinion, Common Currency

The Political Economy of Public Support for EMU

MATTHEW GABEL[1]

Abstract

A common approach to the study of Economic and Monetary Union (EMU) is to use the distributional consequences of EMU to account for the pattern of political conflict over EMU. This chapter examines empirically whether this approach explained variations in voters' support for EMU in the 1990s. Using Eurobarometer data from 1993–94, this chapter analyzes whether individual-level support for EMU was consistent with several common theoretical claims about the distributional effects of EMU. The results indicate that citizens adopted attitudes toward EMU that were consistent with their economic interests related to exchange-rate stability, enhanced capital mobility, and low inflation. But, surprisingly, the economic implications of the convergence criteria did not appear to influence voters' support for EMU.

A common approach to the study of international political economy (IPE) and, in particular, the study of monetary unification in the European Union (EU) is to use the distributional consequences of international economic policies to account for the pattern of political conflict over these policies. Baldwin (1989) refers to this as the "economic self-interest approach"—the basic tenet being that individuals favor or oppose particular international economic policies depending on whether the policy increases or decreases their real income. Eichengreen (1998b) describes the "interest group" models of international political economy along the same lines. In this chapter, I will address several issues relevant to the application of these models to the politics of economic and monetary union (EMU), and ultimately the politics of managing an EU single currency. In particular, I will examine empirically whether these IPE models accounted for variation in mass support for EMU.

Economic self-interest models have two theoretical components: a theory of the distributional consequences of international economic policies and a political theory of how the distributional consequences relate to policymaking via political agents. In general, IPE scholars identify the distributional consequences through relevant theories of economic welfare for that policy. For example, Frieden (1991) used a specific factors model to identify the distributional consequences of international financial integration.

On the politics side, there are a variety of different theories of democratic policymaking that identify which political agents' interests are relevant. Of particular interest for this chapter is how these theories treat the mass electorate. For contrast, we can divide these models into two camps. On one side, scholars assume that voters are generally incapable of holding elected officials accountable for international economic policies and are thus, as an electorate, irrelevant for policymaking (e.g. Magee, Brock, and Young 1989). Much evidence from public opinion research supports this assumption, showing that on most international policy issues citizens demonstrate little interest or sophistication (Nincic 1992). As a result, these scholars assume that organized interest groups are the primary domestic political actors.

On the other side, scholars posit that the threat of electoral penalty endows voters with a strong influence on elected officials and thus policymaking (e.g., Cassing, McKeown, and Ochs 1986). Although little of this theoretical literature has attended to the issue of voter interest and sophistication, there are both theoretical and empirical reasons to believe that uninformed voters can form meaningful opinions about international economics and pose a credible electoral threat. Several scholars argue that voters do not necessarily need a sophisticated understanding of government policy to identify their economic interests and adopt appropriate political attitudes.[2] Through cues from like-minded elites, citizens may infer sufficient information about the consequences of a policy to adopt political attitudes consistent with their economic interests. And, for elected officials with affected constituents, the economic interests of their voters may influence policy. Consequently, these types of political models assume that the distributional consequences of international economic policies across voters (the mass public) are relevant for policymaking.

There are several reasons to believe that the politics of EMU were consistent with the latter family of political models. First, EMU has been far from an obscure issue to EU citizens. In most EU member states, recent survey evidence shows that the majority of the mass public felt well informed about EMU.[3] In addition, considerable recent media attention and public controversy focused on questions of EMU and membership in a single European currency.

Second, even if interest groups and parties are the primary political agents, one can argue that their political behavior is endogenous to public opinion. Particularly in the EU context, there are good reasons to believe that interest groups and political parties adopted positions toward EMU that reflected their mass constituents' preferences over policy. For one, while organized interests may play a powerful role in policymaking, one source of that influence is their ability to threaten elected officials with electoral penalties for their decisions. For these threats to work, organized interests must be able to deliver the votes of those who share their economic interests. Thus, an interest group's political influence may depend fundamentally on its affiliated voters adopting political attitudes and behavior consistent with their economic interests from international economic policy. Furthermore, there is theoretical and empirical support for the claim that political parties in the EU adopt positions on European integration in response to the economic interests of their electorates (Carrubba, forthcoming). To the extent that parties adopted positions on EMU in a similar manner, we would expect public support to influence policymaking regarding EMU.

Thus, in order to apply the economic self-interest model to the politics of EMU, it seems reasonable to model mass voters as relevant political agents. But for this IPE model to apply to EMU, we must address a second issue: whether the relevant political agents—in this case mass voters—adopted positions on EMU that are consistent with theoretical expectations regarding the distributional consequences of EMU. This chapter focuses on this question.

It is worth noting that the answer to this question is also relevant for understanding the current politics of the European monetary unification. Public perceptions of a currency are crucial to its credibility (Barro 1986; Barro and Gordon 1983). If European citizens lack support for the euro, it may influence their investment decisions and the value of the currency. Also, the political viability of the euro will depend on generating and maintaining public support (Cameron 1997). Anticipating how and why EU citizens will vary in their support for the euro is thus important for understanding euro-related political cleavages, changes in public attitudes, and political difficulties. This study of EMU can inform our expectations about these public attitudes toward the euro. For example, consider the scenario where the findings of this study indicate that political attitudes toward EMU were structured by its distributional consequences. Since the euro and EMU share several distributional consequences, then this would suggest that citizens differ in their attitudes toward the euro in a similar fashion.

Finally, whether or not public support for EMU was related to its distributional consequences is an important question for EU monetary policymakers. If variation in public support for the euro reflects the distributional consequences of a single currency, policymakers can identify compensatory policies to buttress public support for the currency. In contrast, consider the scenario where there is no link between distributional consequences and mass attitudes. And, instead, support is due to a fairly fixed personal characteristic, such as ethnocentrism. In this scenario a successful compensatory policy may not exist. In sum, investigating whether economic interests underlie EU citizens' support for EMU is important for understanding the politics of the euro.

This chapter is divided into five sections. In the first section I discuss previous research on public support for European integration and support for EMU. In the second section, I draw on the political economy literature regarding monetary unification to identify the distributional consequences of EMU and specify hypotheses regarding individual-level variation in public support for EMU. I then test these hypotheses statistically using Eurobarometer survey data from 1993/94. In the third section, I describe these data and the statistical methods of analysis. I present the results of the analysis in section four and end by discussing their implications for the politics of European monetary unification in the last section.

Public Support for Economic and Monetary Union

Recent research on public attitudes toward European integration suggests that economic self-interest shapes public support for European policy integration. Gabel (1998a, 1998b, 1998c), Anderson and Reichert (1996), and Gabel and Palmer (1995) provide evidence that variation in individual-level public support for integration—which correlates highly with support for particular policies, such as EMU—is consistent with the distributional consequences of the internal market. However, the literature on individual-level public support for specific policies, particularly EMU, is scant.[4] A recent study by Kaltenthaler and Anderson (1999) provides the only systematic and cross-national study of individual-level EU citizen support for EMU.

Kaltenthaler and Anderson posited that support for EMU was based on two economic factors: citizens' perceptions of their national and personal economic situations and their level of human capital. They hypothesized that, since citizens' general support for integration reflects their economic evaluations, that their support for a single currency would also be positively related to these evaluations. Also, they hypothesized that citizens with high human capital were better able to adapt to and exploit economic opportunities provided by a common currency. Thus, they expected support for EMU to increase with a citizen's level of human capital—measured by level of education. The only corroborating evidence they found was that citizens' prospective sociotropic (national) economic evaluations and level of education were positively related to support for EMU.

In addition, Kaltenthaler and Anderson posited that citizens viewed EMU as a threat to their national political cultures. But the extent to which this threat reduced a citizen's support for EMU depended on how strongly that citizen identified with her nation. Specifically, they hypothesized that the greater a citizen's national pride, the greater her sense of threat from EMU, and the lower her support for EMU. They also argued that, for a complex issue such as EMU, citizens tempered their support by their domestic political attitudes, particularly their support for the current government and their satisfaction with how democracy works in their country. They hypothesized that citizens who supported their government were more supportive of EMU than citizens that did not support the government. Finally, they contended that as citizens' satisfaction with democracy increased, they were less willing to cede authority to the EU and thus were less supportive of EMU. For these hypotheses, the only corroborative evidence was that national pride was inversely related to support for EMU.

Research on aggregate (national) level variation in support for EMU has been more successful in identifying systematic determinants of support. Even though this research is not directly relevant to the focus of this paper—that is, testing hypotheses about individual-level support—it is worth describing, since it will inform the choice of control variables in the empirical analysis.

Of particular note, Gartner (1997) provides a theory of national-level public support for EMU and has tested it on Eurobarometer survey data. Gartner argued that variation in national-level support for EMU reflected the net gains the country's public expected from the move to a single currency. He modeled the public's preferences in terms of a loss function over inflation and income. Focusing particularly on the convergence requirements for entry into EMU, Gartner posited that the fiscal and monetary disciplinary gains from EMU were most beneficial for national economies with the lowest fiscal and monetary discipline. Thus, as the past inflation and the public debt/GDP ratio of a nation increased, that nation's public support for EMU increased.

Finally, Gartner took into consideration ERM membership. After the Treaty on European Union, national publics really had three choices: EMU membership, ERM (or ERM2) membership, or independence. Since the cost of EMU membership was higher in terms of national sovereignty than ERM membership, some national publics might have preferred the discipline associated with the ERM to that associated with EMU. Gartner argued that for a given observed inflation history, the more time the nation spent outside the ERM, the less utility its public expected from adopting the euro. Indeed, for a country like Greece with no ERM experience, the public could reasonably have expected that it could reduce inflation by moving into the ERM but without completely abandoning national sovereignty over monetary policy. Thus, Gartner expected public support for EMU to have increased with the number of years of ERM membership.

Gartner (1997) and Kaltenthaler and Anderson (1999) provided impressive evidence that national public support increased with the number of years in the ERM, the level of public debt/GDP, and the average level of inflation (since 1980).[5] Indeed, Gartner's model explained about 80 percent of the cross-national variance in public support for EMU.

In sum, previous research provides little evidence or theoretical guidance as to whether or how individual-level support for EMU varied with the distributional consequences of monetary integration. The primary question at issue in this chapter therefore remains open. In the next section, I use recent theoretical work to develop several hypotheses about how the distributional consequences of EMU related to variation in individual-level support; these are then tested in section three.

Theoretical Expectations

The economic self-interest approach to the politics of EMU assumes that political agents promote or oppose a policy depending on whether the policy increases or decreases their income. As I argued in the introduction, there are several reasons to consider EU citizens as relevant political actors for the politics of EMU. Thus, I am interested in testing the assumption that members of the general public adopted political attitudes (and, presumably, political behavior) consistent with their economic interests related to EMU. To construct an appropriate test, we must first determine theoretical expectations about the distributional consequences of EMU, which will identify which citizens were expected to support or oppose EMU.

There is a vigorous debate about the extent of national and EU-wide economic gains from EMU, as well as about the potential for asymmetric shocks and regional disparities.[6] What I will focus on are theoretical arguments about the distributional implications of EMU at the individual level (as opposed to the national or EU level). At the time of the survey data analyzed here (1993/94), joining EMU represented two different types of policies: a future fixed exchange rate policy with the other EMU member states and a commitment to attain (or maintain) low levels of public debt, public deficits, and inflation. Several scholars offer arguments about the distributional consequences of these policies across EU citizens. Below I briefly describe these theoretical arguments and identify testable hypotheses that connect the purported distributional consequences of EMU with variation in public support for EMU.

Trade-Related Distributional Consequences of Exchange Rate Stability

Several scholars have explored the distributional consequences of exchange rate stability. The basic story is that the value of exchange rate stability differs between producers of tradable goods and producers and consumers of nontradable goods (Eichengreen 1998b, p. 1005; Frieden 1994a). Frieden (1994a, p. 83) argues that, in a financially and commercially open economy such as the EU of the 1990s, monetary policy operates through the exchange rate, thereby changing the relative prices of tradable and nontradable goods and services. Thus, those employed in tradable and nontradable sectors will view differently the trade-off between national monetary policy independence and exchange rate stability. Specifically, those citizens' whose welfare depends on trade will support a fixed exchange rate with their trading partners because it eliminates exchange rate volatility. As Frieden (1996, p. 203) argues, "those involved in cross-border investment, traders and exporters of specialized manufactured products all tend to favor exchange-rate stability to reduce the risk associated with their business interests in other countries." In contrast, those citizens whose welfare does not depend on trade will prefer national monetary policy independence, since their fortunes depend on domestic business conditions. This latter group includes import-competing traded goods producers and nontradable producers.

In the context of EMU, these distributional effects should have translated into the following patterns of support for EMU. First, those citizens employed in sectors that export to other EU member states should have been more supportive of EMU than those employed in sectors that did not produce tradable goods. And, among those in tradable sectors, support for EMU should have increased with the amount of production for intra-EU export.

Due to data availability, I can only test this claim in an indirect fashion. The Eurobarometer surveys generally did not ask respondents in which sector of the economy they worked. However, in the three surveys I analyze, respondents were classified into four categories: public sector, nationalized industry, private industry, and private services. Applying the theoretical expectations to these groups, I hypothesize that members of the public sector (which is a nontradable sector) were less supportive of EMU than those employed in an industrial sector with at least some intra-EU exports. And, to the extent that services are largely domestically produced and consumed, I expect those respondents employed in services to have been less supportive than those employed in industry.[7]

Although I cannot identify which respondents from the industrial sector worked for firms that were involved in intra-EU exports, I can infer differences in sensitivity to intra-EU trade across industrial sector employees in different member states at the time of the survey. As I describe in the next section, I have constructed an indicator of the percent of total domestic industrial production that was exported to other EU member states.[8] I expect support for EMU to have increased with this indicator because, according to Frieden's argument, greater production for intra-EU export increases the value to industrial employees of fixed exchange rates between the EU member states. That is, respondents employed in national industrial sectors whose production was largely exported to other EU member states should have been more supportive of EMU than those employed in national industrial sectors whose production was consumed domestically and/or exported outside the EU.

The Politics of Inflation: Class-Based
Distributional Consequences of EMU

Oatley (1997) argues that the distributional consequences of EMU were related to the politics of inflation. The politics of inflation pit the interests of labor and Left political parties against the interests of capital and parties of the Right. The Left supports monetary policy that accommodates wage pressures and tight labor markets. The Right supports slack labor markets and restrictive monetary policy designed to preserve price stability. EMU, by institutionalizing price stability as the goal of monetary policy, settled this political conflict decidedly in the favor of capital and parties of the Right.

This argument has clear implications for connecting the distributive consequences of EMU membership with variation in public support for EMU. First, citizens who are employed as manual workers (labor) should have been less supportive of EMU than citizens employed in management/ownership occupations (executives and professionals). Second, since class conflict has traditionally defined the Left–Right dimension, citizens' placement on this spectrum should have related to their support for EMU. Specifically, citizens' support for EMU should have declined as their placement moved toward the Left end of the spectrum and support should have increased as their ideological placement moved toward the Right pole.

The Distributional Consequences of
Cross-Border Shopping and Price Transparency

Those citizens involved in cross-border commerce through cross-border shopping also stand to gain from a fixed exchange rate and a single currency. The elimination of barriers to the movement of goods and people in the EU created cross-border commercial opportunities that are enhanced by a single currency. Consumers residing near intra-EU borders can exploit price differences across nations due to VAT and excise tax rates. Retailers and the border economies in relatively low-tax nations gain from increased demand. EMU was therefore beneficial to these border residents by eliminating commissions on currency exchange and, probably most importantly, facilitating comparative shopping through price transparency.[9]

Thus, I expect residents of border regions to have been more supportive of EMU, on average, than nonborder residents. Also, I expect residents of border regions where price differentials are relatively large to value cross-border commerce (and thereby the single currency) more than border residents where price differences are relatively small. Consequently, among border residents, I expect support for EMU to have increased with the value of cross-border shopping.

The Distributional Consequences of Capital Market Liberalization

EMU also had distributive effects through its liberalization of capital markets. For Scheve (1999, p. 3), the primary economic consequence of EMU for EU citizens was the reduction in transaction costs for cross-border capital investments, thereby completing the capital mobility liberalization of the Single European Act. Scheve developed a formal model of redistributive policymaking (based on that of Persson and Tabellini 1992) that showed how monetary union reduces the amount of national government transfers. Wildasin (1995, 1998) reaches a similar conclusion based on models of factor mobility under economic integration. The result is a greater return on citizens' occupational skills and financial assets in an integrated capital market and lower spending on government programs.

Consequently, monetary union works to the advantage of those citizens with relatively high occupational skills and asset endowments but to the detriment of likely recipients of redistributive policies (for example, the poor). Applied to EMU, Scheve (1999, p. 8) predicted positive relationships between a citizen's support for EMU and (a) her income relative to the national income distribution, (b) her amount of capital assets, and (c) her occupational skills.

The Distributional Consequences of the Convergence Criteria

The convergence criteria required EMU applicants to attain a low level of inflation, public debt, and public deficit before entry into EMU. In 1993/94, the period I analyze, several member states needed to drastically reduce their national debt and deficits in order to qualify for EMU. While there was no common formula for rectifying the public deficits and debts, clearly there were several groups of citizens more likely to be disadvantaged by any reforms. First, the relatively poor citizens in each nation were more likely to depend on government spending for their income and welfare. The poor therefore stood to lose from their government's attempts to meet the convergence criteria. Consequently, I would expect a citizen's support for EMU to be positively related to her financial position relative to other citizens in her nation. This is the same distributional consequence as described by Scheve (1999).

Second, public employees and those in nationalized industries were likely targets for reductions in government spending through privatizations and restraints on public wages and benefits. This threat to employees of the public sector and nationalized industries increased with the size of their nation's public debt and public deficit. Thus, I expect these economic concerns related to EMU to vary with the size of the national public debt, with support for EMU among respondents in public jobs and nationalized industries inversely related to the size of their public debt.

Data and Measurement

To test these hypotheses, I analyze data from three Eurobarometer surveys merged with several economic indicators. The Eurobarometer survey is conducted in the fall and spring of each year in each member state and consists of roughly 1,000 respondents in each EU member state.[10] I use Eurobarometers 39 to 41, which cover spring 1993 to spring 1994. These were the only surveys with the necessary sectoral occupation question. Also, due to the availability of responses to necessary questions, I will restrict the analysis to citizens from the original twelve member states.

Ideally, I would prefer more recent surveys. It seems likely that the diffusion of information and cues about the costs and benefits of EMU to citizens grew over the 1990s. Thus, examining the hypotheses in the 1993/94 time period may pose a particularly difficult test.

These survey data were pooled into one dataset. The national surveys are analyzed together because I expect the hypotheses to have applied to the EU population and because testing several of the hypotheses requires cross-national variation. The pooling over time is due to the fact that, although the overall sample is large, the number of respondents in key categories (for example, residence in particular border areas) was often very small for any one survey and in any one country.

Dependent Variable

For the dependent variable, I use the following question:

> There should be a European Monetary Union with one single currency replacing by 1999 [National Currency] and all other national currencies of the Member States of the European Community.
>   Response: for; against; don't know

TABLE 3.1   Descriptive Statistics (full sample N = 26042)

Variable	Mean	Standard Deviation	Minimum	Maximum
Support for EMU	0.59	0.49	0	1
Consumer price difference[a] (ECU/1000 L unleaded motor fuel)	101.28	81.77	20	230
Retailer price difference[b] (ECU/1000 L unleaded motor fuel)	61.50	30.06	20	230
Private services	0.18	0.38	0	1
Private industry	0.24	0.43	0	1
Public employment	0.21	0.41	0	1
Nationalized industry	0.04	0.21	0	1
Trade sensitivity	0.23	0.24	0.01	0.8
Education	4.44	3.03	1	10
Income (quartiles)	1.56	1.12	0	3
Inflation average (1980–93)	5.67	1.11	4.25	7.97
Public debt (% of GDP for 1993)	73.11	27.46	10	138.4
Years in ERM	9.84	5.21	0	14
Left ideology	0.48	0.97	0	4
Right ideology	0.34	0.84	0	4

[a]N = 8415
[b]N = 3904

In the analyses reported here, I excluded responses of "don't know," which represented about 6 percent of the sample. However, the results of an analysis that included these respondents as an intermediate response category support very similar statistical inferences to those drawn here.[11] Descriptive statistics for this variable are presented in Table 3.1.

Explanatory Variables

To distinguish respondents according to their sector of the economy, I created four dummy variables based on the following survey question.

To those who do or did paid work, are you/were you in . . . ?[12]
   1. Public Employment
   2. Nationalized Industry
   3. Private Industry
   4. Private Services

To test whether, among respondents in industry, support for EMU increased with the sensitivity of their national industrial sector to intra-EU trade, I created an interaction term. To measure the sensitivity of the national industrial sector to intra-EU trade, I divided the total value of manufacturing exports to the EU in the survey year for each member state by the total value of manufacturing production in the survey year in that member state.[13] This indicator, called *trade sensitivity*, was then interacted with a dummy for industrial employment—called *industry*, which included respondents in both nationalized and private industry. The expectation is that, across those employed in industry, support for EMU increased with *trade sensitivity*.

To test the class-conflict hypothesis, I created three occupational dummy variables: *manual worker, executive*, and *professional*. I expect manual workers to represent unskilled workers, which are a key component of the working class. I expect executives and professionals to represent interests of capital and management. The theoretical expectation is that manual laborers were less supportive of EMU than professionals or executives.

I also created two variables to measure Left–Right ideology, which Oatley identifies as indicative of class conflict. The Eurobarometer survey includes a question asking respondents to place themselves on a ten-point Left–Right scale. Previous studies have shown that respondents understand the meaning of this scale and that it translates effectively across nations (Huber 1987; and see Gabel and Huber 2000). The first variable, *left ideology*, is coded zero if a respondent self-identified at five and the variable is coded so that it increases as scores approach one, the left-most position. Similarly, the variable *right ideology* is coded zero for a response of six and is coded so that it increases as the scores approach ten, the right-most position. Thus, both variables range from zero to four, with higher scores representing more extreme ideological positions. The theoretical expectation is that *left ideology* is negatively associated with support for EMU and that *right ideology* is positively related to support for EMU.

To test the hypothesis related to cross-border shopping, I first distinguished respondents by whether or not they resided in a region along an intra-EU land border.[14] I created a dummy variable, *border resident*, coded one for border residents, zero otherwise. The expectation is that border expressed greater support for EMU than nonborder residents.

Second, I created a proxy variable to distinguish among border residents according to the value of cross-border shopping at their border. A 1993 Price Waterhouse study demonstrated that the most important determinant of cross-border shopping was the difference in the price of motor fuel at that border. Specifically, the frequency of cross-border shopping was positively related to the difference in the price of motor fuel at the border. From this finding, I infer that the value to border residents of cross-border shopping increases with the price differential for motor fuel at that border.

I created two variables, based on the absolute value of the difference in the price (in ecu) of 1,000 liters of unleaded motor fuel in the bordering nations in 1993.[15] The first variable, *consumer price difference*, is coded as this price differential only for residents of the relatively high-price side of the border, and zero otherwise. The second variable, *retailer price difference*, is coded as this price difference for residents of the relatively low-price side of the border, and zero otherwise. The reason for creating two variables is to avoid imposing an assumption that the consumer and retailer effects are equal. These variables were then interacted with the variable *border resident*. I expect a positive coefficient for both interaction terms, as I expect support for EMU to have increased with the value to consumers and retailers of cross-border shopping.

To test the hypotheses due to Scheve (1999) about the effects of capital market liberalization on support for EMU, I constructed two variables. First, Scheve predicted that support for EMU increased with a respondent's income relative to the national distribution of income. Relatively poor respondents in a nation faced fewer fiscal transfers due to EMU and wealthier respondents benefited from higher returns on their assets. To test this hypothesis, I include a variable called *income*, which ranges from zero (lowest quartile) to three (highest quartile) according to where the respondent's income falls in the national income distribution. The expectation is that *income* had a positive relationship with support for EMU. Note that this is also a prediction consistent with the expected distributional consequences of the convergence criteria.

Second, Scheve argued that support for EMU increased with occupational skills.[16] Following Scheve, I use the respondent's level of education as a proxy for occupational skills. I created the variable *education*, which indicates the age at which the respondent finished his formal education. This variable is coded 1 for respondents who finished their education before age fifteen. The variable increases with each year of further education (for example, age 15 is coded as 2). The highest value for this variable is 10, indicating the respondent finished his education after age 22 or is still studying.[17] I expect respondents' support for EMU to have increased with their years of education.

Finally, to capture the distributional effects of the convergence criteria, I created variables to capture the differential effects of the convergence criteria across members of the public sector and nationalized industries. I created two interaction terms. First, I interacted a respondent's national public debt as percent of GDP in the survey year with the dummy variable for public sector employment. Second, I interacted a respondent's national public debt as percent of GDP in the survey year with the dummy variable for nationalized industry employment. The expectation is that, as the size of the public debt increased across members of these economic sectors, support for EMU decreased.

Control Variables

As described in the second section, there are theoretical and empirical reasons for expecting national-level factors to have influenced support for EMU. This is an important issue for this research design because all respondents in Luxembourg and Denmark are coded as border residents. Thus, any results on the *border region* variable or its interaction effects could be confounded by national-level factors. In addition, I want to be sure that the interaction terms measuring cross-national differences within economic sectors are not simply capturing national differences. Consequently, I include the variables identified by Gartner (1997) to account for national-level variation in support: the average national inflation performance from 1980 through the survey year; the national public debt as percent of GDP in the survey year; and the number of years the nation has been in the ERM as of the survey year.[18]

I also control for a variety of socioeconomic characteristics (for example, gender, age, and occupation) found in previous studies to relate to support for European integration and that might confound the relationships between the explanatory variables and support for EMU. (The coefficients for these variables from the analyses presented here are available from the author upon request.) The coding of these variables is described in the appendix. Finally, I should note that I would like to control for national pride, which if correlated with particular occupational sectors could confound the relationships estimated here. Unfortunately, the surveys I analyze did not provide appropriate questions.

Model Estimation

To examine the hypothesized relationships I estimated a heteroskedastic probit model. The probit model is appropriate since the dependent variable is dichotomous, coded one if the respondent is in favor of EMU, and zero if against. Note that I do not account for any time-series issues with the data. The data consist of individual-level, nonpanel observations. Moreover, the data cover only three time points.

I am concerned, however, with the assumption of homoskedasticity: a common error variance across respondents. Because citizens may have diverged in their informational environment and/or their ability to process information about EMU, they may have differed in the variability or ambivalence of their opinions on EMU. These differences would have resulted in heteroskedasticity in the survey data analyzed here. If not accounted for, heteroskedasticity causes misleading standard errors for the parameter estimates.

There are two basic responses to this problem in this data setting (see Beck and Tucker 1996). First, I can attempt to model the heteroskedasticity by specifying the sources of differences in error variance across respondents. As just mentioned, EU citizens may have differed systematically in the stability of their survey responses due to their ability to process political information and their exposure to relevant information (Zaller 1992; Alvarez and Brehm 1995). Specifically, a citizen's level of political awareness and her national media/information environment may have influenced her ability to identify her economic interests and to convey these interests in her survey responses. Zaller (1992) emphasizes the importance of political awareness in opinion formation and indicates that citizens' survey responses are less ambivalent or variable as their level of political awareness increases. Zaller (1992, p. 65) states:

> More aware persons are more likely to possess the cueing messages necessary to respond to incoming information in a critical manner. As a result, they are more likely to accept only information that is consistent. This will tend to increase the homogeneity of the considerations from which politically aware persons sample, which will tend to increase their response stability.

Thus, we would expect the error variance to have decreased systematically with the level of a respondent's political awareness.

In addition, citizens may have differed in the variability of their survey responses due to the quality and quantity of information about EMU that their national media environments provide. In particular, since France and Denmark had recently held referenda on the Maastricht Treaty at the time of the survey, their citizens may have been exposed to a particularly rich informational environment regarding EMU. Consequently, respondents from France and Denmark may have expressed attitudes toward EMU that were less ambivalent (less variable) than the attitudes of respondents from other countries. For these reasons, it appears unrealistic to assume homoskedasticity in this probit model. Thus, I need to test for and model the heteroskedasticity to generate consistent parameter estimates.

Following Alvarez and Brehm (1995) and Greene (1993, p. 649), I address this problem by modeling a multiplicative heteroskedastic error variance (Harvey 1976). Specifically, I estimate an error variance model such that respondents from France and Denmark have separate parameters. Also, I estimate a parameter for the level of the respondent's political awareness, which I will measure by level of education.[19] According to Zaller (1992), political awareness is positively related to level of education. The expectation is that the higher education levels and Danish and

French citizenships will be associated with smaller error variances than the rest of the sample.

A second solution to the problem of heteroskedasticity is to estimate robust standard errors. Since the aforementioned model of the error variance may be insufficient to account for all heteroskedasticity, I have also adopted this second solution and estimated Huber (1967) robust standard errors for all parameters.

Statistical Results

Table 3.2 reports the results for two heteroskedastic probit models. The first model includes the explanatory and control variables described above. The second model includes controls for nationality. While I have attempted to include theoretically meaningful variables to control for national factors that might influence support for EMU, there is always the chance that some national effects remain. The advantage of this second specification is that it ensures that no unmeasured national effects bias the results. The main disadvantage of this specification is that, the parameter estimates exclusively reflect the impact of the independent variables on intranational variation in support for EMU.

For some hypotheses, this effectively excludes much of the variation in the independent variables from the analysis. For example, some nations (for example, Denmark) have no intranational variation in the price differential for gasoline in a given year, and little difference in the price differential between 1993 and 1994. Thus, the parameter estimates for the independent variables designed to test for the effects of cross-border commerce are based almost exclusively on observations in the nations with border regions that vary in price differentials. And these intranational differences are generally much smaller than the cross-national differences. Similarly, cross-national differences in public deficit and trade sensitivity are also ignored. Since the only intranational variation in these variables is over time and is generally quite small, the bulk of the variation in these variables is omitted from analysis. Consequently, this model specification provides a poor test of the hypotheses related to these variables.

In contrast, the hypotheses for income, education, occupation, and ideology apply to intranational comparisons. The variables designed to test these hypotheses demonstrate considerable intranational variation. Moreover, given the measurement of these variables, the hypotheses call for intranational comparisons. A particular number of years of education may not represent the same level of occupational skills across nations, but within a nation human capital should increase with years of education. Similarly, income is measured in national quartiles, calling for intra-

TABLE 3.2 Heteroskedastic Probit Models of Public Support for EMU

Choice Model	Model 1	Model 2
Constant	−0.60*	−3.76*
	(0.057)	(0.62)
Private industry	−0.23*	−0.073*
	(0.035)	(0.022)
Industry* trade sensitivity	0.84*	0.20*
	(0.079)	(0.072)
Public employment	−0.17*	−0.065
	(0.058)	(0.048)
Public employment* public debt	0.0014	0.0004
	(0.0007)	(0.0006)
Nationalized industry	−0.25	0.022
	(0.12)	(0.11)
Nationalized industry* public debt	−0.0005	−0.0016
	(0.002)	(0.0018)
Private services	−0.050	−0.034
	(0.022)	(0.020)
Border resident	−0.88*	−0.042
	(0.052)	(0.047)
Border resident* consumer price difference	0.0085*	0.0007
	(0.0004)	(0.0004)
Border resident* retailer price difference	0.013*	0.0012
	(0.0009)	(0.0008)
Income	0.035*	0.028*
	(0.007)	(0.006)
Education	0.012*	0.013*
	(0.0026)	(0.0028)
Manual laborer	−0.040	−0.021
	(0.040)	(0.035)
Executive	0.056	0.071
	(0.042)	(0.039)
Professional	0.11	0.15*
	(0.053)	(0.051)
Right ideology	0.007	0.012
	(0.009)	(0.0077)
Left ideology	−0.030*	−0.020*
	(0.0077)	(0.0072)
Inflation history	0.0085*	−0.044*
	(0.003)	(0.0092)
Public debt	0.014*	0.0024
	(0.0006)	(0.0034)
Years in ERM	−0.017*	0.25*
	(0.0019)	(0.047)

(continues)

TABLE 3.2   *(continued)*

Choice Model	Model 1	Model 2
France	–	0.59*
		(0.054)
Belgium	–	0.67
		(0.31)
Netherlands	–	0.57*
		(0.11)
United Kingdom	–	2.56*
		(0.48)
Italy	–	1.27*
		(0.26)
Denmark	–	0.062
		(0.12)
Ireland	–	1.03*
		(0.17)
Luxembourg	–	0.83*
		(0.17)
Spain	–	3.02*
		(0.45)
Portugal	–	4.10*
		(0.60)
Greece	–	4.41*
		(0.72)
Germany	–	–
Variance Model		
France	13.87*	–0.52*
	(0.12)	(0.18)
Denmark	–1.00*	–1.16*
	(0.13)	(0.16)
Education	–0.005	–0.007
	(.006)	(.005)
Heteroskedasticity Test		
Likelihood ratio (x^2)	15103.31*	53.72*
Goodness of Fit Test		
Percent correctly predicted	67%	71%
N	26042	26042

*0.01 significance level

national comparison. And the comparison of ideological positions is probably most appropriate in a national political system, which defines that range and content of the Left–Right dimension. Consequently, the model specification provides appropriate tests of these hypotheses.

Results

Across both models, the results are consistent with several hypotheses based on the distributional consequences of capital market liberalization. As expected, respondents from the lowest quartile of their national income distribution expressed less support for EMU than those from the highest income quartile. For example, in Model 1 the likelihood of supporting EMU increased from 0.64 to 0.68 due to a change from lowest to highest quartile.[20] This is consistent with the expectations of Scheve (1999) and the distributional consequences of the convergence criteria. Also, support for EMU was positively related to level of education, which serves here as a proxy for occupational skills. In Model 1, a respondent who finished her education before age fifteen had, on average, a 0.66 probability of supporting EMU while a respondent who finished education after age 22 had a 0.70 probability of supporting EMU. Thus, public support for EMU varied consistently with the distributional consequences of capital market liberalization identified by Scheve (1999). However, these effects are not substantively large.

The results are also consistent with the hypotheses based on the distributional consequences of exchange rate stability. The expectation that employees of industry were more supportive of EMU than employees in either the public sector or in private services is difficult to assess because of the interaction of private and nationalized industry with trade sensitivity. The average private industrial employee was employed in an economy where 24 percent of manufacturing production went to intra-EU exports. Thus, for the average private industrial employee, the combined parameter estimate in Model 1 is $(0.24)(0.84) + (-0.23) = -0.028$. The average employee of nationalized industry was employed in an economy where 15 percent of manufacturing production went to intra-EU exports. Thus, for the average employee of nationalized industry, the combined parameter estimate is $(0.15)(0.84) = 0.13$.

Now, we can compare the estimated probability of being in favor of EMU across employees of private and nationalized industry, the public sector, and private services. The probability that a private industrial employee favored EMU is 0.66, that a nationalized industry employee favored EMU is 0.72, that a public sector employee favored EMU is 0.61, and that a private services employee favored EMU is 0.67. Clearly, there is no strong distinction here between the industrial employees and those in the public and services sectors.

However, recall that the hypothesis of sectoral differences in support was predicated on the assumption that industrial sector employees were more sensitive to intra-EU trade than those in the public and services sector.[21] If we compare the industrial sector employees who were the most sensitive to intra-EU trade, the sectoral difference in support for EMU was clearly consistent with expectations. As trade sensitivity increased across industrial sector employees, support for EMU rose. At the upper limit (trade sensitivity = 0.80), a private sector industrial employee had a probability of 0.89 of favoring EMU in Model 1. An employee of a nationalized industry had a 0.87 probability of favoring EMU. Thus, the sectoral differences were apparent when comparing the members of the industrial sector who were the most sensitive to intra-EU trade with those in nontradable sectors. As expected, these sectoral differences were considerably smaller when calculated for Model 2, but the results are consistent with the same conclusions. Thus, variation in public support for EMU—particularly of Model 1—was consistent with the distributional consequences of exchange rate stability identified by Frieden (1994a).

The results for the class-conflict variables are generally consistent with the hypotheses based on the distributional consequences of EMU related to the inflation. In both models, respondents who identified themselves as ideologically Left were less supportive of EMU than self-identifiers of the Right. In Model 1, the strongest Left respondent had a 0.63 likelihood of supporting EMU while respondents who were in the middle of the ideological dimension or on the Right had a likelihood of 0.67. It is also worth noting that the coefficient for Right ideology is in the expected direction in both models, but is only significant at about the 0.10 level. The results for the occupational dummy variables provide little supporting evidence for the class-based hypothesis. Across both models, professionals were more supportive (at the 0.05 level) of EMU than manual workers. However, there was no difference in the level of support between executives and manual workers.

As for the effects of cross-border commerce, the results provide some evidence consistent with expectations. In Model 1, support for EMU increased with the value of cross-border shopping for residents of both the "consumer" and "retailer" sides of the border. This is consistent with expectations. Note that in Model 1 the coefficient for *border resident* is negative, but the effect of border residence on support for EMU depended on the price differential at the border where the respondent resides. A border resident of a border with the lowest observed price difference (20 ecu/1,000 l.) was, on average, less supportive of EMU than a nonborder resident.[22] This is inconsistent with expectations. However, residents of border regions with the highest price difference (230 ecu/1,000 l.) were much more supportive of EMU than nonborder residents. At this price difference in Model 1, a "consumer" border resident had a 0.94 probability of supporting EMU and a "retailer" border resident had a 0.99 probability of supporting EMU. A nonborder resident had a 0.67 probability of supporting EMU. This finding is consistent with the expectation that support for EMU varies with the benefits of cross-border commerce due to a single currency.

This border effect disappears in Model 2, since the coefficients lose statistical significance. As discussed earlier, this was expected due to the inclusion of national dummy variables, eliminating cross-national variation in border effects from the analysis.

Other results are not consistent with expectations. First, for employees of the public sector and nationalized industries, support for EMU was not related to the size of their public debt as a percentage of GDP, as expected due to the convergence criteria.[23] Second, manual workers did not show a statistically significant difference in support for EMU from executives, although they were on average less supportive of EMU than professionals in Model 2.

The results are partially consistent with the expectations for the national-level control variables. In Model 1, support for EMU increased with the average historical level of inflation and the size of the public debt in the respondent's nation. However, the number of years in the ERM was negatively related to support for EMU. When controls are included for nationality, the results for these variables change dramatically. This is understandable, given that the model effectively includes multiple proxy variables for the same national effects and there are only three time points (Achen 1985).

Finally, it is important to note that, for each model, the likelihood-ratio test indicates that we can reject (at the 0.01 level) the null hypothesis that the error variances are homoskedastic. Thus, the error variance model is capturing at least some of the heteroskedasticity. In addition, the results of the error variance model meet some of the theoretical expectations. The error variance is smaller for the Danish than the baseline respondent in both models and is smaller for the French than the baseline respondent in Model 2.[24] It is important to note that in a heteroskedastic probit model, the effects of the explanatory variables increase as the error variance decreases. Thus, in Model 2, the effects of the explanatory variables are larger for French and Danish respondents than for respondents from other member states.

However, inconsistent with expectations, the error variance does not vary across respondents with their level of education. The coefficients for the education parameter in the variance models are all negative, as expected. But these coefficients do not reach conventional levels of statistical significance.

Discussion

A commonly assumed, yet rarely tested, claim in the study of international political economy is that domestic political agents behave so as to further their economic goals related to international economic policy. In particular, some scholars assume that voters connect their economic interests to their political attitudes and behavior regarding international economic policies. Yet there is little evidence to that effect, due largely to the lack of empirical study. This chapter has empirically examined this assumption in the context of public support for economic and monetary union. Based on several theoretical claims about the distributional consequences of EMU, I have examined the relationship between variation in citizens' support for EMU and differences in their expected economic gains/losses from EMU. The analysis reveals that EU citizens did indeed vary in their support for EMU consistent with their economic interests related to the distributional consequences of EMU. These results have important implications for our theoretical conception of the politics of monetary unification in Europe.

Many studies of international economic policy in general and European monetary unification in particular suffer from a level-of-analysis problem (Eichengreen 1998b, p. 1002).[25] Scholars who employ the economic self-interest model in the study of international economic policymaking often assume that a government's preference in international negotiations reflects its nation's economic interests. However, scholars often leave unopened the black box of how this national preference is formed. Instead, they rely on an assumption that the relevant political actors in the national context pursue their economic interests regarding the international economic policy at issue, thereby endowing the national government with a preference that represents an aggregation of economic interests concerning that policy.

This chapter, by providing a test of this assumption, supports the application of the economic self-interest model to the politics of EMU. The analysis presented here provides evidence at the individual level that citizens adopted political attitudes (and, presumably, behavior) that were consistent with their economic self-interest regarding international economic policy. Moreover, these results obtain in a time period (1993/94) that provides a particularly difficult test of the hypotheses.

In addition, the results contribute to resolving the theoretical debate about which distributional effects of EMU were politically relevant—at least at the mass level. Some scholars contend that the reduced risk in cross-border commerce from a fixed exchange rate accounted for intranational variation in support for EMU. Others argue that EMU was politically divisive because of the consequences of capital market liberalization for redistributive policies and returns on citizens' assets. Still another scholar posits that the politically salient aspect of EMU was that the fixed exchange rate regime imposed restrictive monetary policy on its members, which benefits capital at labor's expense. The empirical analysis provides fairly robust evidence for all three of these claims.

The empirical analysis also indicates that the convergence criteria, particularly the requirement of reduced public debt, had no effect on support for EMU among citizens employed in the public sector. This is a surprising result given that some national governments instituted dramatic reforms of public spending in order to meet the convergence criteria.

It is important to note that the theoretical expectations of the distributional consequences of EMU are also applicable to the politics of the euro. Distributional issues related to a fixed exchange rate, exchange rate stability, inflation, capital market liberalization, and price transparency are all relevant for a European single currency. Thus, to the extent that citizens form attitudes toward the euro in a similar fashion to their attitudes toward EMU, these results have several implications for the politics of the euro. For one, these findings suggest that variation in the distribution of trade by EU member states could upset the balance of domestic political coalitions favoring a single currency. For example, if German industrial exporters were to shift their trade from the EU eastwards (particularly if EU enlargement is postponed), then the analysis indicates that German public support for fixed exchange rates (and thus a single currency) with other EU member states will decline.[26] Specifically, support for the euro among Germans working in the industrial sectors would decline. In contrast, if commercial integration (intra-EU trade as a portion of EU GDP) in the EU continues to increase, then the number of citizens supporting the euro should also increase.

Second, the empirical results indicate that efforts toward tax harmonization may influence the level of public support for the euro. Recent efforts at tax harmonization, particularly harmonization of VAT and excise taxes, may cause a reduction in national price differences for consumer goods. Reduced price differences, in turn, diminish the incentives for cross-border shopping and the value of price transparency provided by a single currency. The results of the analysis suggest that residents of border regions are sensitive to these incentives for cross-border shopping when evaluating a common currency. Specifically, border residents were increasingly supportive of EMU as the price difference at their border increased. Consequently, any reduction in price differences due to tax harmonization is likely to decrease support for the euro among border residents. Since border regions represent significant portions of some nations (for example, Luxembourg is border region), this may have a significant effect on national public support for the euro in some countries.

Appendix: Control Variables

I included control variables for age (in years), gender (female = 1), education (see note 14), and the following occupational categories based on the Eurobarometer survey question concerning the occupation of the respondent:

1. homemaker
2. student
3. service job
4. fisherman
5. supervisor
6. clerical worker
7. retired
8. farmer
9. unemployed

Notes

1. The author thanks John Hajner for assistance with data collection, Steve Voss for methodological advice, and participants at the PEEI Meeting at UC-Berkeley, March 5, 1999 for helpful comments and suggestions on an earlier version of this chapter.

2. On low-information opinion formation, see Lupia and McCubbins (1998). See Gabel (1998a, 40) for a discussion more specific to the context of European integration.

3. On public opinion trends, see *European Public Opinion on the Single Currency*, January 1999. Special Edition of *Europinion*, DG X/A2.

4. But see Dalton and Eichenberg (1998) for a descriptive assessment of support for integration in a variety of policy areas, including EMU.

5. Kaltenthaler and Anderson (1999) also considered central bank independence as an independent variable. Gartner (1997) demonstrated that inflationary history (1980–1995) is a better indicator of the public's expectation of inflationary performance than central bank independence. Thus, in my empirical analysis I will not include central bank independence.

6. There is an extensive literature on these issues. See, for example, Hall and Franzese 1998; Eichengreen 1998a; Eichengreen and Frieden 1997; Goodhart 1995; Bean 1992; and Eichengreen 1992.

7. The survey question is not detailed in defining "services." Thus, it probably included respondents working as waiters and barbers, as well as international financial consultants.

8. I am implicitly assuming here that survey respondents, on average, assumed that EMU involves fixed exchange rates with all other EU member states, not a subset.

9. Some cross-border shoppers avoid paying commission on exchange by using credit cards. But, according to *The Economist* (September 25, 1999, p. 92), a significant currency transaction cost for cross-border retail shopping remains. Indeed, this cost is sufficiently large to attract the concern of the European Central Bank.

10. As will be apparent in the analysis, a considerable number of respondents are deleted from the analysis due to missing data.

11. Results from ordered probit analyses of the models estimated in the next section are available from the author upon request.

12. About 5 percent of respondents answered "don't know."

13. I was not able to find industrial data comparably coded so as to create a more general measure of industry sensitivity to intra-EU trade. The data used to construct this measure were from *Eurostat: External and Intra-EU Trade 1994* and *Eurostat Yearbook 1997*. Both the industrial production and the trade data were measured in 1994 ecus.

14. I used the smallest geographic unit available in the Eurobarometer. In most cases that was a province. But for Denmark and Luxembourg it was the entire nation.

15. The price data are from the *Excise Duty Tables* 1993.

16. Scheve also posited that support for EMU would increase with a respondent's amount of capital assets. A measure of capital assets was not available, so I do not test this hypothesis.

17. Note that if a respondent was currently studying, she was assigned the level of education corresponding to her age.

18. Economic data were collected from *Eurostatistics* (various years).

19. Zaller (1992) concluded that level of education is an appropriate proxy for political awareness, in the absence of information concerning a respondent's objective political knowledge. Education is coded the same as the variable *education*, described above.

20. For this and all ensuing calculations, I estimated the probabilities at the median value for all continuous variables and at the modal category for all dummy variables.

21. I do not take into account the interactive effect of public employment or nationalized industry with public debt because the coefficients on the interaction terms are not significantly different from zero.

22. The net border effect for the "retailer" residents is $(20)(0.013) - 0.88 = -0.62$ and the net border effect for "consumer" residents is $(20)(0.0085) - 0.88 = -0.71$.

23. This is also true when public deficit as percent of GDP is used in place of public debt.

24. The baseline is citizen of a nation other than France or Denmark.

25. See Frieden (1996) for an example of such aggregate-level analysis based on assumptions about domestic politics consistent with the economic self-interest approach. Frieden (1996) offers evidence from within France and Italy to describe how affected interests behave in the domestic arena to promote their interests regarding European monetary policy.

26. Of course, it also depends on the exchange rates between the euro and the currency of the trading partner.

Bibliography

Achen, Christopher, 1985, Proxy variables and incorrect signs on regression coefficients. *Political Methodology* 11, 299–316.

Alvarez, Michael and John Brehm, 1995, American ambivalence towards abortion policy: Development of a heteroskedastic probit model of competing values. *American Journal of Political Science* 39:4, 1055–1082.

Anderson, Christopher J., and M. S. Reichert, 1996, Economic benefits and support for membership in the E.U.: A cross-national analysis. *Journal of Public Policy* 15, 231–249.

Baldwin, Robert, 1989, The political economy of trade policy. *The Journal of Economic Perspectives* 3:4, 119–135.

Barro, Robert, 1986, Reputation in a model of monetary policy with incomplete information. *Journal of Monetary Economics* 17:1, 1–20.

Barro, Robert, and David Gordon, 1983, Rules, discretion, and reputation in a model of monetary policy. *Journal of Monetary Economics* 12:1, 101–120.

Bean, Charles, 1992, Economic and monetary union. *The Journal of Economic Perspectives* 6:4, 31–52.

Beck, Nathaniel, and Richard Tucker, 1996, Conflict in space and time: Time-series-cross-section analysis with a binary dependent variable. Paper presented at the 1996 Annual Meeting of the American Political Science Association, San Francisco, August 29–September 1, 1996.

Cameron, David, 1997, Economic and monetary union: Underlying imperatives and third-stage dilemmas. *Journal of European Public Policy* 4, 455–485.

Carrubba, Clifford, 1997, Net financial transfers in the European union: Who gets what and why? *Journal of Politics* 59, 469–496.

_____, forthcoming, The electoral connection in European union politics. *Journal of Politics*.

Cassing, James, Timothy McKeown, and Jack Ochs, 1986, The political economy of the tariff cycle. *American Political Review* 80, 843–862.

Dalton, Russell, and Richard Eichenberg, 1998, Citizen support for policy integration, in: Wayne Sandholtz and Alec Stone Sweet, eds., *European integration and supranational governance* (Oxford: Oxford University Press).

Davidson, Russell, and James G. MacKinnon, 1993, *Estimation and inference in econometrics* (New York: Oxford University Press).

Eichenberg, Richard, 1998, Measures, methods, and models in the study of public opinion and European integration, 1973–1997. Paper presented at the Annual Meeting of the American Political Science Association, Boston, Mass., September 3–6.

Eichengreen, Barry, 1992, Should the Maastricht treaty be saved? Princeton Studies in International Finance 74 (Princeton: International Finance Section). Located at http://ideas.uqam.ca/ideas/data/fthprinfi.html.

_____, 1998a, *European monetary unification* (Cambridge. Mass.: MIT Press).

_____, 1998b, Dental hygiene and nuclear war: How international relations looks from economics. *International Organization* 52:4, 993–1012.

Eichengreen, Barry, and Jeffry Frieden, eds., 1997, *The political economy of European monetary integration* (Ann Arbor, Mich.: University of Michigan Press).

Eurostatistics, Excise Duty Tables: Situation at 1–1–93 (Luxembourg: Commission of the European Communities).

Frieden, Jeffry, 1991, Invested interests: The politics of national economic policies in a world of global finance. *International Organization* 45, 425–451.

_____, 1994a, Exchange rate politics: Contemporary lessons from American history. *Review of International Political Economy* 1, 81–102.

_____, 1994b, Monetary populism in nineteenth-century America: An open economy interpretation. *The Journal of Economic History* 57, 367–395.

_____, 1996, The impact of goods and capital market integration on European monetary politics. *Comparative Political Studies* 29, 193–222.

Frieden, Jeffry, Daniel Gros, and Erik Jones, eds., 1998, T*he new political economy of EMU* (New York: Rowman and Littlefield).

Gabel, Matthew, 1998a, *Interests and integration: Market liberalization, public opinion, and European union* (Ann Arbor, Mich.: University of Michigan Press).

_____, 1998b, Economic integration and mass politics: Market liberalization and public attitudes in the European union. *American Journal of Political Science* 42:3, 936–953.

_____, 1998c, Public support for European integration: An empirical test of five theories. *Journal of Politics* 60:2, 333–354.

Gabel, Matthew, and John Huber, 2000, Putting parties in their place: Inferring party left-right ideological positions from manifestos data. *American Journal of Political Science* 44:1, 94–103.

Gabel, Matthew, and Harvey D. Palmer, 1995, Understanding variation in public support for European integration. *European Journal of Political Research* 27, 3–19.

Gartner, Manfred, 1997, Who wants the euro—and why? Economic explanations of public attitudes towards a single European currency. *Public Choice* 93, 487–510.

Goodhart, Charles, 1995, The political economy of monetary union, in: Peter Kenen, ed., *Understanding interdependence* (Princeton: Princeton University Press).

Greene, William H., 1993, *Econometric analysis*, 3rd ed. (Upper Saddle River, N.J.: Prentice Hall).

Hall, Peter, and Robert Franzese, 1998, Mixed signals: Central bank independence, coordinated wage bargaining, and European monetary union. *International Organization* 52:3, 505–533.

Harvey, Andrew, 1976, Estimating regression models with multiplicative heteroskedasticity, *Econometrica* 44, 461–465.

Henning, Randall, 1998, Systemic conflict and regional integration: The case of Europe. *International Organization* 52:3, 537–573.

Huber, John, 1989, Values and partisanship in left-right orientations: Measuring ideology. *The European Journal of Political Research* 17, 599–621.

Huber, Peter J., 1967, The behavior of maximum likelihood estimates under nonstandard conditions, in: *Proceedings of the Fifth Annual Berkeley Symposium on Mathematical Statistics and Probability*, Vol. 1 (Berkeley: University of California Press, 221–233).

Kaltenthaler, Karl, and Christopher Anderson, 1999, Europeans and their money: Explaining public support for the common European currency. Working Paper, Department of Political Science, SUNY-Binghamton.

Lupia, Arthur, and Mathew D. McCubbins, 1998, *The democratic dilemma: Can citizens learn what they need to know?* (New York: Cambridge University Press).

Magee, Stephen, William Brock, and Leslie Young, 1989, *Black hole tariffs and endogenous policy theory*. (New York: Cambridge University Press).

McNamara, Kathleen, 1998, *The currency of ideas* (Ithaca, N.Y.: Cornell University Press).

Nincic, Miroslav, 1992, A sensible public. *Journal of Conflict Resolution* 36, 772–789.

Oatley, Thomas, 1997, *Monetary politics* (Ann Arbor, Mich.: University of Michigan Press).

Persson, Torsten, and Buido Tabellini, 1992, The politics of 1992: Fiscal policy and European integration. *Review of Economic Studies* 59, 689–701.

Price Waterhouse, 1993, VAT and excise duties: Changes in cross-border purchasing following the abolition of fiscal frontiers on January 1993. Final report prepared for the Commission of the European Union DG XXI: C–3.

Scheve, Kenneth, 1999, European economic integration and electoral politics in France and Great Britain. Paper presented at the Annual Meetings of the American Political Science Association, Atlanta, August.

Wildasin, David, 1995, Factor mobility, risk, and redistribution in the welfare state. *Scandinavian Journal of Economics* 97:4, 527–546.

_____, 1998, Factor mobility and redistributive policy: Local and international perspectives, in: Peter Sorensen, ed. *Public finance in a changing world* (London: Macmillan).

Zaller, John, 1992, *The nature and origins of mass opinion* (Cambridge: Cambridge University Press).

4

A Retrial in the Case
Against the EMU

Local-Currency Pricing and
the Choice of Exchange Rate Regime

CHARLES ENGEL[1]

Abstract

Feldstein (1992, 1997) invokes Friedman's (1953) classic case for flexible exchange rates to argue that the single currency of the European
Monetary Union will hinder adjustments that might have occurred
through real exchange rate movements under a more flexible exchange rate system. The extent of local-currency pricing among European countries undermines this view. The prices that consumers pay
for imported goods are not much influenced by changes in nominal
exchange rates in the short run. The channels for adjustment through
relative price changes are considerably narrowed when local-currency
pricing predominates. New evidence is presented that reaffirms the
predominance of local-currency pricing for consumer prices in Europe. The optimum currency area analysis is reexamined in a
Mundell-Fleming framework with local-currency pricing.

There is little consensus among economists that Europe is well suited for
a single currency. Frequently, commentators offer the opinion that the
chief benefits of currency union for Europe are political, but that more

flexible exchange rates are preferable if the choice of monetary system were based solely on economic considerations. Feldstein (1992, 1997) perhaps most prominently expresses those views. If indeed Europe is not an "optimum currency area," the prospects for survival of the euro area may be dim. Europe might find the macroeconomic costs of maintaining the euro area too high, and may wish to revert back to a system of independent currencies with more flexible exchange rates.

But the case for flexible rates may be overstated. One of the pillars of the argument for floating exchange rates is that it allows for relative national price levels to adjust quickly even when goods prices adjust sluggishly. However, the existing body of empirical evidence (supplemented by some new work in this chapter) indicates that consumer prices do not react quickly to exchange rate changes. The critics of the euro have contended that eliminating national currencies will abolish a tool for macroeconomic adjustment. The evidence that exchange rates have little impact on consumer prices in the short run undermines that position.

The argument for more flexible rates in Europe is straightforward. Suppose there is some shock to the economy that requires prices of German goods to rise relative to the prices of French goods. For example, Eichengreen and Wyplosz (1993) argue that the fiscal expansion that followed German unification necessitated an increase in the price of German goods relative to other EMS countries. Such a relative price change has an automatic stabilizing effect on output. It leads to a trade balance deficit as Germans and other Europeans shift demand away from German goods toward goods produced in other countries.

How is this increase in the price of German goods to be achieved? In the traditional view of the macroeconomic adjustment process, the "law of one price" holds. Let P_G be the price of a good produced in Germany and sold in Germany. The price of that German-produced good sold in France is denoted $\Pi_G = P_G/E$, where E denotes the German currency price of French currency (that is, the mark price of francs in the pre-euro currency arrangement.) According to the traditional view, if an increase in Π_G relative to the price of the French good (Π_F) is required, there are two means by which that could be achieved: P_G could increase (or Π_F could fall); or, the exchange rate could decline. Friedman (1953) comments:

> If internal prices were as flexible as exchange rates, it would make little economic difference whether adjustments were brought about by changes in exchange rates or by equivalent changes in internal prices. But this condition is clearly not fulfilled. The exchange rate is potentially flexible in the absence of administrative action to freeze it. At least in the modern world, internal prices are highly inflexible.

Friedman advocates allowing exchange rates to remain floating on the grounds that relative price adjustment is less costly if it can occur through changes in the exchange rate rather than through changes in "internal prices." The latter change sluggishly and at differing speeds across different types of goods, resulting in "a distortion of adjustments in response to changes in external conditions." Friedman makes the following famous analogy:

> The argument for flexible exchange rates is, strange to say, very nearly identical with the argument for daylight saving time. Isn't it absurd to change the clock in summer when exactly the same result could be achieved by having each individual change his habits? All that is required is that everyone decide to come to his office an hour earlier, have lunch an hour earlier, etc. But obviously it is much simpler to change the clock that guides all than to have each individual separately change his pattern of reaction to the clock, even though all want to do so. The situation is exactly the same in the exchange market. It is far simpler to allow one price to change, namely, the price of foreign exchange, than to rely upon changes in the multitude of prices that together constitute the internal price structure.

Feldstein (1992) makes a similar argument when he advocates flexible exchange rates for Europe:

> A currency union means, of course, that nominal exchange rates cannot adjust to achieve a needed change in the real exchange rate. The local price level must, therefore, adjust to bring about the change in the real exchange rate. Thus a 10 percent fall in the real value of a currency can be achieved either by a 10 percent fall in the nominal exchange rate or by a 10 percent fall in local wages and prices.
>
> Either form of adjustment can bring the real exchange rate to its equilibrium value, but a decline in domestic prices is likely to require a period of increased unemployment. It would certainly be better to have a decline in the nominal exchange rate. The shift to a single currency in Europe would preclude such nominal exchange rate adjustments and force real exchange rate reductions to be achieved through lower local wages and prices.

In a similar vein, Obstfeld (1997) argues that Europe is not an optimum currency area, as defined by Mundell (1961). Floating exchange rates, he argues, would make adjustment to shocks much easier:

> Imagine, for example, an unexpected permanent fall in Spanish aggregate demand that the other EMU countries escape. An idiosyncratic national real shock such as this would not cause much depreciation of the euro against

other currencies, nor would it trigger monetary easing by the ECB [European Central Bank]. If EMU were an optimum currency area, Spanish workers would migrate to other EMU countries rather than facing unemployment at home. In reality, however, out-migration would be minimal, and unemployment would therefore persist until Spanish prices and costs had fallen enough to create an export-led recovery. The deflation process is a lengthy one. With its own currency, Spain would have the option of altering relative international prices more quickly through depreciation, at lower costs in terms of unemployment.

However, the Friedman-Feldstein analysis of the benefits of floating exchange rates is dependent on their view of how prices are set. In particular, it pays insufficient attention to the recent evidence of significant local-currency pricing.

Consider the simple law-of-one-price model that underlies the Friedman-Feldstein analysis. In this formulation, the German producer sets its price in deutsche marks. The price P_G is charged to German consumers and is unresponsive to changes in demand. When the mark appreciates the French franc price of the good sold to French consumers increases. The empirical evidence suggests that a better model of reality, at least for a large number of goods, is that German producers treat the German market for their goods separately from the French market. They choose a mark price, P_G, for the good sold in the German market, and a franc price, Π_G, for the good sold in the French market. Both of these prices are inflexible—neither responds when the exchange rate changes. The automatic stabilizing property of exchange rates vanishes when there is no "exchange-rate pass-through" to local prices. Likewise, the price of French goods does not fall for the German consumer, because the French firm sets a price in marks for selling its good to German consumers, at P_F (and a price in francs for French consumers, Π_F.)

There are, of course, real effects of the nominal exchange rate changes. When the mark appreciates, but Π_G, the French franc price of German-produced goods, does not change, the revenue (in mark terms) for the German firm declines. Conversely, the franc revenue for the French firm selling goods in Germany increases. There can be a channel through which the changes in firms' profits stabilize swings in aggregate demand. The decline in profits of German firms, and increase in profits of French firms, will have the effect of lowering demand in Germany and raising it in France.

But this channel for stabilization is likely to be much weaker than the one posited by Friedman and Feldstein. The exchange rate change does not induce consumers to switch demand away from German goods toward French goods. Instead, there is an income effect. Lower profits for German firms reduce income for German owners of those firms, and conversely in France. To the extent that spending in each country is biased toward goods produced in that country, there will be a relative increase in demand for French products resulting from the mark appreciation. This effect is likely not to be strong unless profits are a relatively large fraction of income, and there is a strong home-country bias in spending.

In fact, there are several considerations that weaken this profit channel for influencing aggregate demand. First, firms can hedge their foreign exchange exposure. By selling francs forward for marks at a sufficient number of horizons into the future, or making use of other derivative markets, the German firm can insulate its profits from short-run fluctuations in the exchange rate. Second, the firms may not need to protect their bottom line from foreign exchange fluctuations because firm owners might do the diversification. Our assumption so far has been that German consumers own German firms and French consumers own French firms. In fact, while there is a home bias in asset holdings, there has been an increasing degree of internationalization of financial markets. Particularly within Europe, in which there are few barriers to capital flows, international diversification of portfolios is on the rise. The income of a German who owns shares of both German firms and French firms will not be affected much by exchange rate changes.

Another consideration is the fact that many of the firm's costs are incurred in the foreign currency. In order to sell its product in France, the German firm must pay for advertising, distribution, and retailing in French francs. Particularly for consumer goods, these marketing and distribution costs can account for a significant fraction of the cost of the good. So the amount of exposure the German firm has to foreign exchange rate changes depends on the fraction of its costs that are in marks versus francs. Finally, a practical consideration is one of information. In the short run, the firm's foreign exchange profits or losses are not observed by shareholders who are not completely informed of the firm's foreign exchange exposure because the amount of hedging by the firm is not continuously reported. Frequently, the markets are not aware of significant gains or losses on foreign exchange markets until annual reports are compiled. So, even if the firm has not fully protected itself against foreign exchange fluctuations, the shareholders may not realize this and fail to adjust fully their assessment of the value of the firm.

Recent empirical studies suggest that consumer prices are not very responsive to exchange rate changes. For example, Engel (1993) finds that for differentiated consumer products, there is virtually no response of consumer prices to exchange rate changes, while the law of one price appears to hold much better for simple homogenous products such as fresh fruits and vegetables. Engel (1999) finds that well over 95 percent of real exchange rate movements among major industrialized countries are attributable to failures of the law of one price. However, studies of consumer prices suffer from the problem that the data do not distinguish the location of the producer of the products. Thus, the data do not account for the differences in the mix of products by location of producer in each buyer location. (That is, German consumer price indexes are likely to reflect a preponderance of German-produced goods, as compared to price indexes in other countries that give smaller weight to German-produced goods.) Keeping in mind that caveat, the greater unresponsiveness of consumer prices as compared to export prices suggests that the marketers and distributors of goods in the consumers' locale also must cushion the effect of exchange rate changes on prices by allowing their profit margins to vary with exchange rates.

To be clear, consideration of the implications of local-currency pricing do not constitute an argument for fixed exchange rates or for a single currency in Europe. It merely weakens the case for flexible exchange rates. Under the traditional argument, when regions are struck by asymmetric demand shocks, there may be large output responses in the regions if they share a common currency. So, according to this position, if Germany suffers an adverse fiscal shock, for example, then under the euro it will bear most of the burden in terms of reduced employment and output in the short run. Floating rates would, the reasoning goes, quickly lower prices of German output and encourage other economies in Europe to import German goods and boost their economy. But, the evidence presented indicates that consumer prices in Europe are not much affected by exchange rate changes. National currencies with adjustable exchange rates do not in practice offer such a strong and automatic stabilizing effect on the European economy. Of course, there are other arguments for national currencies, such as the fact that national currencies allow countries independence to conduct monetary policy.

In the section that follows, I present some new evidence on the failure of the law of one price in Europe. The evidence indicates there is local-currency pricing for consumer goods, and that consumer goods prices do not respond to exchange rate changes. Then in the next section, I formally review the argument for flexible exchange rates in the traditional Mundell-Fleming model, and demonstrate how that argument is refuted when there is little exchange-rate pass-through. The concluding section summarizes some of the shortcomings of this analysis and points to directions for future research.

Empirical Evidence

How do consumer prices in Europe respond to exchange rate changes? Consider the log of the price of a good, call it good i, p_{it} in one country relative to the log of the price of the same good in another country, π_{it}. Under the law of one price assumption, changes in $p_{it} - \pi_{it}$ should exactly match changes in the log of the exchange rate, e_t. Here, we examine that proposition taking two different approaches. If exchange rate changes worked their way into prices relatively rapidly, then annual changes in p_{it} − π_{it} should be highly correlated with annual changes in e_t; or, equivalently, annual changes in e_t should be nearly uncorrelated with annual changes in $e_t + \pi_{it} − p_{it}$. Alternatively, if there are short-term deviations from the law of one price that are eliminated over time, then $p_{it} − \pi_{it}$ should adjust when there are deviations from the law of one price.

We present evidence on both of these concepts of the law of one price using price index data for twenty-two categories of goods for nine European countries: Belgium, Denmark, Germany, Spain, France, Italy, the Netherlands, Portugal, and the United Kingdom. The data are monthly. The length of the series varies. The longest runs from January 1977 to December 1995, and the shortest runs from April 1982 to July 1995. Many of the series are monthly from January 1981 to July 1995. The data were obtained from Eurostat's consumer price database.[2]

The categories of consumer goods involve different levels of aggregation. Some of the series are highly aggregated: food, clothing and footwear, household equipment. Other categories are substantially more disaggregated: fruit, books, hotels. Clearly, none of the data is so disaggregated that it actually compares prices of identical products across countries.

Another shortcoming of the data, for our purposes, is that the data are indexes rather than price level data. Hence, we cannot examine directly the degree of failure of the law of one price. Instead, we can only infer failures by examining changes in $p_{it} − \pi_{it}$ and e_t.

First, consider the behavior of nominal exchange rates and relative prices. If the law of one price holds, there should be no correlation of the nominal exchange rate and the relative price, $p_{it} − \pi_{it}$. No economist would expect instantaneous changes in nominal prices in response to market changes. We interpret the short-run law of one price as saying that annual changes in the exchange rate are uncorrelated with annual changes in $e_t + \pi_{it} − p_{it}$. The upper triangle of the matrices in Table 4.1 report these correlations. In fact, these correlations are generally very high. For all but a few goods, the vast majority of correlation coefficients are over 0.70. Approximately half are over 0.90 for most goods. So the pattern of correlations is much closer to what one would expect in the extreme case of no exchange-rate pass-through than to the zero correlation predicted by the law of one price.

For some simple goods sold in relatively competitive markets (fruit and fuel and energy being notable examples), the correlations are lower—in the neighborhood of 0.30 to 0.40 for many country pairs. But for the categories of goods that include differentiated products sold by

TABLE 4.1 Correlations of Twelve-month Changes in Relative Prices and Nominal Exchange Rates; Estimated Response of Prices to Deviations from the Law of One Price

A) Food—Series 1110 (1/77–2/95)

	be	dk	de	es	fr	it	nl	pt	uk
be	–	0.432	0.725	0.888	0.613	0.836	0.726	0.673	0.926
dk	0.461*	–	0.53	0.921	0.773	0.932	0.554	0.671	0.938
de	0.513*	0.383*	–	0.853	0.583	0.811	0.572	0.615	0.961
es	0.347*	0.273*	0.338*	–	0.919	0.891	0.843	0.728	0.896
fr	0.652*	0.334	0.329*	0.303*	–	0.945	0.597	0.725	0.934
it	0.219	0.106	0.18	0.279	0.121	–	0.827	0.76	0.936
nl	0.4*	0.228	1.94*	0.224*	0.101	0.0909	–	0.615	0.955
pt	0.189	0.178	0.174	0.318*	0.215	0.3*	0.111	–	0.754
uk	0.0999	0.0387	0.034	0.205	0.00791	0.0152	–0.00188	0.103	–

B) Bread and Cereals—Series 1111 (1/81–7/95)

	be	dk	de	es	fr	it	pt	uk
be	–	0.623	0.823	0.96	0.826	0.965	0.589	0.944
dk	0.729*	–	0.548	0.919	0.478	0.902	0.495	0.939
de	0.101	0.121	–	0.927	0.659	0.883	0.514	0.956
es	0.405*	0.424*	0.334*	–	0.954	0.958	0.461	0.927
fr	1.12*	0.314	0.0883	0.566*	–	0.973	0.541	0.914
it	0.138	0.000481	–0.0119	0.561*	0.0017	–	0.684	0.907
pt	0.935*	0.936*	0.885*	0.891*	0.843*	0.51*	–	0.641
uk	0.0916	0.102	0.0454	0.224	0.16	0.124	0.659*	–

C) Meat—Series 1112 (1/81–7/95)

	be	dk	de	es	fr	it	nl	pt	uk
be	–	0.317	0.763	0.901	0.82	0.945	0.814	0.312	0.934
dk	0.513*	–	0.552	0.832	0.428	0.862	0.671	0.167	0.917
de	0.0352	0.426*	–	0.8	0.702	0.899	0.631	0.187	0.95
es	0.673*	0.468*	0.251	–	0.88	0.865	0.827	0.495	0.808
fr	0.276*	0.532*	0.0593	0.658*	–	0.973	0.764	0.192	0.934
it	0.0639	0.0832	0.0095	0.613*	0.0123	–	0.922	0.445	0.932
nl	0.0496	0.45*	1.11*	0.273	0.0416	0.0566	–	0.223	0.956
pt	0.21	0.389*	0.12	0.63*	0.264	0.0982	0.149	–	0.457
uk	0.0281	0.00224	–0.014	0.242	0.0365	0.0727	0.0143	0.16	–

D) Dairy Products—Series 1114 (1/81–7/95)

	be	dk	de	es	fr	it	nl	uk
be	–	0.471	0.672	0.88	0.76	0.947	0.62	0.899
dk	0.67*	–	0.404	0.859	0.543	0.877	0.438	0.879
de	0.0713	0.544*	–	0.862	0.705	0.842	0.55	0.977
es	0.174	0.343*	0.105	–	0.909	0.896	0.848	0.833
fr	0.396*	0.957*	0.184*	0.311*	–	0.953	0.669	0.911
it	0.0226	0.295*	–0.0026	0.169	0.0796	–	0.826	0.906
nl	0.108	0.728*	1.15*	0.137	0.18	0.0699	–	0.969
uk	0.0611	0.227	0.0642	0.0804	0.122	0.0658	0.132	–

E) Fruit—Series 1116 (1/81–7/95)

	be	dk	de	es	fr	it	nl	uk
be	–	0.18	0.169	0.544	0.344	0.527	0.257	0.74
dk	1.43*	–	0.0243	0.653	0.214	0.704	–0.00169	0.753
de	2.73*	2.76*	–	0.603	0.237	0.515	0.176	0.67
es	1.74*	1.52*	2.56*	–	0.642	0.434	0.465	0.663
fr	2.67*	1.66*	2.58*	1.73*	–	0.678	0.0545	0.723
it	1.28*	0.699*	2.04*	1.21*	0.855*	–	0.636	0.612
nl	1.82*	1.11*	2.94*	1.25*	0.99*	0.577*	–	0.723
uk	1.47*	0.771*	1.55*	1.78*	0.987*	0.563*	0.531*	–

F) Alcoholic and Nonalcoholic Drinks—Series 1150 (1/81–7/95)

	be	de	es	fr	it	nl	pt	uk
be	–	0.803	0.916	0.817	0.973	0.788	0.647	0.968
de	0.169	–	0.909	0.731	0.926	0.416	0.65	0.947
es	0.13	0.111	–	0.896	0.912	0.886	0.402	0.917
fr	0.536*	0.0698	0.133*	–	0.98	0.693	0.592	0.959
it	0.0646	–0.00168	0.0994	0.0138	–	0.915	0.649	0.964
nl	0.266	0.908*	0.102	0.261*	0.0687	–	0.639	0.944
pt	0.234*	0.218*	0.246*	0.242*	0.209*	0.251*	–	0.629
uk	0.124	0.107	0.144	0.135	0.0582	0.156	0.189*	–

G) Clothing and Footwear—Series 1200 (1/77–10/95)

	be	dk	de	es	fr	it	nl	pt	uk
be	–	0.675	0.862	0.834	0.631	0.833	0.794	0.797	0.942
dk	0.65*	–	0.744	0.889	0.764	0.868	0.772	0.858	0.954
de	0.195	0.413	–	0.867	0.722	0.845	0.225	0.818	0.957
es	0.0906	0.208	0.0302	–	0.924	0.939	0.916	0.912	0.903
fr	0.377*	0.598	0.0521	0.113	–	0.945	0.767	0.882	0.908
it	0.145	0.341	0.093	–0.00299	0.212	–	0.902	0.909	0.877
nl	0.885*	1.01*	1.56*	0.269	0.876*	0.35	–	0.866	0.942
pt	0.076	0.101	0.0355	0.0702	0.154	–0.0142	0.201	–	0.841
uk	0.136	0.147	0.0929	0.127	0.152	0.116	0.408*	0.131	–

(continues)

TABLE 4.1 *(continued)*

			H) Clothing—Series 1210 (1/81–7/95)					
	be	de	es	fr	it	nl	pt	uk
be	–	0.882	0.956	0.737	0.932	0.877	0.778	0.952
de	0.209	–	0.939	0.708	0.902	0.122	0.759	0.97
es	0.195	0.00537	–	0.986	0.971	0.95	0.857	0.909
fr	1.07*	–0.0125	0.0943	–	0.983	0.765	0.843	0.896
it	0.236*	0.0496	–0.0411	0.172	–	0.924	0.892	0.904
nl	1.35*	1.9*	0.449	0.935*	0.356	–	0.827	0.941
pt	0.191	0.0614	0.0887	0.164	0.0387	0.275	–	0.816
uk	0.18	0.146	0.159	0.213	0.152	0.575*	0.118	–

				I) Footwear—Series 1220 (1/81–7/95)					
	be	dk	de	es	fr	it	nl	pt	uk
be	–	0.617	0.946	0.966	0.769	0.969	0.813	0.784	0.937
dk	0.673*	–	0.863	0.893	0.195	0.888	0.779	0.736	0.959
de	0.118	0.405	–	0.932	0.763	0.898	0.617	0.832	0.956
es	0.0735	0.0936	0.0161	–	0.981	0.988	0.899	0.811	0.848
fr	0.325	0.233	0.0172	0.13	–	0.983	0.598	0.834	0.873
it	0.0598	0.136	0.015	–0.0513	0.118	–	0.885	0.891	0.877
nl	1.06*	1.73*	3.15*	0.237	0.764*	0.377	–	0.782	0.911
pt	0.205	0.224	0.118	0.13	0.395*	0.089	0.438	–	0.817
uk	0.0625	0.0582	0.0418	0.0836	0.0729	0.0925	0.504	0.117	–

				J) Rents—Series 1300 (5/78–12/95)					
	be	dk	de	es	fr	it	nl	pt	uk
be	–	0.427	0.654	0.917	0.411	0.87	0.743	0.479	0.813
dk	0.668*	–	0.268	0.936	0.723	0.809	0.398	0.511	0.886
de	0.157	0.245	–	0.914	0.594	0.696	0.5	0.52	0.824
es	0.107	0.0991	0.101	–	0.939	0.856	0.936	0.458	0.791
fr	0.638*	0.639*	0.133	0.08	–	0.853	0.696	0.446	0.841
it	0.265	0.493*	0.149	0.266	0.196	–	0.771	0.757	0.738
nl	0.707*	0.455*	1.78*	0.279	0.482*	0.502*	–	0.552	0.833
pt	0.335	0.359	0.289	0.334	0.447*	0.487*	0.339	–	0.502
uk	0.382*	0.383*	0.314*	0.438*	0.38*	0.367*	0.456*	0.341*	–

K) Fuel and Energy—Series 1330 (1/80–7/95)

	be	dk	de	es	fr	it	nl	pt	uk
be	–	–0.0855	0.383	0.567	0.159	0.766	0.452	0.0786	0.739
dk	0.67*	–	–0.0371	0.535	0.311	0.59	0.0455	0.143	0.862
de	0.36	0.788*	–	0.664	0.265	0.627	0.0207	0.148	0.836
es	0.491*	0.365	0.326	–	0.665	0.811	0.737	0.0177	0.816
fr	0.955*	0.912*	0.435*	0.503*	–	0.852	0.431	0.286	0.846
it	0.515*	0.451*	0.35	0.592*	0.518*	–	0.663	0.599	0.866
nl	0.95*	0.48	1.42*	0.508*	0.785*	0.451*	–	0.299	0.809
pt	0.337	0.389*	0.284	0.49*	0.395	0.301	0.282	–	0.495
uk	0.203	0.294	0.0561	0.393*	0.243	0.3*	0.133	0.27	–

L) Household Equipment—Series 1400 (1/77–12/95)

	be	dk	de	es	fr	it	nl	pt	uk
be	–	0.525	0.84	0.841	0.657	0.847	0.824	0.863	0.946
dk	0.167	–	0.682	0.906	0.882	0.948	0.699	0.865	0.966
de	0.0294	0.126	–	0.841	0.707	0.848	0.822	0.841	0.964
es	0.0593	0.00753	0.0508	–	0.909	0.876	0.84	0.894	0.927
fr	0.0803	0.168	0.0614	0.0769*	–	0.966	0.702	0.843	0.949
it	0.0565	0.043	0.0449	0.0487	0.1	–	0.851	0.876	0.934
nl	0.0215	0.123	0.406*	0.0207	0.0289	0.0101	–	0.834	0.968
pt	0.227*	0.152	0.163	0.118	0.191	0.0637	0.101	–	0.874
uk	0.0421	0.0075	0.00384	0.0443	0.0812	0.0506	–0.00208	0.0904	–

M) Furniture—Series 1410 (1/81–9/94)

	be	dk	de	es	fr	it	nl	pt	uk
be	–	0.883	0.923	0.971	0.849	0.961	0.896	0.833	0.972
dk	0.5*	–	0.737	0.985	0.887	0.981	0.724	0.9	0.957
de	0.0407	0.0204	–	0.947	0.856	0.918	0.717	0.826	0.972
es	–0.0101	0.00363	0.013	–	0.991	0.981	0.938	0.906	0.922
fr	0.282	0.205	0.0369	0.0498	–	0.991	0.79	0.874	0.934
it	0.0703	–0.0456	0.0293	–0.0371	0.0587	–	0.895	0.932	0.932
nl	0.0837	0.0503	0.617*	0.0183	0.039	0.0267	–	0.817	0.979
pt	0.05	0.0688	0.0326	0.0325	0.0825	0.079	0.0437	–	0.864
uk	0.142	0.154	0.183	0.088	0.215*	0.155	0.145	0.0772	–

(continues)

TABLE 4.1 *(continued)*

N) Domestic Appliances—Series 1420 (1/81–9/94)

	be	de	es	fr	it	nl	pt	uk
be	–	0.818	0.963	0.823	0.956	0.849	0.681	0.957
de	0.122	–	0.893	0.694	0.848	0.457	0.625	0.981
es	0.00795	0.0391	–	0.974	0.96	0.904	0.592	0.894
fr	0.335*	0.0566	0.086	–	0.98	0.751	0.56	0.937
it	0.0865	0.0855	0.0682	0.0756	–	0.865	0.742	0.937
nl	0.0396	0.793*	0.0121	0.0515	0.0215	–	0.629	0.989
pt	0.137	0.0749	0.13	0.131	0.0586	0.0322	–	0.724
uk	–0.0362	–0.00274	0.0146	0.0393	0.0626	–0.000946	0.0239	–

O) Transport and Communications—Series 1600 (1/77–12/95)

	be	dk	de	fr	it	nl	uk
be	–	0.607	0.933	0.859	0.97	0.936	0.972
dk	0.686*	–	0.819	0.846	0.975	0.853	0.979
de	0.161	0.231*	–	0.936	0.97	0.251	0.981
fr	0.334*	0.387*	0.137*	–	0.968	0.948	0.961
it	0.0689	0.0731	0.081	0.14	–	0.974	0.906
nl	0.122	0.227	1.01*	0.0885	0.053	–	0.982
uk	0.00739	0.0818	0.0593	0.0572	0.299*	0.0152	–

P) Vehicles—Series 1610 (1/81–7/95)

	be	de	es	fr	it	nl	uk
be	–	0.632	0.898	0.632	0.902	0.694	0.923
de	0.292*	–	0.912	0.618	0.75	0.287	0.97
es	0.36*	0.191	–	0.906	0.89	0.923	0.928
fr	0.439	0.276*	0.21	–	0.909	0.743	0.915
it	0.371	0.158	0.152	0.22	–	0.777	0.864
nl	0.132	0.989*	0.214	0.182	0.154	–	0.981
uk	0.178	–0.0146	0.25	0.123	0.0698	0.128	–

Q) Public Transport—Series 1630 (4/82–7/95)

	dk	de	es	fr	it	nl	uk
dk	–	0.236	0.903	0.749	0.838	0.44	0.816
de	0.715*	–	0.909	0.659	0.779	–0.492	0.935
es	0.196	0.124	–	0.94	0.938	0.938	0.83
fr	1.15*	0.285	0.193	–	0.894	0.784	0.88
it	0.466*	0.283	0.742*	0.287	–	0.852	0.791
nl	0.994*	0.905*	0.136	0.782*	0.189	–	0.869
uk	0.163	0.246*	0.133	0.158	0.261*	0.202*	–

R) Recreation—Series 1700 (1/77–12/95)

	be	dk	de	es	fr	it	nl	uk
be	–	0.697	0.837	0.913	0.74	0.899	0.886	0.951
dk	0.192	–	0.577	0.961	0.92	0.937	0.731	0.971
de	0.236	0.253*	–	0.889	0.689	0.836	0.417	0.961
es	0.126	0.108	0.168	–	0.962	0.933	0.92	0.952
fr	0.186	0.265	0.0874	0.134	–	0.949	0.766	0.963
it	0.11	0.201	0.113	0.0818	0.134	–	0.875	0.945
nl	0.291*	0.256	1.37*	0.128	0.132	0.109	–	0.969
uk	0.0414	0.00512	0.142	0.00887	0.0169	0.103	0.0654	–

S) Sound and Photographic Equipment—Series 1710 (1/81–7/95)

	be	de	es	fr	it	nl	uk
be	–	0.672	0.933	0.775	0.956	0.806	0.955
de	0.41*	–	0.907	0.809	0.861	0.212	0.965
es	0.164	0.0742	–	0.96	0.958	0.934	0.947
fr	0.678*	0.0506	0.116	–	0.964	0.846	0.972
it	0.162	0.0551	0.0738	0.0321	–	0.914	0.943
nl	0.423*	0.861*	0.157	0.158	0.0438	–	0.971
uk	0.128	0.00923	0.0211	−0.00159	0.0145	0.049	–

T) Leisure—Series 1720 (1/81–7/95)

	be	es	fr	nl	pt	uk
be	–	0.953	0.778	0.853	0.804	0.906
es	0.203	–	0.941	0.96	0.664	0.893
fr	0.683*	0.321*	–	0.734	0.695	0.875
nl	0.1	0.096	0.356*	–	0.734	0.954
pt	0.139	0.203	0.188	0.0396	–	0.712
uk	0.0214	0.0772	0.291	0.121	0.0789	–

U) Books—Series 1730 (1/81–7/95)

	be	dk	de	fr	it	nl	uk
be	–	0.785	0.892	0.696	0.889	0.907	0.952
dk	1.12*	–	0.589	0.629	0.89	0.593	0.961
de	0.225	0.21	–	0.695	0.8	0.239	0.944
fr	0.4*	0.655*	0.163	–	0.915	0.739	0.96
it	0.317	0.287	0.274	0.358*	–	0.833	0.89
nl	0.567*	0.396	1.47*	0.199	0.176	–	0.946
uk	−0.00644	0.0361	0.0243	0.123	0.0465	0.148	–

(continues)

TABLE 4.1 *(continued)*

	be	dk	de	es	fr	it	nl	pt	uk
			V) Hotels—Series 1830 (1/81–7/95)						
be	–	0.837	0.925	0.928	0.646	0.932	0.947	0.782	0.973
dk	1.05*	–	0.563	0.963	0.818	0.965	0.73	0.876	0.94
de	0.289	0.0416	–	0.91	0.75	0.87	0.536	0.806	0.984
es	0.155	0.167	0.0344	–	0.958	0.982	0.923	0.896	0.907
fr	0.433*	0.281	0.096	0.128	–	0.972	0.788	0.838	0.929
it	0.212	0.186	0.137	0.0872	0.112	–	0.903	0.945	0.919
nl	0.189	0.152	1.96*	0.12	0.114	0.228*	–	0.819	0.979
pt	0.305	0.281	0.14	0.164	0.267	0.177	0.157	–	0.877
uk	0.134	0.0597	0.0631	0.13	0.111*	0.179*	0.0867	0.137	–

Legend:
be = Belgium
dk = Denmark
de = Germany
es = Spain
fr = France
it = Italy
nl = Netherlands
pt = Portugal
uk = United Kingdom

NOTE: The upper triangle of each table is the correlation of the log of the nominal exchange rate between the indicated pair of countries, s_t, and the log of the relative price, $s_t + p_{it}^* - p_{it}$, where p_{it}^* and p_{it} are the nominal prices in each country.

The lower triangle of each table reports the coefficient β from the error-correction regression:

$$\Delta(p_{it} - \pi_{it}) = \alpha - \beta(p_{it} - \pi_{it} - e_t) + \sum_{j=0}^{k} \lambda_j \Delta e_{t-j} + \sum_{j=1}^{k} \gamma_j \Delta(p_{it-j} - \pi_{it-j}).$$

The * next to the coefficients in the lower triangle means significant at 95% level.

monopolistically competitive firms—for example, domestic appliances, sound and photographic equipment, furniture, books—the correlations are extremely high. One exception to these generally high correlations is for relative prices between Germany and the Netherlands. Here, the correlations are much lower than for other country pairs, suggesting that the German-Dutch market is much more unified than other markets.

A different approach to the law of one price is that price differentials may crop up between locations, but they are eliminated over time through price adjustment. This approach can be expressed in the error-correction equation:

$$(1) \quad \Delta(p_{it} - \pi_{it}) = \alpha - \beta(p_{it} - \pi_{it} - e_t) + \sum_{j=0}^{k} \lambda_j \Delta e_{t-j} + \sum_{j=1}^{k} \gamma_j \Delta(p_{it-j} - \pi_{it-j}),$$

where Δ refers to the monthly change. This equation states that when the relative price $e_t + \pi_{it} - p_{it}$ is above its mean or long-run value, $p_{it} - \pi_{it}$ adjusts to eliminate those deviations from the law of one price. The parameter β is a measure of how much of the deviation is eliminated after one month.

Equation (1) is estimated for each relative price series—for each good and each country pair. The lag length k was chosen by an iterative procedure. Initially the equation is estimated with eight lags of Δe_{t-j} and $\Delta(p_{it-j} - \pi_{it-j})$. If the sixteen estimated lag parameters (λ_j and γ_j, $j = 1, 2, \ldots, 8$) are not jointly significant, the eighth lag is dropped and the equation is reestimated with seven lags. This procedure is repeated until the k lags are jointly significant.[3]

The values of the estimated parameter β are reported in the bottom triangle of the matrices in Table 4.1. If adjustment to the law of one price were rapid, the estimated β coefficient would be close to unity. For a few goods—again, fruit and fuel and energy stand out—the estimated values of β are near to unity. In fact, many of the estimated coefficients in the fruit regression exceed one. But for most goods, the β coefficients are much smaller, frequently between 0.10 and 0.25. Again, exceptions to this general rule are the coefficients for the Germany-Netherlands regressions, which tend to be much closer to unity.

The table reports tests of the null hypothesis that $\beta = 0$. Under this null, there is no adjustment in prices toward the long-run law of one price. The relative price in this case has a unit root. The test of $\beta = 0$ is a test of cointegration between $p_{it} - \pi_{it}$ and e_t. Zivot (1995) develops this single-equation cointegration test (when the cointegration vector is known to be (1,–1).) Critical values are derived in Hansen (1995).

The null that $p_{it} - \pi_{it}$ and e_t are not cointegrated should not be taken literally. Failure to reject the null should be interpreted as meaning that the test does not have sufficient power to reject the null in our samples. Still, Zivot (1995) shows his test has quite good power in general. So the surprising result is that convergence to the law of one price is so slow that we cannot reject the null of no cointegration for most relative prices even with fifteen to eighteen years of monthly data. For most relative price series, we fail to reject the null for a majority of country pairs. The exceptions to this are bread and cereal products, dairy products, fruit, fuel and energy, rent and public transportation.[4]

So for most categories of goods, there is not even evidence that deviations from the law of one price tend to be eliminated. The evidence from both types of tests for the law of one price demonstrate that, especially for categories of differentiated consumer products, price differentials do not respond much to exchange rate changes.

The Model

We will demonstrate how local-currency pricing reduces the desirability of floating exchange rates in a simple Mundell-Fleming model. The fixed versus floating debate for Europe has largely been carried out (sometimes implicitly) in the context of the Mundell-Fleming model, so this model is the appropriate venue to consider the implications of local-currency pricing. However, in this model, behavior is not based explicitly on optimization. Problems that arise with assessing the value of a floating exchange rate system in such a model are discussed in the concluding section. Recent models (for example, Obstfeld and Rogoff (1995, 1998) and Corsetti and Pesenti (1998)) replicate many of the features of the Mundell-Fleming model in optimizing frameworks. Betts and Devereux (1996, 2000) and Devereux and Engel (1998) examine some of the implications of pricing to market and sticky nominal prices in models of dynamic utility maximization.

We compare the short-run volatility of output in response to aggregate demand shocks in two models: the standard Mundell-Fleming model and the Mundell-Fleming model with local-currency pricing. Feldstein and Friedman cast their argument in terms of short-run volatility; in the long run, nominal prices adjust so the choice of nominal exchange rate regime is immaterial.

The essence of the argument is that when there are asymmetric demand shocks (for example, an increase in demand for one country's output and a decrease in demand for another country's), in the long run there must be some adjustment in the relative prices of the countries' outputs. In the short run, there is some stickiness in the adjustment of prices to shocks to demand. The standard Mundell-Fleming model implies that flexible exchange rates facilitate adjustment of relative prices internationally. It assumes that prices set by producers in their own currency respond slowly to demand shocks, but prices faced by importing consumers change instantly as the exchange rate changes. So, the change in the nominal exchange rate allows relative prices to adjust even when goods prices adjust sluggishly. But, the empirical evidence contradicts the assumption of the standard Mundell-Fleming model that prices of imported goods respond instantly when exchange rates change. In fact, there is little short-run response of consumer prices to exchange rates, so flexible exchange rates do not facilitate relative price changes in the short run. That is, the prices that importing consumers pay are not much influenced by short-term exchange rate movements.

The standard Mundell-Fleming model (under the law of one price) assumes that demand for domestic output, y, comes from consumption less imports $(c - m)$, exports (x), investment and an exogenous shift factor (g).

(2) $\quad y = c(y) - q \cdot m(y, q) + f(i) + x(y^*, q) + g.$

with $0 < c' < 1$. The real exchange rate is defined as the relative price of foreign goods, so import demand falls as q rises (and import demand increases with income): $m_q < 0; 0 < m_y < c' < 1$. Investment demand depends inversely on the interest rate i: $f' < 0.5$ Foreign demand for exports from the home country depends directly on foreign income and the real exchange rate: $x_y > 0; x_q > 0$.

The IS curve in the foreign country is analogous:

(3) $\quad y^* = c^*(y^*) - \frac{1}{q} x(y^*, q) + m(y, q) + f^*(i^*) + g^*.$

In financial markets, there is perfect capital mobility so uncovered interest parity holds:

(4) $\quad i = i^* + \Delta e^e / e,$

where e is the nominal exchange rate, so that $\Delta e^e / e$ is the expected percentage change in the exchange rate.

In each country, real money demand falls as the interest rate rises, and rises with increases in income. So, in the home country

(5) $\quad h / p_h = \lambda(i, y), \lambda_i < 0$ and $\lambda_y > 0.$

where h is the home money supply, and p_h is the home currency price of home goods. In the foreign country is an analogous money demand equation:

(6) $\quad h^* / \pi_f = \lambda^*(i, y), \lambda_i^* < 0$ and $\lambda_y^* > 0$

where π_f is the foreign-currency price of foreign-produced goods.

The real exchange rate is defined as:

(7) $q = e\pi_f/p_h$.

There are two periods in the model. The second period represents the long run in which nominal prices are completely flexible and output is produced at the full-employment levels, which are exogenously given as $\bar{y}$ and $\bar{y}^*$. We will not consider changes in the money supply, so there is no permanent inflation or depreciation. There is no expected change in the exchange rate in the long run, so $i = i^*$. Equations (2) and (3) determine the long-run real exchange rate level and the long-run interest rate. Note, then, that money is neutral in the long run. From equation (5), p_h is proportional to h, and from equation (6), π_f is proportional to h^*. We will consider effects of shocks that affect the composition of aggregate demand between the home and foreign country, but not the level of aggregate demand. That is, we will assume

(8) $dg + q \cdot dg^* = 0$,

where dx ($x = g, g^*$) refers to the differential of x.

The appendix presents algebraic derivations. The text demonstrates the results graphically. The line labeled HH in Figure 4.1 represents the locus of interest rates and real exchange rates that maintain aggregate demand at the full-employment level. An increase in the interest rate depresses demand for domestic goods, which must be offset by an increase in q in order to maintain demand at $\bar{y}$. The FF curve is the locus of interest rates and real exchange rates that maintain demand for the foreign good at $\bar{y}^*$. It is downward sloping because an increase in q reduces demand for the foreign good.

An exogenous increase in domestic aggregate demand (a rise in g) shifts the HH curve downward. If the interest rate is held constant, so that investment is constant, and income is constant at $\bar{y}$, then an increase in g must be offset exactly one-for-one by a drop in the trade balance in order to maintain demand at $\bar{y}$.

An exogenous decrease in foreign aggregate demand shifts the FF curve downward. Note that if the value of the reduction in foreign aggregate demand exactly equals the value of the increase in domestic aggregate demand (that is, if $-q \cdot dg^* = dg$), then the vertical shift in the FF curve is exactly the same as the vertical shift in the DD curve (as depicted in Figure 4.2). The vertical shifts are equal because the foreign trade balance must improve by exactly the same amount that the domestic trade balance declines (since their sum is zero). So an identical real exchange rate decline is

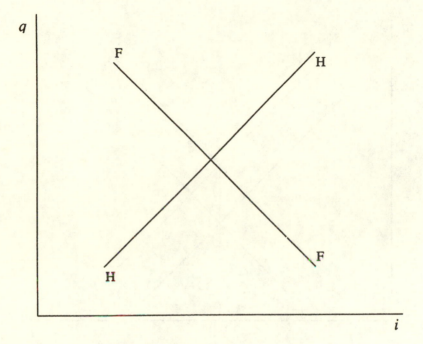

FIGURE 4.1   Long-Run Equilibrium in the Goods Market

needed to offset the exogenous decline in foreign aggregate demand to keep foreign demand at $\bar{y}^*$ and the exogenous increase in domestic aggregate demand that keeps domestic demand at $\bar{y}$. There is a real depreciation of the domestic currency, but no change in the interest rate.

Intuitively, the interest rate is the price of current consumption relative to future consumption, while the real exchange rate is the price of foreign goods relative to domestic goods. When the change in domestic aggregate demand is offset by a decline in foreign aggregate demand so that restriction (8) holds, there is no change in the demand for current consumption relative to future consumption. So there is no change in the interest rate. But the relative price of foreign goods declines because of the shift in the pattern of demand.

Now consider the short run in the standard Mundell-Fleming model. Nominal prices do not adjust immediately in response to changes in aggregate demand. But the key assumption in this type of model is that prices are fixed in the sellers' currencies. That is, p_h and π_f are fixed. The law of one price holds for each good, so that the foreign currency price of domestic goods is p_h/e and the domestic currency price of foreign goods

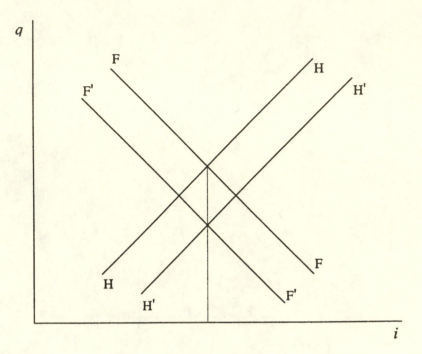

FIGURE 4.2   An Increase in Domestic Aggregate Demand and Equal Decrease in Foreign Aggregate Demand in the Long Run

is $e\pi_f$. With p_h and π_f fixed, the real exchange rate q moves one-for-one with changes in the nominal exchange rate, e.

We assume that expectations are rational, so that investors expect the exchange rate to equal its long-run value next period:

(9) $$\frac{\Delta e^e}{e} = \frac{\bar{e} - e}{e}$$

where $\bar{e}$ represents the long-run exchange rate.

Figure 4.3 represents this model graphically. In the upper right quadrant is the traditional IS-LM graph for the home country. Note, however, that the IS curve is not determined independently from the foreign country. Changes in foreign income and the real exchange rate each influence the domestic IS curve through their effects on the trade balance. An increase in foreign income leads to greater export demand and a shift up in the IS curve. An increase in the exchange rate (a depreciation of the domestic currency) reduces the relative price of domestic goods, and so also leads to a shift out in the domestic IS curve.

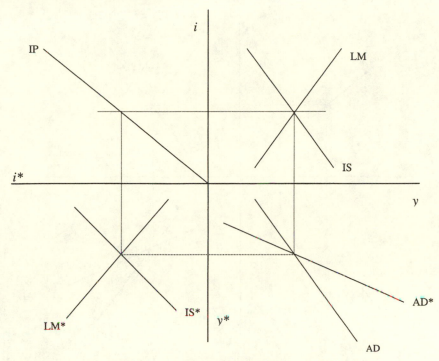

FIGURE 4.3   Equilibrium in Standard Mandell-Fleming Model

The lower-left quadrant is the IS-LM graph for the foreign country. Here, an increase in domestic income shifts the foreign IS curve out. A decrease in e (a depreciation of the foreign currency) also causes the foreign IS curve to shift out.

The interest rates at home and abroad are not determined independently. The uncovered interest parity relation, equation (4), links them. That relation is charted in the upper-left quadrant. The IP (for interest parity) line is a (negative) 45-degree line. A change in expectations of exchange rate changes shifts the IP curve. From equation (4), if there is an increase in the expected change in the exchange rate (that is, if $\Delta e^e/e$ rises), the IP curve shifts up as i increases relative to i^*. Using our model of expectations from equation (9), if e declines relative to its long-run value, $\bar{e}$, then $\Delta e^e/e$ rises and the IP line shifts up.

The lower-right quadrant shows equilibrium in the international market for goods. The AD curve represents domestic aggregate demand as a function of foreign income. Note that an increase in foreign income has a relatively small effect on the demand for the domestic good through ex-

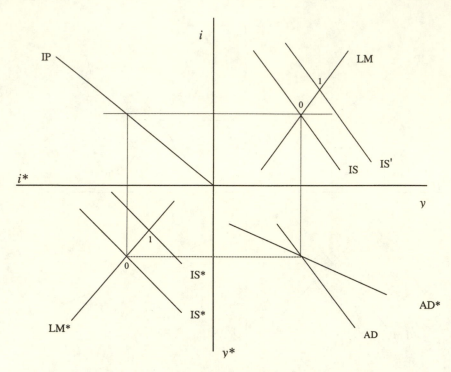

FIGURE 4.4   Shift in Demand in Traditional Mandell-Fleming Model

port demand. Likewise, the AD* curve shows foreign aggregate demand as a function of domestic income. For the curves to have the relative slopes depicted in Figure 4.3, we must have $m_y + x_y < 1$.

Either a decline in the domestic interest rate or an increase in the real exchange rate will cause domestic aggregate demand to increase, shifting the AD curve up to the right. Likewise, a decline in the foreign interest rate or a decrease in the real exchange rate cause foreign aggregate demand to increase, which translates to a shift down to the left of the AD* curve.

In Figure 4.3, the economy is resting at its long-run equilibrium. Domestic output, y, and foreign output, y^*, are at their long-run full-employment values $\bar{y}$ and $\bar{y}^*$, respectively. Since the exchange rate is at its long run value, there is no expected change in the exchange rate. Hence, the IP line cuts through the origin, and $i = i^*$.

Figure 4.4 depicts the short-run response of these economies to a shift in aggregate demand—an increase in domestic aggregate demand, matched by an equal decline in foreign aggregate demand. There is an incipient shift out in the domestic IS curve and inwards in the foreign IS curve. That is depicted in Figure 4.4 as a shift to point 1 in the upper-right quadrant and lower-left quadrant. However, those initial shifts cannot represent an equilibrium. The domestic interest rate at point 1 in the upper-right quadrant is higher than the foreign interest rate at point 1 in the lower-left quadrant. The shift in demand will also cause a change in the real exchange rate.

In fact, in the new equilibrium the domestic currency has appreciated just enough to shift both IS curves back to their original positions. The exogenous expansion in demand at home is completely offset by a worsening of the domestic trade balance. The foreign decline in demand is completely offset by an improvement of the foreign country's trade balance. Note that when both IS curves have shifted back to their initial positions, there is no change in the interest rates at home and abroad. So we have $i = i^*$, as in the initial long-run equilibrium. That means $e = \bar{e}$, so the initial appreciation of the domestic currency equals the long-run appreciation: there is no overshooting or undershooting of the exchange rate. The economy has moved directly to its long-run equilibrium, even though nominal prices are sticky, because the fiscal shock we are considering does not require any changes in nominal prices in the long run. Even in the long run, all of the adjustment in relative prices is accomplished through a change in the nominal exchange rate.

The adjustment shown in Figure 4.4 is the underpinning for Mundell's conclusion that a floating exchange rate system best suits countries that are not highly integrated in the goods market. The shock we are considering is one in which the home country and foreign country are hit by opposite demand shocks as we would witness in a pair of economies that are not well integrated. The change in the exchange rate cushions the shock in both countries. When there is no change in world aggregate demand, the exchange rate change completely eliminates any idiosyncratic output changes.

In this example, demand shocks across the countries are negatively correlated. In country pairs that are more integrated, local demand shocks would be more positively correlated. The more positively correlated, the larger would be changes in world aggregate demand. Floating exchange rates can do nothing to stabilize shocks to world aggregate demand. So, floating exchange rates are most beneficial when goods markets are not highly integrated.

Now consider the alternative view of short-run pricing behavior by firms. Under this view, there is a large degree of local-currency pricing, and not much exchange-rate pass-through. In other words, firms consider the different countries in which they sell their goods to be separate markets. They set their prices in the local currency, and do not quickly adjust those prices in response to exchange rate changes.

We take the opposite extreme from the Mundell model (which assumes 100 percent exchange-rate pass-through) and assume no exchange-rate pass-through. Prices are sticky in the buyers' currencies. So, import demand is a function of income, z, and the relative price of foreign goods:

(10) $m = m(z, p_f/p_h)$,

where p_f is the domestic currency price of the foreign good paid by home residents, and p_h is the domestic currency price of the home good paid by home residents. (Note that income, z, is not necessarily equal to the value of output, y. That will be discussed in more detail momentarily.) Since in the short run p_f and p_h are fixed, changes in the nominal exchange rate have no direct influence on import demand.[6] The real value of imports, expressed in terms of units of the home good, is given by $p_f m/p_h$, which also is not directly influenced by the nominal exchange rate.

Similarly, demand for exports from the home country are influenced by foreign income and the prices faced by foreigners:

(11) $x = x(z^*, \pi_f/\pi_h)$,

where z^* is foreign income, π_f is the foreign currency price of the foreign good paid by foreigners, and π_h is the foreign currency price of the home good paid by foreigners. Since π_f and π_h are fixed, there is no direct influence of changes in the exchange rate on foreigners' demand for exports.

The quantity of goods produced domestically is given by y. If the law of one price held, it would be simple to evaluate sales of goods in real terms. As in the Mundell model, the real value of sales is simply the quantity of goods sold. But, in our model, output sold to foreigners is sold at a different price than identical output sold to domestic residents. The domestic currency value of exports is equal to $e\pi_h x$, so the real value of exports, valued at domestic prices is $e\pi_h x/p_h$. Accordingly, real home income evaluated at domestic prices is:

(12) $z = y - x + \dfrac{e\pi_h}{p_h} x = y - x \cdot (1 - \dfrac{e\pi_h}{p_h})$.

As we discussed in the introductory section, firms may hedge their exchange rate gains and losses in various ways. They might use derivatives to protect themselves from foreign exchange fluctuation. Alternatively, some of their costs may be borne in the currency of the location where the good is sold. For example, the firm might do some production or assembly in the buyer's country. At the least, marketing and distribution costs may be denominated in the buyer's currency. In that case, a change in the exchange rate changes costs and revenues in the same direction, so that the impact on profits is diminished. Furthermore, to the extent that domestic firms are in part owned by foreigners (and vice versa), the effect of the exchange rate change on the relative income of domestic and foreign residents is mitigated. Finally, as we noted earlier, in practice, firm owners may not have full information on how foreign exchange gains and losses affect the firm's profits in the short run. So individual firm owners may not treat short-run changes in profits from foreign exchange exposure the same as other income.

For all of these reasons, we modify our definition of income so that only a fraction k of foreign exchange earnings are considered to be part of income in the short run:

$$(13) \quad z = y - k(1 - \frac{e\pi_h}{p_h})x$$

where $0 < k < 1$. Foreign income is defined analogously:

$$(14) \quad z^* = y^* - k^*(1 - \frac{p_f}{e\pi_f})m.$$

The equilibrium condition in the domestic goods market is now given by:

$$(15) \quad y = c(z) - \frac{p_f}{p_h} \cdot m(z, \frac{p_f}{p_h}) + f(i) + x(z^*, \frac{\pi_f}{\pi_h}) + g.$$

Similarly, the equation for the foreign IS curve is given by:

$$(16) \quad y^* = c^*(z^*) - \frac{\pi_h}{\pi_f} x(z^*, \frac{\pi_f}{\pi_h}) + f^*(i^*) + m(z^*, \frac{p_f}{p_h}) + g^*.^7$$

How does this economy react to a demand shock such as the one that we described for the Mundell economy: one in which the increase in domestic aggregate demand is matched by an equal decline in foreign aggregate demand? In the long run, nominal prices fully adjust, so, the long-run response is the same as described above. The relative price of domestic goods falls in the long run, but interest rates are not affected. The law of one price holds for each good in the long run, so $p_h = e\pi_h$ and $pf = e\pi_f$. Because the domestic and foreign money supplies do not change, interest rates do not change. With constant interest rates and output in each country fixed at full-employment levels, from equations (5) and (6) we have that p_h and π_f do not change in the long run. The change in the nominal exchange rate equals the change in the relative price p_f / p_h.

So in response to the aggregate demand shift, agents expect a long-run appreciation of the domestic currency.

The short-run adjustment of the economy depends on how changes in the exchange rate affect aggregate demand. Changes in the exchange rate do not directly affect demand, because neither the prices faced by domestic nor those by foreign consumers are affected by changes in the exchange rate. However, there is an indirect effect of exchange rate changes on demand—an effect that works through income. An appreciation of the domestic currency (a decline in e) reduces the home-country value of home-country goods sold in the foreign country. So there is a decline in domestic income. Conversely, there is an increase in foreign income. The decline in domestic income leads residents to demand less of both domestic and foreign goods, and foreigners demand more of both foreign and domestic goods. Assuming that residents of each country have expenditure biased toward their own country's good, the net effect is to reduce demand for domestic goods and increase demand for foreign goods.

However, the magnitude of this effect depends on how much fluctuations in revenues from overseas sales coming from exchange rate changes is evaluated as a change in income. That is, the effect depends on the size of k and k^* in equations (13) and (14). We have argued in the introduction that k and k^* are likely to be quite small, so that the exchange rate change has a small effect on income and demand.

Figure 4.5 illustrates the short-run equilibrium when k and k^* are small. Initially, the IS curve in the home country shifts out, while in the foreign country it shifts in. These initial shifts are represented by point 1 in the upper-right and lower-left quadrants of Figure 4.5. This is not the full equilibrium, however. The IS curve in the domestic country will be further affected from two sources. First, the decline in foreign income will reduce demand for home country exports, and shift the IS curve in. Further, there will be an appreciation of the domestic currency in the short run (as we shall demonstrate momentarily), which shifts the IS curve in further through its effect on domestic income. Similarly, the overall increase in domestic income leads to an increase in import demand, which helps to shift the foreign IS curve back outward (downward and leftward in the lower-left quadrant of Figure 4.5.) And the decline in the exchange rate increases foreign income, leading to a further shift back outward of the foreign IS curve.

In the Mundell-Fleming model, these secondary movements were quite significant. Indeed, the exchange rate effect was strong enough that both IS curves shifted back to their initial locations, so that there was no change in output levels. But in this model, the channel for the exchange rate to affect aggregate demand is much weaker in the short run. So the curves may not shift very far back toward their initial positions.

At points 2 in the upper-right quadrant and lower-left quadrant, i has risen relative to i^*. From uncovered interest parity (equation [4]) and our model of expectations (equation [5]), this implies that e falls relative to $\bar{e}$. That is, there is overshooting of the exchange rate. The IP line in the upper-left quadrant shifts upward.

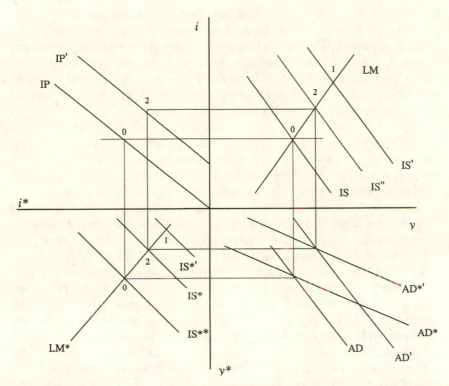

FIGURE 4.5   Shift in Demand in Mandell-Fleming Model with Local-Currency Pricing

Note that the equilibrium configuration in Figure 4.5 was geometrically impossible in the standard Mundell-Fleming model. If there were exchange rate overshooting, then the trade balance would change more in the short run than in the long run. That is because in the Mundell-Fleming model, the channel through which the exchange rate affects the trade balance is the same in the short run and the long run. But if the trade balances adjusted more in the short run than in the long run, then the shift back in the IS curves would overshoot, not undershoot, the long-run equilibrium points.

However, in this model, the exchange rate works on the trade balance through a much different channel in the short run than in the long run. In the long run, the exchange rate movement raises the relative price of domestic to foreign goods for both home and foreign country residents. So agents in both countries substitute away from the domestic good to the foreign good. But in the short run, the exchange rate works on the trade balance only because it affects income in both countries. The appreciation of the home currency lowers income for home country residents as the value of exports falls since the foreign currency price of the exports is unchanged. Similarly, the appreciation increases income for foreign residents. That redistribution of income affects the relative demand for home and foreign goods. But as we have argued, this short-run effect may be much smaller than the long-run substitution effect.

The fact that our model predicts short-run overshooting of the exchange rate is consistent with the extreme volatility of modern floating exchange rate regimes. The exchange rate change has very little effect on the goods market in the short run. Hence, in order to achieve financial market equilibrium, large swings in the exchange rate are required.

In this model, Mundell's argument in favor of floating exchange rates is very much mitigated. The insulating properties of flexible exchange rates is much smaller when there is a substantial amount of local-currency pricing. In the Mundell model, exchange rate changes effectively completely offset the relative demand shock, so that there are no output effects. But, when there is local-currency pricing, and very little exchange-rate pass-through, floating exchange rates are not much of a stabilizer. In this case, changes in the exchange rate have little effect on goods markets in the short run, so they are not a channel through which adjustment to shocks to the real sector can occur.

In evaluating fixed versus flexible exchange rates, we must weigh the pros of fixed exchange rates—mostly the enhanced stability when monetary shocks are preponderant—against the pros of floating exchange rates—which are supposed to be the enhanced stability when real shocks are preponderant. But when there is little exchange-rate pass-through, the advantages of floating rates are greatly diminished.

Conclusions

The Friedman-Feldstein case for flexible exchange rates must be reexamined in light of the evidence of local-currency pricing. The stabilizing role of flexible exchange rates may not be so strong when producers set prices in the consumer's currency.

In practice, exchange-rate pass-through is not the same for all goods, nor for producers in all countries. Even the limited evidence we have presented suggests there is more pass-through for simple, homogeneous goods than for complex goods produced by monopolists or monopolistic competitors. Evidence from Goldberg and Knetter (1997) seems to indicate there is more pass-through directly to export prices than there is to prices of finished goods sold to consumers. A complete analysis requires consideration of the causes of these varying pricing practices.

The Mundell-Fleming model assigns labor markets a secondary role. But many authors have noted that labor market behavior is key to the understanding of adjustment in European economies. It has been observed that Europe is characterized by a high degree of real-wage rigidity, which leads to very slow adjustment of Europe's labor markets. Obstfeld (1997), for one, investigates the implications of this real-wage rigidity for the choice of exchange rate regime.

Our concern with the viability of floating exchange rates has been mainly with the stability of output. A more comprehensive analysis would compare overall economic welfare with varying degrees of pricing in local versus producer's currencies under fixed and floating exchange rates. Devereux and Engel (1998) have recently compared fixed and floating exchange rate regimes in intertemporal optimizing models with uncertainty. Their concern is how welfare comparisons between the two exchange rate regimes are affected by price-setting behavior. They find that local-currency pricing strengthens the case for flexible exchange rates. However, their concern is solely with transmission of monetary shocks. They do not consider the goods-market shocks that Feldstein puts at the center of his analysis. Indeed, it would seem that monetary transmission is not so relevant an issue for the EMU, where it is generally presumed that overall monetary stability will be enhanced under the European Central Bank.

Devereux and Engel (1998) assume a complete market of state-contingent nominal bonds. When markets are complete in this way, the marginal utility of consumption relative to prices across countries are equalized:

$$(17) \quad \frac{u'(c)}{p} = \frac{u'(c^*)}{ep^*}.$$

Here, u represents the instantaneous utility function, c (c^*) is per capita consumption in the home (foreign) country, and p (p^*) is the price index for consumption in the home (foreign) country. When the law of one price holds, and under the assumption of identical preferences made by Devereux and Engel, purchasing power parity holds as well. In that case $p = ep^*$, and so equation (17) indicates that there is complete consumption insurance: $c = c^*$. On the other hand, when prices are set in consumers' currencies, the law of one price and purchasing power parity fail. In that case, consumption is not equalized across countries. This leads us to similar conclusions as we found in our ad hoc IS-LM model. We can conclude that under floating rates and the law of one price, consumption is stabilized across countries. In response to shocks, there are no idiosyncratic fluctuations in consumption across countries, only fluctuations in world consumption. This is exactly what we found in the IS-LM model, where we examined offsetting demand shocks at home and abroad so there were no fluctuations in world output. We found that local fluctuations in output (and hence consumption) are completely eliminated when PPP holds. On the other hand, if there is pricing in producers' currencies and the law of one price holds, equation (17) shows that there will be idiosyncratic differences in home and foreign consumption, which corresponds to the results we found in the IS-LM model with local-currency pricing.

There are some important differences in IS-LM models and the models based on intertemporal optimization of Obstfeld and Rogoff (1995, 1998) and Devereux and Engel (1998). The IS-LM models are not genuinely forward-looking and ignore budget constraints facing consumers, firms, and governments. Both sets of models, however, retain the central feature explored here: with local-currency pricing, nominal exchange rate changes do not affect relative prices faced by consumers.

The opponents of the euro have contended that the single currency for Europe will increase regional macroeconomic instability. If that were the case, the euro might be doomed. But, since the evidence indicates that exchange rates do not appear to alter relative national prices in the short run, then national currencies may not naturally lead to smoother regional adjustments. The European economy may adjust regionally almost as well under a single currency, so Europe may not notice any deterioration in economic performance under the euro.

Appendix

First, we will show the change in the long-run real exchange rate when there are shocks to domestic and foreign demand. In the long run there is no expected change in the exchange rate. (We are assuming money supplies are constant. Our interest is in real demand shocks, rather than monetary shocks.) So from equation (4), we have $i = i^*$. Also, in the long run, output in both countries is at full employment levels. So, in taking the total differentials of equations (2) and (3), we will assume $dy = 0$, $dy^* = 0$, and $di = di^*$. We will take the initial real exchange rate as $q = 1$, and evaluate derivatives at this point.

(A.1) $0 = -m \cdot dq - m_q dq + f_i di + x_q dq + dg.$

(A.2) $0 = x \cdot dq - x_q dq + m_q dq + f_i^* di + dg.$

Assume that trade is balanced initially, so that $x = m$. Using the fact that we are assuming the net aggregate demand shock is zero, so that $dg + dg^* = 0$, we have, adding equation (A.2) to equation (A.1):,

$0 = (f_i + f_i^*)di.$

which implies $di = 0$ in the long run. Then, using (A.1) we have that the long-run change in the real exchange rate for the switch in demand from the foreign good toward the domestic good is given by:

(A.3) $\quad \dfrac{dq}{dg} = \dfrac{-1}{x\Omega}$,

where $\Omega = E_x + E_m - 1$, and $E_x = x_q/x$ is the elasticity of demand for exports, and $E_m = -m_q/m$ is the elasticity of import demand. We assume $\Omega > 0$, which is the Marshall-Lerner condition.

Since y and i do not change in the long run, and the money supply, h, of the domestic country is constant, then from equation (5), p_h does not change in the long run when there is a change in aggregate demand. Likewise, from equation (6), π_f does not change. So the real exchange rate adjustment is achieved completely through an adjustment of the nominal exchange rate. The change in the long-run nominal exchange rate is given by:

(A.4) $\quad \dfrac{d\bar{e}}{dg} = \dfrac{-1}{x\Omega} < 0.$

It follows very directly that the solution in the short run in the Mundell-Fleming model is the same as the solution in the long run for a change in g, when we impose the condition that $dg + dg^* = 0$. In the long run, y and y^* are assumed to be constant, but p_h and π_f are free to adjust. Nonetheless, there was no change in p_h and π_f when g changed. In the short run, but p_h and π_f are fixed, and y and y^* are able to change. We claim, however, that in the short-run solution, y and y^* do not change.

To see this, suppose there is no change in the domestic or foreign interest rate, so that $di/dg = di^*/dg$. Then from equation (9), the short-run change in the exchange rate equals the long-run change: $de/dg = d\bar{e}^*/dg$. From equations (5) and (6), since p_h and π_f are fixed, and y and y^* do not change. But then from equations (2) and (3), if y and y^* do not change, then the change in the short-run exchange rate is the same as the long-run change.

The modified version of the Mundell-Fleming model is given by equations (4), (9), (15), and (16), and the following two equations, which replace equations (5) and (6):

(A.5) $\quad h/p_h = \lambda(i, z),$

(A.6) $\quad h^*/\pi_f = \lambda^*(i^*, z^*),$

In this model, p_f, p_h, π_f, and π_f are all fixed in the short run. For simplicity, we set those prices equal to one.

We totally differentiate equations (4), (13), (14), (15), (16), (A.5), and (A.6), evaluating the derivatives at $e = \bar{e} = p_h = p_f = \pi_h = \pi_f = 1$, and $x = m$:

(A.7) $\quad di = di^* + d\bar{e} - de.$

(A.8) $\quad dz = dy + xkde.$

(A.9) $\quad dz^* = dy^* - xk^*de.$

(A.10) $\quad dy = c_z dz - m_z dz + f_i di + x_z dz^* + dg.$

(A.11) $\quad dy^* = c_z^* dz^* - x_z dz^* + f_i^* di^* + m_z dz^* + dg^*.$

(A.12) $0 = \lambda_i di + \lambda_z dy + \lambda_z x k de.$

(A.13) $0 = \lambda_i^* di^* + \lambda_z^* dy^* + \lambda_z^* k^* x de.$

For simplicity, consider the symmetrical case in which $c_z = c_z^*$, $f_i = f_i$, $\lambda_i = \lambda_i^*$, $\lambda_z = \lambda_z^*$, and $k = k^*$. Then, add equations (A.8) and (A.9) together to get

$$dz + dz^* = dy + dy^*.$$

Then, recalling we are examining the case in which $dg + dg^* = 0$, add together equations (A.10) and (A.11) to get

(A.14) $(1 - c_z)(dy + dy^*) = f_i(di + di^*).$

Add equations (A.12) and (A.13) to get

(A.15) $0 = \lambda_i(di + di^*) + \lambda_y(dy + dy^*).$

Equations (A.14) and (A.15) imply $dy + dy^* = 0$, and $di + di^* = 0$, which in turn imply $dz + dz^* = 0$. So the effects on the two countries are symmetric—the change in output and interest rates in the home country are exactly the opposite of the change in the foreign country. We can then reduce the system to one of three equations that will solve for dz, de, and di:

(A.16) $dz - kx de = (c_z - m_z - x_z)\, dz + f_i di + dg.$

(A.17) $2di = d\bar{e} - de.$

(A.18) $0 = \lambda_i di + \lambda_z dz.$

From these equations we find,

$$\frac{\partial e}{\partial g} = \frac{-(\Sigma - \Omega x)}{x\Omega(\Sigma - kx)} < 0.$$

where

$$\Sigma = \frac{\lambda_i(1 - c_z + m_z + x_z) + f_i \lambda_z}{2\lambda_z} < 0.$$

and Ω is defined above. Note that as long as $\Omega > k$ there is short-run overshooting of the exchange rate:

$$\frac{\partial e}{\partial g} - \frac{\partial \bar{e}}{\partial g} = \frac{\Omega - k}{\Omega(\Sigma - kx)} < 0.$$

In this case, the home country interest rate will increase,

$$\frac{\partial i}{\partial g} = \frac{k - \Omega}{2\Omega(\Sigma - kx)} > 0.$$

and income and output will increase:

$$\frac{\partial z}{\partial g} = \frac{\lambda_i\,(\Omega - k)}{2\lambda_y\Omega(\Sigma - kx)} > 0$$

and,

$$\frac{\partial y}{\partial g} = \frac{\partial z}{\partial g} - kx\,\frac{\partial e}{\partial g} > \frac{\partial z}{\partial g} > 0.$$

Notes

1. I thank John Rogers and participants in the Symposium on the Political Economy of European Integration for helpful comments. I also thank two referees for helpful suggestions. This research is supported in part by a National Science Foundation grant to the National Bureau of Economic Research.

2. There were quite a few data entry errors in the dataset obtained from Eurostat. In cases where there were more than a few errors in one series, the series was dropped. Hence, there is not data for all nine countries for all of the goods. In cases where data entry errors were near the beginning or end of the series, the series were truncated. In some cases, the data was corrected from other sources. In some cases the entry error involved a transposition of digits, which was corrected. In the remaining cases, the data points were replaced using interpolation from adjacent data points. The total number of data points used in the tables that are corrected data is 99 (out of a total of approximately 40,000 data points.) A list of corrections is available on request from the author. The original data is sold by Eurostat.

3. This is the procedure advocated by Ng and Perron (1995).

4. Public transportation refers to transport that is shared, such as rail and air travel. It is generally a traded good.

5. Investment depends on the nominal interest rate for simplicity. In the examples we will look at, in which there are changes in relative demand, nominal prices turn out not to change in equilibrium. So, there is no difference between the real and nominal interest rates.

6. Though changes in the exchange rate directly influence income, z, as discussed below.

7. For simplicity of exposition of the graphical model, we will continue to assume money demand is a function of y in the home country (rather than z), and of y^* in the foreign country (rather than z^*). The Appendix derives the results in which money demands depend on z and z^*.

References

Betts, Caroline, and Michael B. Devereux, 1996, Exchange rate dynamics in a model of pricing to market. *European Economic Review* 40, 1007–1021.

————, 2000, The international monetary transmission mechanism: A model of real exchange rate adjustment under pricing-to-market. *Journal of International Economics*, forthcoming.

Corsetti, Giancarlo, and Paolo Pesenti, 1998, Welfare and macroeconomic interdependence. Working paper, Yale University.

Devereux, Michael B., and Charles Engel, 1998, Fixed vs. floating exchange rates: How price setting affects the optimal choice of exchange rate regime. National Bureau of Economic Research, working paper no. 6867.

Eichengreen, Barry, and Charles Wyplosz, 1993, The unstable EMS. *Brookings Papers on Economic Activity* 1, 51–124.

Engel, Charles, 1993, Real exchange rates and relative prices: An empirical investigation. *Journal of Monetary Economics* 32, 35–50.

_____, 1999, Accounting for U.S. real exchange rate changes. *Journal of Political Economy* 107, 507–538.

Engel, Charles, and John H. Rogers, 1996, How wide is the border? *American Economic Review* 86, 1112–1125.

Feldstein, Martin, 1992, The case against the EMU. *The Economist* (June 13, 1992), 19–22.

_____, 1997, The political economy of the European economic and monetary union: Political sources of an economic liability. *Journal of Economic Perspectives* 11, 23–42.

Friedman, Milton, 1953, The case for flexible exchange rates, in Milton Friedman, *Essays in Positive Economics* (Chicago: University of Chicago Press), 157–203.

Gagnon, Joseph E., and Michael M. Knetter, 1995, Markup adjustment and exchange rate fluctuations: Evidence from panel data on automobile exports. *Journal of International Money and Finance* 14, 289–310.

Goldberg, Pinelopi K., and Michael M. Knetter, 1997, Goods prices and exchange rates: What have we learned? *Journal of Economic Literature* 35, 1243–1272.

Hansen, Bruce E., 1995, Rethinking the univariate approach to unit root testing: Using covariates to increase power. *Econometric Theory* 11, 1148–1171.

Harrigan, James, 1996, Openness to trade in manufactures in the OECD. *Journal of International Economics* 40, 23–40.

Knetter, Michael M., 1989, Price discrimination by U.S. and German exporters. *American Economic Review* 79, 198–210.

Marston, Richard, 1990, Pricing to market in Japanese manufacturing. *Journal of International Economics* 29, 217–236.

Mundell, Robert A., 1961, A theory of optimum currency areas. *American Economic Review* 51, 657–665.

Ng, Serena, and Pierre Perron, 1995, Unit root tests in ARMA models with data dependent methods for the truncation lag. *Journal of the American Statistical Association* 90, 268–281.

Obstfeld, Maurice, 1997, Europe's gamble, *Brookings Papers on Economic Activity* 2, 241–317.

Obstfeld, Maurice, and Kenneth Rogoff, 1995, Exchange rate dynamics redux. *Journal of Political Economy* 103, 624–660.

_____, 1998, Risk and exchange rates. National Bureau of Economic Research, working paper no. 6694.

Rangan, Subramanian, and Robert Lawrence, 1993, The response of U.S. firms to exchange rate fluctuations: Piercing the corporate veil. *Brookings Papers on Economic Activity* 2, 341–369.

Zivot, Eric, 1995, The power of single equation tests for cointegration when the cointegrating vector is known. Department of Economics, University of Washington.

5

The Politics of Maastricht

GEOFFREY GARRETT[1]

Abstract

The Economic and Monetary Union (EMU) treaty signed at Maastricht did not guarantee that Euroland would be a zone of German-style monetary rectitude. Membership was not limited to countries that mimicked the German commitment to price stability nor that plausibly constitute an optimal currency area in Europe. National representatives can outvote inflation-averse members of the Executive Board of the European Central Bank in monetary policy decisions. The Council of Ministers has the power to set exchange rate policy vis-à-vis third currencies. The treaty did not provide binding constraints against fiscal profligacy in member states; neither does the subsequent Growth and Stability Pact. The German government agreed to this suboptimal outcome because, in the wake of the demise of the Soviet Union and German unification, it had broader political interests in maintaining the pace of European integration—through the creation of the euro.

The creation of an Economic and Monetary Union (EMU) by 1999 was the principal objective of the 1992 Maastricht Treaty on European Union.[2] The common wisdom about the EMU agreement at the time was that it would recreate at the European Community (EC) level the German monetary regime: a central bank that is immune from tampering by politicians and that can impose the goal of price stability, even at the cost of higher unemployment (at least in the short term). Two central pieces of evidence were used to support this position. First, the rules governing the creation and operation of the new European Central Bank (ECB) appear to give it at least as much autonomy from political tampering as those for the German Bundesbank. Second, the convergence criteria were supposed to limit admission to countries that already mimicked German economic policies and outcomes. From this perspective, the Maastricht treaty was expected to entrench Germany's preferred set of institutions and macroeconomic policies at the European level.

This chapter offers a very different interpretation of the treaty that helps explain monetary politics in Europe since 1992. Instead of a small euro bloc comprising Germany, France, the Benelux countries (and new member, Austria), Euroland today comprises all European Union (EU) members that wanted to join except Greece. In its first year of existence, the euro depreciated by more than 10 percent against the dollar, at least in part the product of a relatively loose monetary stance by the ECB. I argue that the seeds for these eventualities were sown in the Maastricht treaty itself.

There is no doubt that the institutional details of the ECB closely resemble those of the Bundesbank. But the success of the German inflation-fighting model was contingent upon much more than the institutional structure of the central bank (Hall 1993; Scharpf 1991). The memory of Nazism rendered price stability a more important objective for all actors in Germany—political parties, trade unions, and voters, as well as central bank officials—than for other countries. Moreover, coordination between organized business and labor mitigated wage-price spirals more effectively than in other member states (Soskice 1990).

Thus, the correspondence between the institutions of the ECB and the Bundesbank is not sufficient to generate price stability in Europe. Rather, low inflation would only be the norm in the euro-zone if:

- membership in the union were limited to countries that have demonstrated a strong commitment to price stability;
- all decisions affecting macroeconomic policy were made by actors with Bundesbank-like aversion to inflation; or
- the Bundesbank itself were allowed to set European macroeconomic policy—as was the case, de facto, under the exchange rate mechanism (ERM) of the European Monetary System (EMS).

The Maastricht treaty did not entrench the Bundesbank's hegemony over monetary policy. Neither did it ensure price-stable members or inflation-averse decisionmakers. The convergence criteria were merely guidelines for determining membership in the monetary union, which ultimately was settled by a qualified majority vote among member governments. Deals could thus be struck in which governments displaying less than rigid macroeconomic discipline could vote one another into the monetary union. If membership in the EMU were not restricted to a narrow deutsche mark zone, the only other guarantor of price stability would be a macroeconomic policymaking procedure that eliminates the influence of less inflation-averse actors. The Maastricht treaty did not do this. Decisions in the ECB are by simple majority, permitting national representatives to outvote the ECB's Executive Board to accommodate other objectives with looser monetary policies. Furthermore, the governments of member states retain significant influence over European macroeconomic policy through their power to establish guidelines for external exchange rates—irrespective of ECB decisions over monetary policy. Finally, EMU generates strong incentives for members to free-ride on the union by running large budget deficits, and the treaty does not provide automatic and binding sanctions against this. Even the apparently stringent rules subsequently written into the Growth and Stability Pact contain significant loopholes, and few analysts believe that the letter of the law will ever be enforced.

This interpretation suggests that the fundamental puzzle of Maastricht is not why the other members acquiesced in the institutionalization of German macroeconomic hegemony, but rather why the German government agreed to an EMU that weakened its position in Europe and threatened a cherished set of domestic outcomes. My answer is that the German government accepted an economically suboptimal EMU because after the implosion of the former Soviet bloc and German unification, it had a very strong interest in maintaining the momentum for ever greater European integration. Helmut Kohl simply was unwilling to allow the Maastricht summit to fail.

In turn, this implies a reading of post-Maastricht politics that does not concentrate on the anti-Brussels reaction of mass publics across Europe. Rather, it suggests that the major struggles over the path to the completion of Stage III of EMU should have taken place on two levels. The first was between the German interest in a small euro-zone and the larger vision championed by France—most importantly, including Italy in the monetary union. The second dimension was within Germany, between Helmut Kohl and the Bundesbank. The empirical record shows that France won the battle for an encompassing monetary union because the German government preferred this outcome to no euro at all. At the same time, Kohl won the domestic battle with the Bundesbank, paving the way for the inclusion of Italy in the monetary union.

In the following sections, I elaborate on this analysis of the pre- and post-Maastricht politics of monetary union. I put the EMU treaty under the microscope, so to speak, to determine precisely what the governments agreed to; to explain the outcome of the treaty negotiations; to explore the aftermath of Maastricht; and finally, to lay out my conclusions.

Interpreting the Maastricht Treaty

The part of the Treaty of European Union pertaining to EMU can be divided into two components: provisions regarding the transition to monetary union, and those governing macroeconomic policy in the completed union. The former include the convergence criteria; the latter set forth decisionmaking structures.

The protocols attached to the treaty outlined the following economic preconditions for EMU membership:

- for one year prior to membership, an inflation rate that was less than 1.5 percentage points higher than that of the three lowest national inflation rates in the EC;
- for one year prior to membership, long-term interest rates that were less than 2 percentage points higher than those of the three EC countries with the lowest inflation rates;
- for two years prior to membership, no devaluations within the narrow band (± 2.25 percent) of the exchange rate mechanism of the EMS;
- a national budget deficit of less than 3 percent of GDP; and
- a public debt of less than 60 percent of GDP.

These convergence criteria, however, were not hard-and-fast rules for admission. All decisions about membership in the union must ultimately be made under the qualified majority voting rule described in the Single European Act of 1987 (Article 109i). Moreover, the Maastricht treaty explicitly directed governments to base their decisions on whether members had made good faith efforts to meet the criteria. Article 109j, paragraph 1, states that eligibility for EMU is contingent upon "the achievement of a high degree of sustainable convergence" and that "this will be apparent from a rate of inflation which is *close to* that of at most the three best performing Member States." The treaty also asserts that the relevant deficit criterion is whether it has "*declined substantially and continuously* and has . . . reached a level that comes *close to the reference value*" (Article 104c, para. 2a). The appropriate consideration with respect to the public debt is "whether the ratio is not *sufficiently diminishing* and not *approaching the reference value at a satisfactory pace*" (Article 104c, para. 2b; all emphases added).

When the EC governments agreed to the reference values for the convergence criteria in December 1991, only France and Luxembourg satisfied them all. In the years that followed, convergence in inflation and interest rates was so pronounced that these criteria were scarcely mentioned in the debate about EMU members. The exchange rate criterion was rendered moot because of the EMS crises in 1992 and 1993 that resulted in the creation of broad ± 15 percent bands for members. Budget deficits rose considerably in the face of a stubborn and deep recession. Due to a combination of hard work and creative accounting in both national capitals and Brussels, almost all would-be euro members had deficits that were remarkably close to the 3 percent level in 1998. But no sleights of hand could conceal the fact that many member states had accumulated public debts in excess of the 60 percent threshold specified at Maastricht. To take the extreme examples, public debt was well over 100 percent of GDP in Belgium, Greece, and Italy.

But violating the debt ceiling clearly did not stop Belgium and Italy becoming founding members of the euro. How was this possible? The formal answer is that a qualified majority of EU member governments voted to let them in. To take the most important case, the member states decided that the costs of excluding Italy were greater than the costs of including it. A simple but not unreasonable rendering of the bargaining that made this possible goes like this: France wanted Italy in the EMU to eliminate the possibility of competitive devaluations of the lira, which were perceived to have harmed the French economy for years, and to create a powerful counterweight to German thinking on monetary policy. Romano Prodi's government made Italy's case for membership stronger through a series of domestic reforms committing the country to macroeconomic rectitude. Helmut Kohl, with the support of German exporters interested in stopping the competitiveness costs of an appreciating deutsche mark (DM), was strong enough to overcome the Bundesbank's opposition to a large euro-zone (and declining support among the mass public). Moreover, German opposition to Italian membership came to be seen as somewhat hypocritical given Germany's own fiscal difficulties in the mid-1990s. All of this politicking was made possible by the loopholes built into the Maastricht treaty.

What about the course of monetary policy inside the euro-11? The formal rules are clear. The Executive Board of the ECB and the national central bank governors of participating countries together constitute the ECB's Governing Council. According to the Maastricht treaty, the Council is fully independent (i.e., immune from political intervention) (Protocol on ESCB/ECB, Article 7). The primary objective of the ECB is price stability. Other goals, such as promoting employment and output, may be pursued only where they do not prejudice price stability (Article 105, para. 1). The ECB cannot monetize national deficits through the provision of credit to member governments (Article 104). The treaty also reinforces the independence of the ECB with appointment rules designed to reduce the influence of governments, not only collectively over the members of the Executive Board, but also individually over national central bank governors sitting on the Governing Council.[3]

It is these provisions that lead to the characterization of the ECB as a "super-Bundesbank." But does this institutional structure ensure stable and low rates of inflation in the euro-zone? There are at least three reasons to be skeptical about such a conclusion.

First, the Maastricht treaty is ambiguous as to who determines exchange rate policy. Article 105 delegates authority to the ECB not only to control monetary policy, but also to manage external exchange rates. However, this provision is qualified—if not contradicted—by Article 109, paragraph 1, which declares that the Council of Ministers—which comprises relevant government ministers from the member states, may (acting unanimously) "conclude formal arrangements for an exchange rate system for the ECU now the euro with respect to non-Community currencies." Paragraph 2 goes further, declaring that the Council of Ministers (voting by qualified majority) may "formulate general guidelines for exchange rate policy vis-à-vis these currencies." Paragraph 2 then states that these guidelines should be "without prejudice to the primary objective of the ESCB to maintain price stability," but it is unclear how in practice the tension between monetary policy—controlled by the ECB—and exchange rate policy—determined by the Council of Ministers—should be resolved.

Second, even assuming that effective control of monetary and exchange rate policies rests with the ECB, its decisions are by simple majority, with each member of the Governing Council having one vote (Protocol on ESCB/ECB, Article 10.2). In the euro-11, the Governing Council has seventeen members: six members of the Executive Board of the ECB and the governors of the eleven national central banks of countries in the union (Article 109a). Simple majority voting allows a coalition of nine national governors interested in looser monetary policies to outvote members of the Executive Board and the remaining central bank governors (even if the latter always pursue "sound money").

The Maastricht treaty anticipated this problem by mandating reforms for national central banks intended to ensure their independence, but there is no guarantee—and as yet no evidence—that this will be sufficient to turn all central bankers into would-be members of the Bundesbank. Looking to the future, the larger the membership of EMU becomes, the more likely that more members of the Governing Council will wish to stray from the path of price stability. For example, if Greece and Sweden are the next members of the euro-zone, this would most likely tilt the Governing Council in the direction of looser, not tighter, monetary policy.

Third, other things being equal, the creation of the single currency lessened the constraints on national fiscal policies by decoupling them from national money supply growth and exchange rate movements, thereby creating strong temptations for individual governments to free-ride on the monetary union as a whole by running large national deficits. If governments and economic actors within a member country believed that others would view their national economy as "too big to fail" (and hence would cover their debts, rather than allow them to default on loans), this would generate even stronger temptations to pursue expansionary fiscal policies. Thus, national governments that wished to engage in deficit spending would be constrained only by their ability to raise capital in international markets. Governments undoubtedly would have to pay higher interest rates when borrowing, but it is unlikely that the disparities in real interest rates across member states would be more than a couple of percentage points.[4]

The Maastricht treaty responded to these incentives for fiscal profligacy by providing that governments with "excessively" loose fiscal policies may be fined or required to maintain non-interest-bearing deposits in the ECB (Article 104c). But the structure for enforcing these sanctions is weak and indeterminate.[5] Most significantly, the decision to take any action against a high-deficit or high-debt government rests with a qualified majority in the Council of Ministers, not with the ECB (Article 104c). Thus a blocking coalition in the Council of Ministers could make it impossible to sanction EMU members who were using the protection of the single currency to pursue expansionary fiscal policies.

The weakness of these provisions led fiscal hawks in the EU successfully to push for the Growth and Stability Pact that would impose much tighter constraints on deficit spending.[6] The pact allows for the imposition of severe fines for countries that exceed 3 percent budget deficits—except when their economies are in recession. There are, however, two important loopholes in the stability pact that will likely reduce the probability of fines actually being imposed. First, governments are given a grace period (of two years) for running excessive deficits before any fines can be levied. Second, the provisions of the pact may be vitiated where there are "special circumstances." Decisions concerning what this means, and when fines should be imposed, will be made by a qualified majority vote in the Council of Ministers.

In sum, the formal independence granted to the ECB in the Maastricht treaty does not guarantee that EMU will generate low inflation across Europe. While it would be patently false to assert that the treaty mandates macroeconomic laxity in the EC, it is equally clear that neither will the monetary union necessarily be a paragon of price stability. For this to transpire, actors in all participating countries—not only central bank governors, but also government leaders—will have to behave in ways that mimic the stance of the Bundesbank. Based on the first year of the euro's existence, there is little reason to believe that this scenario will soon materialize. Further expansion of the euro-zone will make a hard-money scenario even less likely.

Intergovernmental Bargaining over the Treaty

Why did the member governments agree to this form of EMU at Maastricht? Conventional economic accounts are not particularly helpful. There is an extensive literature on optimal currency areas (McKinnon 1963) and on the desirable consequences of central bank independence (Barro and Gordon 1983; Rogoff 1985). It is doubtful, however, that the EC represents an optimal currency area, and this significantly weakens the putative benefits of central bank independence (Eichengreen 1992). The monetary union eliminates currency transaction costs and the uncertainty associated with the possibility of exchange rate movements for members. But it is not clear that these benefits outweigh the large costs associated with asymmetries in economic shocks, the limited prospects for efficient adjustment to them by less mobile factors (such as fixed capital and labor), and the likely responses of governments to these conditions.

The absence of a compelling economic justification for EMU led economists quickly to conclude that the prime motivating force behind the Maastricht treaty was "politics" (Fratianni, von Hagen, and Waller 1992). But what does this mean? A political explanation should start with the preferences of the governments who signed the treaty, and then move on to an analysis of the bargaining among them.

Government Preferences

Let us begin with the preferences of the critical player in EMU negotiations: the German government of Helmut Kohl. The most important point to note here is that the government was quite satisfied with the EMS status quo. Germany possessed considerable macroeconomic autonomy in the ERM as the nth currency in a de facto "$n - 1$" fixed exchange rate regime. So long as the currency markets viewed the deutsche mark as "good as gold"—and this seemed not to have been shaken by the massive economic costs of German unification—the German government could set its own fiscal policy, and the Bundesbank could maintain its preferred monetary policy, while policymakers in other ERM member states were constrained to follow the German lead.[7]

There were, nonetheless, two economic incentives for the German government to contemplate EMU. The government believed that the stability of the EMS would be prejudiced within Europe by the removal of capital controls, as mandated by the Single European Act, and stability in the external environment is very important to the exporters and multinationals that form the base of the German economy (Frieden 1992). With respect to the rest of the world, the government believed that the creation of a single European currency (dominated by Germany) would create a counterweight to the U.S. dollar and the yen, which in turn would lessen the effects of U.S. and Japanese policy choices on Germany (Scharpf 1991).

These reasons for German support of EMU should not conceal the fact that the government had very clear preferences as to the precise form the monetary union should take (and these preferences were faithfully followed by the governments of the Benelux countries, and later Austria, whose economies and policies were already inextricably connected with Germany). First, it wanted membership limited to countries whose economic policies and outcomes mirrored those in Germany ("convergence before union"). In the negotiations over Maastricht, German representatives opposed the qualified majority voting rule for membership in EMU, favoring instead a unanimity rule, under which Germany could veto the admission of any country (Woolley 1991, p. 16). Second, the German government believed that the operating rules for EMU should generate policies wholly consonant with the preeminence of price stability. Indeed, the government proposed that the ECB should be given complete control over both monetary and exchange rate policies, with no role at all for the Council of Ministers (Cameron 1992b, pp. 38–39; Woolley 1991, p. 18). The Germans also advocated the automatic imposition of large fines on union members whose budget deficits and public debts exceeded specific, previously determined levels (Cameron 1992b, p. 39).

The preferences of the other EU member governments were quite different from those of Germany and the other existing members of the de facto deutsche mark zone. There is little doubt that all the other governments sought to appropriate some of the German reputation for monetary stability. This was the basic impetus after the demise of the Bretton Woods regime for the creation of the "snake" exchange rate system and subsequently the EMS. However, by the end of the 1980s, it had become apparent to a number of EU members that large costs were associated with participation in the ERM. By far the most important was being forced to acquiesce in the Bundesbank's hard line on macroeconomic policy even if this generated very high levels of unemployment during national recessions. Thus, for the EC members outside the deutsche mark zone—France, Italy, and the four less industrialized countries, Greece, Ireland, Portugal, and Spain—the primary objective in moving to EMU was to "soften" the EMS. They sought to maintain a credible commitment to low inflation through participation in an international institution with a strong reputation for price stability, but without having to suffer the full consequences of the Bundesbank's uncompromising policy stance.

France's president, François Mitterrand, was in the vanguard of moves to limit Bundesbank power. Mitterrand and his advisers believed that the government's "socialism in one country" experiment of the early 1980s had been undermined by German unwillingness to accommodate the

French expansion within the ERM (Cameron 1992a). This position was strongly supported by the Italian government, as a result of the large economic costs associated with ERM membership, even though Italy did not join the narrow band until 1990 (Giavazzi and Spaventa 1989). Ireland, too, suffered within the ERM in the 1980s (Dornbusch 1989). The other European less industrialized countries realized that they, too, would in all likelihood soon have to join the narrow band of the ERM, and bear the consequences. For the governments in all these countries, the deleterious consequences of participating in the ERM were underlined in the period after German unification in 1990. High German interest rates greatly reduced the scope for other governments in the ERM to ease monetary policy, even though most were in the middle of deep domestic recessions. It is thus not surprising that Mitterrand was able to find strong allies for his basic position in other EC members.

These governments also disagreed with the German insistence that economic convergence precede union. All the governments—with the probable exception of Mitterrand's French administration—needed to transform their reputations for macroeconomic laxity by attaching themselves quickly to an international institution with strong counterinflation credentials. Obviously, this could be achieved by stable participation in the narrow band of the ERM, but the costs of attaining some of the Bundesbank's reputation were very high. EMU offered a more attractive prospect so long as its rules allowed some room for using countercyclical policies during deep recessions or, alternatively, provided some compensation for adhering to the dictates of macroeconomic rectitude. France and Italy pushed most strongly on the former front, whereas the European less industrialized countries, led by Spain, argued persistently that agreement on EMU should be coupled to the creation of a large new program for financial assistance to the poorer countries, in the name of cohesion.

The only government that did not neatly fall into either the deutsche mark zone or what might be called the "countercore"[8] group was the conservative British government under John Major. Major's government was not—at least initially—as inveterately anti-European as was Thatcher's. Nonetheless, protecting British sovereignty was still a fundamental element in the government's calculus. In the run up to Maastricht, the Major government sided with the German camp on the importance of price stability and on a long transition to EMU. However, Major was constrained from aligning too closely with the German government because of the popular perception that the decision in 1990 to participate in the German-dominated ERM had eroded British sovereignty. The ambivalence of the British government was reflected in Major's bargaining stance at Maastricht: basic support for the German position, but with the proviso that Britain obtain an opt-out clause that would delay the final

British decision on EMU until the membership and form of the union were complete.

In sum, the primary cleavage in the intergovernmental bargaining at Maastricht was between Germany, its Benelux allies, and Britain—who favored convergence before union, a slower transition to EMU, and strict operating rules—and France, Italy, and the southern countries—who preferred union before convergence, a fast transition, and looser operating rules. Given the differences between these two basic camps, what outcome might have been expected?

Bargaining over EMU: A First Cut

During the intergovernmental conferences that culminated at Maastricht, there was no indication that any of the member governments—not even the British one—would consider moving to a more flexible exchange rate regime. Thus, the governments were faced with two decisions. The first was whether to maintain the basic structure of the EMS or to move toward full monetary union. The second was whether the EMU would primarily reflect the preferences of the German government or those of the countercore.

On the basis of the economic dimension of monetary politics in Europe, one would have expected the German government to have been in a very strong position to impose its preferences on the countercore. The German government was quite satisfied with the EMS. It had an economic rationale to support a move to EMU, but these incentives were far smaller than those for the governments of the countercore, which were suffering badly at the hands of the Bundesbank within the ERM. Given this simple bargaining structure, the German government should have been able to hold out for an agreement at Maastricht that would have reflected its primary concerns for convergence before union and for the most stringent possible central bank independence reforms.

As discussed above, however, the final EMU treaty diverged considerably from these German preferences. In addition, the British government secured its opt-out clause. The less industrialized countries also gained agreement to development of a cohesion fund, the details of which were finally settled at the Edinburgh summit in the Delors II package. Thus, the outcome of the intergovernmental bargaining at Maastricht cannot be explained purely in terms of monetary politics. Rather, the bargaining must be understood in a much broader political economic context.

EC Bargaining in Post–Cold War Europe

Why was the German government unable to impose its EMU preferences on the other EC members at Maastricht, given its hegemonic position in

European monetary politics? It is commonly suggested that the German government had a strong federalist impulse—as a result of German history—and that this explained its acquiescence in a suboptimal EMU. However, more tangible reasons can be adduced to explain the government's behavior at Maastricht. There is little doubt that in the period up until the all-Germany election in December 1990, Kohl was prepared to trade acquiescence in a rapid movement towards EMU (and political union) for the acceptance by the other EC members of rapid German unification (such as allowing the new Germany into the EC without any revisions of the EC treaties). Indeed, it was in the calendar year 1990 that the firm pro-EMU (and pro–political union) alliance was formed between Kohl and Mitterrand (Cameron 1992b, pp. 40–43).

But the Maastricht treaty was not signed until December 1991—one year after the process of German unification was formally complete and internationally recognized. Why didn't the Kohl government then push harder for its preferred EMU? An abrupt about-face would have been difficult to manage diplomatically. More important, however, German interests changed significantly in the wake of the implosion of the Soviet bloc in 1989, moving beyond the short-term goal of gaining international acquiescence in German unification (Anderson and Goodman 1993). The clearest manifestation of these new German interests was the importance the government attached to convincing not only its European neighbors but also the U.S. that unification would not be the harbinger of a bellicose remilitarization; creating powerful institutional ties to the EC was viewed as the best way to achieve this end.

The economic consequences of the momentous events of 1989–1990 were at least as significant as these security concerns. In virtue of its geographic location, the historical ties of the former East Germany to the former Soviet bloc, and unified Germany's position as the economic hegemon in Europe, the German government of necessity had to play a central role in dealing with the problems that arose from the revolutions to the east. The government committed itself to a very large aid program to Russia in return for the latter's acquiescence in unification. It made the largest contributions of aid and other forms of economic assistance to the emergent capitalist democracies in Eastern Europe. Germany also bore the brunt of immigration pressures from the east, as hundreds of thousands of people sought to take advantage of the asylum provisions of the Basic Law and of a common cultural and ethnic heritage to migrate to Germany.

Moreover, the internal German economic outlook deteriorated significantly immediately after unification. Projections of the time it will take fully to integrate the former German Democratic Republic into the Federal Republic now run in the decades. In the short run, the official central government deficit increased from 0.5 percent in 1989 to 5 percent in 1991, largely as the result of spending US$83 billion on investment, unemployment benefits, and employment subsidies (Anderson and Goodman 1993, p. 10). The dire economic consequences of unification were layered on top of longer term demographic developments that place ever greater stress on the economy and the government in the coming decades—most significantly the graying of the population and the increasing propensity of Germans to take early retirement.

From this perspective, the German government's commitment to "Europe" could be readily understood. The partial socialization of the costs among all EC members of integrating the old eastern bloc (including the former East Germany) into Europe was very appealing, although the burden the other members are willing to assume has been considerably smaller than the German government would prefer.[9] More important, the most viable route for the German economy to dig its way out of its plight was through exports, and further penetration of EC markets was the best method of achieving this objective. This prospect would be enhanced by further progress toward ever greater European integration at Maastricht, whereas stalemate may have proved very damaging to broader German interests.

In sum, the German government had powerful reasons to hope that the Maastricht summit would result in a clear and significant advance in European integration. Other things being equal, the government would have preferred that this include an EMU based on an ironclad commitment to price stability. However, given its preferences for "more Europe," the government was prepared to compromise. The other member governments understood this, and thus they were able to gain significant concessions from Kohl in the wording of the Maastricht treaty, notwithstanding Germany's monetary hegemony and the bargaining power over EMU one might have expected this to have generated.

Ratification Politics and the Demise of the ERM

In contrast to the relatively straightforward ratification of the Single European Act (SEA) and the success of subsequent moves toward the completion of the internal market, the Maastricht treaty's infancy was a very trying one. As discussed above, the greatest opposition to the treaty was likely to come from economically conservative forces in Germany, particularly the Bundesbank (and finance minister Theo Waigel of the Bavarian Christian Socialist Union). But in 1992, the major problem was populist opposition in other member states (Britain, France, and above all, Denmark) and from the instability in the foreign exchange markets this opposition generated. It is equally clear, however, that the Bundesbank's intransigence with respect to lowering interest rates exacerbated these problems.

Each of the governments seeking to ratify the Maastricht treaty confronted a difficult political problem: how to persuade a majority of its citizens (in the cases of popular referenda) or parliamentarians (in the cases of legislative decisions) that giving up the national currency and formal authority over monetary policy was in their best interests.[10] As discussed above, the countercore governments had good reasons to be content with the economic implications of the EMU treaty. However, the arguments supporting this position were complex, and they required a sophisticated understanding of both open economy macroeconomics and the arcane details of the EMU treaty itself. Governments had to convince mass publics that under the EMS they had very little effective macroeconomic autonomy, and that autonomy would actually be increased under EMU as a result of diminished Bundesbank power, majoritarian decisions over monetary policy, and the like. This task was made all the more difficult by the depth of the recession in Europe in 1992, and the attendant feeling that "Europe" was at least partially to blame for this. In this environment, naive nationalism rather than sophisticated realpolitik was likely to be the dominant force in domestic politics.

The task confronting the French government after Mitterrand decided to tie the treaty's ratification to a popular referendum is illustrative. The Socialists were convinced that France's economic interests would be best served by ratifying the treaty, since it would increase the government's influence over French (and European) macroeconomic policy by mitigating the power of the Bundesbank. For many French voters, however, it was an absurd proposition that the best means of gaining economic independence was giving up the franc.

The ratification problems that plagued the Maastricht treaty were clearly highly significant on their own. But the popular backlash against Maastricht also had very harmful effects on the EMS. After the removal of virtually all controls on capital flows within the EC by 1991, many economists argued that the future stability of the exchange rate mechanism would depend crucially on expectations in the currency markets that the EMS was only a stepping-stone to EMU. So long as speculators believed this, they had little reason to fear prospective devaluations by members—even those whose economies were performing very badly.

Once the treaty's ratification became problematic, however, the markets' confidence in the weaker currencies in the EMS—and the disciplines imposed by the exchange rate mechanism—declined precipitously. The credibility of the ERM was contingent upon the commitment of all participants to defend their currency parities, come what may, and agreement to EMU was the most important tangible evidence of this commitment. As the credibility of the ERM eroded, the probability of speculative runs against the weaker currencies increased significantly. With hindsight, it is clear that some currencies were overvalued in the EMS, most notably, sterling and the lira. But their parities might have been sustainable if the ERM had continued to be perceived as a stepping-stone to EMU. When this connection was called into question, the foreign exchange markets began making speculative runs on currencies whose economic "fundamentals" were not sound. Indeed, even the "sound" franc was subject to extensive speculative attacks, particularly at the time of the French referendum.

In essence, this is the story of September 1992 and its aftermath. For present purposes, however, two elements of the politics of the currency crisis should be highlighted. First, the governments with currencies that were under attack struggled valiantly to maintain their ERM parities, with public pronouncements of commitment to the system, the raising of interest rates, and the spending of reserves in the currency markets. In this context, it should be remembered that both Prime Minister Major and Chancellor of the Exchequer Lamont continued to insist that sterling would remain in the ERM right up until the moment it was announced that, in fact, Britain was suspending its membership. This behavior was consistent with preferences for more, rather than less, monetary integration in Europe. There was little evidence before September 1992 that any of the EC members wished to turn to more flexible exchange rates.

Second, and more important, the Bundesbank was under political pressure—from the German government and from the rest of Europe—to ease interest rates throughout the crisis period. For the German government, the Bundesbank's tight monetary policy was counterproductive with respect to reviving the German economy. The bank argued precisely the opposite: that tight money was the only antidote to the government's fiscal laxity during the euphoric months after the fall of the Berlin Wall. It was also clear to government leaders throughout the EC that the Bundesbank's policy was critical to the economic fortunes of other EC members, to the stability of the EMS, and ultimately to the prospects for the EMU.

In this regard, it should be noted that the Bundesbank studiously adhered to its EMS obligations to intervene in the foreign exchange markets to support currencies that reached their floors against the deutsche mark.[11] For example, the German central bank bought DM24 billion worth of lira in the second week of September to defend the Italian currency. At the same time, however, the bank was not prepared to take the more important step of significantly lowering its interest rates, which would have lessened the speculative pressures that were pushing the weak currencies to their ERM floors. When the lira was devalued by 7 percent on September 12, the Bundesbank cut Germany's Lombard rate by a quarter of a percentage point and its discount rate by half a point, but these cuts were considered far too small and too late. Moreover, in the ensuing months of speculative runs against other currencies, the Bundesbank refused to take any significant action on interest rates, confining its activity to the EMS-mandated interventions in the foreign exchange markets (while speaking out against this practice as encouraging speculation) (Norman 1992).

One might argue that the Bundesbank merely acted myopically, focusing exclusively on the German economy, in 1992, rather than trying willfully to break up the EMS and to lessen the prospects for an EC-wide EMU. However, in the months after September, the three highest officials of the bank—Helmut Schlesinger, the president; his vice president, Hans Tietmeyer; and the Bundesbank's chief economist, Otmar Issing—gave numerous speeches detailing their opposition to the EMU negotiated at Maastricht (Norman 1992). Predictably, their speeches emphasized three points. First, while EMU was a worthwhile objective in theory, it could not under any circumstances prejudice German price stability. Second, membership in the union should have been determined by a monetary survival of the fittest, in which only those economies that matched German performance should have been admitted. Finally, the operating rules of the EMU were not stringent enough to mandate price stability, and the political control that the treaty allowed should be eradicated.

What explains the behavior of the Bundesbank? Here, it must be recognized that even before Maastricht, there was a cleavage in Germany between Kohl and his foreign minister, Hans-Dietrich Genscher, both of whom were prepared to compromise on EMU agreement in the context of broader political and economic objectives, and the Bundesbank, for which domestic price stability was the preeminent concern. Kohl possessed the formal authority to sign the Maastricht treaty to commit Germany to EMU, but this did not guarantee that the Bundesbank would then fall into line. Rather, as had been the case after the government's decision quickly to create a monetary union in Germany (with its hallmark one-to-one deutsche mark–ostmark exchange rate for individuals' savings), the bank used its autonomy with respect to monetary policy to counteract the government's decision. With respect to German monetary union and the government's subsequent fiscal expansion, the Bundesbank's response was ever higher interest rates. This policy carried over to the EC level, where the bank insisted that given the German economy's domestic problems, it was imperative that inflation be held in check, irrespective of the consequences of this policy for the other European economies and for the Maastricht treaty. The signing of the treaty only strengthened the Bundesbank's resolve to hold the line on stable money.

The Birth of the Euro

Given all the turmoil of 1992/93, one might have expected that the transition to Stage III of EMU, the birth of the euro, would have been fraught with pitfalls—any one of which might have led to the collapse of the project. This view could only have been strengthened when the EU governments agreed to shelve plans for a fast track to stage III and to move to the latest possible starting date stipulated in the treaty, December 31, 1998. Moreover, the 1990s European recession was longer and deeper than most people would have anticipated. This could have been expected both further to erode public support for EMU and to make it even harder for governments to satisfy the letter of the law concerning the convergence criteria.

But the euro was born with the dawn of 1999, and its membership was considerably larger than a DM-zone, however broadly defined. Denmark, Sweden, and the United Kingdom exercised their opt-outs, but of the countries that wanted to join the new club only Greece was excluded. In turn, the first year of the euro's existence was one in which its value declined steadily to reach parity with the U.S. dollar. For those interested in turning around Europe's parlous unemployment record in the 1990s, this was a good thing. For others, it is only a sign that the euro is and will always be a much weaker currency than the deutsche mark was.

However, perhaps the notable thing about the birth and infancy of the euro is how "normal" it all was. There was no massive volatility in European currency markets as the New Year approached in December 1998. Euro-denominated bank deposits did not flee Italy in favor of Germany during 1999. All that happened was that the euro depreciated against the dollar—with good reason, given the overheated American economy and double-digit unemployment rates on the continent. Greece and Sweden—and perhaps even Denmark—may join the euro-zone in the next couple of years. Tony Blair wants the United Kingdom to join them, though it increasingly seems that his European ambitions will have to be put on hold for the foreseeable future.

How did we get from the turmoil of 1992/93 to the tranquility of 1999? Two observations stand out. First, Helmut Kohl's political will acted as the midwife of the euro's birth. He acquiesced in an expansive interpretation of the convergence criteria, and he was able to fend off domestic opposition to this stance. To be sure, Kohl was helped by the heroic efforts of Prodi in Italy, the support of the Commission's interpretation of the economic statistics, and numerous other propitious events along the way. But with hindsight, the Chancellor's commitment to the monetary integration project for almost twenty years was surely the most important determinant of the project's success.

The second observation is the mirror image of the first. Euroland does not today look much like the edifice the Bundesbank wanted to create. Italian participation in EMU is a reality. Once Oskar LaFontaine lost his job in the new German social democrat-led government (ending the public cries for monetary expansion), the ECB was able quietly but effectively to cut European interest rates in ways that reinforced relatively expansionary fiscal stances in national capitals. Efforts to coordinate fiscal policy at the European level are likely to strengthen in the coming years.

Conclusion

The history of monetary integration in 1990s Europe is truly remarkable. The creation of the euro was arguably one of the most important peacetime events in twentieth-century Europe, if not the world. One cannot understand this history in terms of traditional economic analyses. The politics of the Maastricht treaty is critical to all that has happened since.

The provisions of EMU were part of the Treaty on European Union, signed at Maastricht in December 1991. It was monetary union, rather than political union, that strengthened the bonds of European integration in the 1990s. The Maastricht treaty did not amount to a plan to re-create the German model at the European level. It did not rule out the admission of less disciplined and lower performing members. Its operating rules were not designed to eliminate political control over monetary policy. How can this be explained? The simple answer is that after the tumultuous events of 1989 and 1990, the German government was prepared significantly to compromise on the details of the EMU treaty in order to make tangible progress on European integration at Maastricht, for both political and economic reasons. Notwithstanding the hegemonic German position in the EMS, the Kohl government acceded to the demands of seemingly less powerful member governments for less stringent admission rules and a less than airtight commitment to price stability.

Notes

1. I would like to thank Peter Hall, Torben Iversen, Peter Lange, David Soskice, Wolfgang Streeck, George Tsebelis, and John Woolley for helpful comments and suggestions on various aspects of this chapter. Special thanks to Barry Eichengreen and Jeffry Frieden for their tireless criticism and enthusiastic support.

2. The other important elements of the treaty included institutional reforms to increase the power of the European Parliament, the extension of qualified majority voting to certain areas of social policy, and agreements for coordinating defense and foreign policies.

3. Article 14 of the Protocol stipulates that all members of EMU must alter their domestic regimes so that the terms of governors of national central banks are at

least five years (i.e., no shorter than electoral cycles in any of the member countries). The term of the president of the ECB shall be eight years; the vice president will serve for five years; and the four other members of the Executive Board (who will also serve on the Governing Council) will have terms from five to eight years. Furthermore, the terms of members of the Executive Board are not renewable (Protocol, Article 50).

4. During the late 1980s, for example, real interest rates in Italy were only two points higher than those in Germany, even though the Italian national debt was very high, and even though a considerable part of the interest rate differential was caused by the risk premium attached to the possibility of a devaluation of the lira.

5. It is instructive that the EC did not choose to follow the practice that has evolved in the U.S. to meet this problem: balanced budget amendments to almost all of the state constitutions.

6. See Eichengreen and Wyplosz (forthcoming) for an excellent analysis.

7. The government and the Bundesbank, of course, may pursue conflicting policies, as has been the case in German unification. However, this does not detract from the central point that German policymakers possess considerably more macroeconomic autonomy than do their counterparts in other European countries.

8. I wish to thank Jeffry Frieden for suggesting this term to me.

9. The EC extended approximately US$4 billion in structural funds to the eastern portion of Germany in 1991, but the Bonn government continues to shoulder the bulk of financial assistance, not only to the former East Germany, but also to Eastern Europe.

10. Referendums were constitutionally mandated only in Denmark and Ireland. In France, Mitterrand decided to seek a referendum in order to capitalize on what he thought to be very strong popular support for the treaty. German Länder have argued that portions of the treaty require revisions of the Basic Law, but this argument was not accepted by the federal government.

11. It is less clear whether the Bundesbank followed the 1987 Basle-Nyborg guidelines for intramarginal interventions.

References

Alesina, Alberto, and Vittori Grilli, 1992, The European Central Bank: Reshaping monetary politics in Europe, in: Matthew Canzoneri, et al., eds., *Establishing a central bank: Issues in Europe and lessons from the U.S.* (Cambridge: Cambridge University Press).

Anderson, Jeffrey, and John Goodman, 1993, Mars or Minerva? A united Germany in a post-cold war Europe, in: Stanley Hoffmann, Robert Keohane, and Joseph Nye, eds., *The post-cold war settlement in Europe* (forthcoming).

Barro, Robert, and David Gordon, 1983, Rules, discretion and reputation in a model of monetary policy. *Journal of Monetary Economics* 12, 101–122.

Cameron, David, 1992a, Exchange rate policy in France, 1981–1983. Paper presented at the Conference on Labor and the Left in France: A Decade of Mitterrand, Wesleyan University.

_____, 1992b, *The Maastricht agreement on Economic and Monetary Union: Initiation, negotiation, implications.* manuscript, Yale University.

Dornbusch, Rudiger, 1989, Credibility, debt and unemployment: Ireland's failed stabilization. *Economic Policy* 4, 173–209.

Eichengreen, Barry, 1992, *Should the Maastricht treaty be saved?* PEEI Working Paper 1.10, University of California, Berkeley.

Eichengreen, Barry, and Charles Wyplosz, forthcoming, The stability pact: more than a minor nuisance? *Economic Policy.*

Fratianni, Michele, Jürgen von Hagen, and Christopher Waller, 1992, *The Maastricht Way to EMU.* Princeton Essays in International Finance 182 (Princeton: International Finance Section).

Frieden, Jeffry, 1992, *European Monetary Union: A political economy perspective.* Manuscript, University of California, Los Angeles.

Giavazzi, Francesco, and Luigi Spaventa, 1989, Italy: The real effects of inflation and disinflation. *Economic Policy* 4, 133–172.

Hall, Peter, 1993, *Independence and inflation: The missing variables.* Manuscript, Harvard University.

Kenen, Peter, 1992, *EMU after Maastricht* (Washington, D.C.: Group of Thirty).

Magee, Stephen, et al., 1989, *Black hole tariffs and endogenous policy theory* (New York: Cambridge University Press).

McKinnon, Ronald, 1963, Optimum currency areas. *American Economic Review* 53, 717–725.

Norman, Peter, 1992, The day Germany planted a currency time bomb. *Financial Times,* Dec. 12–13, 2.

Rogoff, Kenneth, 1985, The optimal degree of commitment to an intermediate monetary target. *Quarterly Journal of Economics* 100, 1169–1190.

Scharpf, Fritz, 1991, *Crisis and choice in European social democracy* (Ithaca, N.Y.: Cornell University Press).

Soskice, David, 1990, Wage determination: The changing role of institutions in advanced industrialized countries. *Oxford Review of Economic Policy* 6, 36–61.

Woolley, John, 1991, *Creating a European Central Bank: Negotiating EMU and the ESCB.* Manuscript, University of California, Santa Barbara.

6

International and Domestic Institutions in the EMU Process and Beyond

LISA L. MARTIN[1]

Abstract

European progress toward monetary union takes place within the highly institutionalized setting of the European Union (EU). This chapter examines the ways in which formal institutions and decisionmaking procedures constrain the Economic and Monetary Union (EMU) process. The EU's structure has both created demands for and facilitated cross-issue linkages, and these linkages characterize the successful bargaining on EMU and its stability in the early stages. However, success also required ratification. Domestic ratification procedures and changes in the EU's context of linkage created challenges for the ratification of the Maastricht treaty. Ratification was also tied to concerns about democratic accountability, which arose from current legislative procedures and are the subject of ongoing institutional reform.

In 1985, members of the European Union (EU) agreed in the Single European Act (SEA) to move rapidly toward completion of the internal market and to use qualified majority voting on questions relating to their commercial relations. In December 1991, in Maastricht, EU members extended the scope of supranational cooperation on economic and monetary issues.[2] The Maastricht Treaty on European Union modestly expanded regional cooperation on social, foreign, and defense policy, but its centerpiece was a timetable for Economic and Monetary Union (EMU). The treaty specified institutional procedures and substantive goals for moving to monetary union and a plan for the management of members' financial affairs through a European Central Bank (ECB). The late stages of moving toward EMU went more smoothly than analysts expected, and the ECB is now in place, with eleven members of the EU using a new currency, the euro.

The Maastricht treaty ran into trouble during the ratification process. Most analyses of the initially troubled progress of EMU focus either on the alleged economic and efficiency problems of the Maastricht treaty or on the conflicts of interest among the most powerful member states.[3] I argue that a full understanding of the EMU process also requires careful attention to the institutional features of regional and domestic politics. I find that outcomes cannot be explained solely in terms of efficiency or by the interests of the most powerful states; they are in large part shaped by the opportunities and constraints created by institutional arrangements.

The institutionalized rules under which the EU operates, and through which member states make decisions about EU affairs, condition the outcomes of regional bargaining. EMU is embedded in a complex, institutionalized pattern of intermember cooperation on many issues. The bargains struck on EMU and the process of implementation are not dependent solely on state power and the potential economic benefits of EMU, but also on the ways in which decisionmaking on EMU is constrained by EU procedures. Foremost among these institutional constraints are the linkages between EMU and other EU issues, the ratification procedures for treaty revisions, and the need for accountability to domestic politicians. Each of these constraints is explored in this chapter.

The first section argues that issue linkages enhanced by the EU's institutional structure are vital to an understanding of the bargains reached at Maastricht and the success of EMU thus far. This structure enhances the value of members' reputations for living up to agreements, allowing them to construct deals that would be more difficult to sustain if undertaken outside of the institutional context. Because the institutionalized framework of the EU offers members benefits in many issue areas, it decreases temptations to renege on agreements and thus increases the level of cooperation. Moreover, issue linkage creates possibilities for mutually beneficial deals that would not be available in single-issue bargaining. Members are able to gain cooperation on those issues of most vital interest to themselves—for example, political unification for Germany—by making concessions on issues of lesser concern. Such deals would be unstable outside a formal institutional framework. Linkage also helps us understand the surprisingly smooth transition to EMU.

The second section turns to the ratification problem. I examine how domestic ratification procedures and the prospect of a multispeed Europe constrained states' decisions on the Maastricht treaty, focusing on Denmark as an illustrative case. Because the EU's rules required ratification of the Maastricht treaty by all members, the bargaining leverage of small states was enhanced relative to what we would expect in typical interstate bargaining. A relevant example is the disproportionate attention paid to satisfying Denmark's demands in late 1992 and early 1993, since its rejection of the treaty created additional questions about the future of EMU. While national representatives, in general, have incentives to construct cross-issue deals, domestic interests often prefer to separate issues from one another, thus threatening to undermine EU agreements, such as the Maastricht plan for EMU. These pressures came into play during the domestic ratification process, when the specific rules governing ratification determine whether domestic interests can reduce the level of cooperation to which government negotiators have agreed. Stringent ratification procedures, such as Denmark's, if not properly anticipated by negotiators, can lead to failure to carry out mutually beneficial deals. If anticipated, they can enhance an individual state's bargaining power. Both domestic rules and the changing context of international linkage constrain both the nature of EU bargains and the probability of successful ratification.

Ratification is also tied to correcting a perceived lack of democratic accountability; in the third section I analyze how the EU's regulatory structure has produced and is attempting to correct this deficit. Accountability problems are more severe in day-to-day EU business than in the treaty ratification process. Ratification requirements give domestic actors the opportunity to influence bargaining on treaty revisions. However, questions have arisen as to the ability of such actors to have a say in the normal EU legislative process. Such concerns are a central part of the debate over Maastricht and thus influence the future of EMU. Analysis of legislative procedures shows that concerns about accountability are valid and that changes in the role of the European Parliament (EP) can increase accountability, but also that such changes are predictably opposed by national parliaments. Accountability issues also directly affect the future of EMU as analysts, politicians, and publics raise concerns about the accountability of the ECB. The future of EMU cannot be divorced from ongoing debates about how to correct the accountability deficit.

Issue Linkage and EMU

International institutions such as the EU play a powerful role through changing the incentives states face. States' incentives change because of stable linkages among issues created by institutions. The Maastricht agreement on the terms of monetary union was influenced and facilitated by a link between EMU and other issues within the EU. Such linkages are unstable and susceptible to reneging if done on an ad hoc basis, thus the EU's institutional framework explains why state leaders are willing to take the risk of committing themselves to such deals as the one reached in Maastricht (Weber and Wiesmeth 1991). In this way, the EU framework contributes to a network of political relationships, identified by Cohen (1994) as necessary for monetary union.

International organizations such as the EU facilitate stable linkages among issues that are not inseparably intertwined for functional reasons. As Robert Keohane put it, "Clustering of issues under a regime facilitates side-payments among these issues: more potential *quids* are available for the *quo*. Without international regimes linking clusters of issues to one another, side-payments and linkages would be difficult to arrange in world politics" (1984, p. 91). The EU has, indeed, linked clusters of issues: commercial policy, agricultural subsidies, social policies, occasional foreign policy initiatives, and so on. Members have been able, at times, to use institutionalized linkage to gain the support of other states on issues on which the latter have no other compelling interest. Since refusal to go along could jeopardize the broad array of benefits provided by the EU, linkages have increased incentives to cooperate.[4] For example, in 1982 Britain used the leverage created by linked issues to generate support from reluctant member states for economic sanctions against Argentina during the Falklands war (Martin 1992). Eichengreen and Frieden (1994) cite the linkage between monetary and broader EU issues as a component of French and Italian decisions to join the EMS.

EU linkage incentives can be strong. Ireland, for example, has received EU aid equivalent to approximately 5 percent of its GDP, channeled through agricultural, social, and regional funds (*The Economist*, Dec. 7, 1991, p. 53). This financial windfall inclines Ireland and similarly positioned recipients to support further moves toward European union, even though such movement is likely to pose real challenges for their national economies and social structures. In the past, side-payments to poorer EU states have been essential to gaining their agreement on social policies that would threaten their competitive edge as low-cost producers (Marks 1992) and their agreement to the SEA in 1985 (Moravcsik 1991, p. 25). Their acquiescence to the Maastricht social protocol and EMU was, according to some, explicitly linked to financial incentives, following this historical pattern (Lange 1993).

In the bargaining over EMU, demands from poorer states for financial compensation in exchange for support of Franco-German plans were unusually explicit. Because EMU proposals implied austerity measures with high short-term economic costs and even higher political costs for the governments of the poor countries, they were unwilling to sign on to EMU without gaining something in return. In 1988, the "structural funds" that provide resources for structural reform to poorer members had been doubled, as anticipated in the SEA deal. In the bargaining over EMU, Spain led a group of the four poorest EU members (the other three were Portugal, Greece, and Ireland) in threatening to veto any treaty unless the group received increased transfers. Beyond increases in the structural funds, the group sought and achieved promises of a "cohesion fund," so that transfers would again double. These initiatives were not enshrined in the Maastricht treaty itself, but in a package known as Delors II, presented by European Commission president Jacques Delors immediately following the summit.

A number of institutional aspects of this deal are particularly intriguing. First is the decision of richer states, particularly Germany, to respond positively to Spanish demands. The German economy, under strain from the demands of unification, was not in a condition in which increases in transfers to poor EU members can be regarded as negligible. Although the increased resources of the cohesion fund represent only a small fraction of Germany's GDP, it is not obvious that Germany would have been willing to commit money for increased transfers unless it saw clear benefits in doing so. From a purely intergovernmental perspective, relying on state power as the key explanatory variable, Germany's decision to increase transfers significantly is puzzling since it involves a significant concession by Germany to weaker states. As one formal analysis of linkage puts the puzzle, "Why offer concessions when you will prevail without them?" (Morrow 1992, p. 164). Considering the institutional setting in which bargaining took place provides insight. Because the Maastricht plan took the form of a treaty requiring ratification by all members, each state had veto power. A veto would have dealt a blow to Germany's efforts to make rapid progress on European integration, an especially urgent agenda since German reunification (Garrett 1994). EU rules that require unanimous approval of the treaty changed the bargaining dynamics from those we would expect in typical, noninstitutionalized interstate bargaining, increasing the leverage of smaller countries such as Spain.[5]

Institutional constraints—here, unanimity requirements—help us understand why Spain was successful in gaining targeted concessions for the four poorer EU members. However, questions remain on the other side of the ledger, in explaining the willingness of the four to sign the treaty while increases in structural funds were left to a separate budget package, on which Germany could, in principle, renege. Here, consideration of institutional factors provides guidance. Deals cut within an institution rather than outside one gain stability because members put increased value on their reputations for living up to agreements. If the richer states were to back down from the understandings reached in Maastricht, their reputations and ability to reach mutually beneficial cross-issue deals within the EU in the future would suffer. Thus, the four could rely on commitments by the other eight to increase transfers in spite of difficult economic conditions in the richer countries. In fact, at the Edinburgh summit in December 1992, after much debate, the rich countries formally committed themselves to budget provisions very close to those of the Delors II package. A focus on the EU's institutional structure provides insight into two related sets of questions about issue linkage: why it was necessary for the richer countries to make side-payments, and why the four poorest found such commitments credible.

The dependence of past patterns of EU cooperation on reliable issue linkages draws our attention to the *acquis communautaire*. New entrants to the EU have been required to accept the *acquis communautaire*, the accumulated set of norms, rules, and obligations developed by the EU. This concept makes explicit the linkages created by the EU, further solidifying them and thus enlarging the scope for jointly beneficial agreements (Tollison and Willett 1979; Sebenius 1983). Because the process of ratification is public and the terms of membership clear and explicit, acceptance of the *acquis communautaire* has served as a signal of members' intentions and linked their reputations to the EU in a way that informal or ad hoc agreements could not (Lipson 1991).

Institutional linkages also appear central to the fact that the EMU process has remained on track, contrary to the predictions of many analysts. One set of concerns that threatened to derail EMU was the fact that Maastricht specified that the primary goal of the ECB was price stability. In the face of persistent high unemployment and sluggish growth in EU members, many states—most prominently France—expressed concern that a single-minded emphasis on keeping inflation low under EMU would exacerbate employment and growth problems. The result was intense bargaining between Germany and France, resulting in the Stability and Growth Pact, reached at the Dublin summit in 1996. Eighteen-hour marathon negotiations between France and Germany resulted in a pact that was dominated by Germany's desire for stringent rules to bolster the convergence criteria specified in the Maastricht treaty (Barnard 1997). France, in contrast, demanded some degree of political oversight and an emphasis on the need for flexibility to pursue growth objectives.

Reflecting German demands for price stability, the pact puts strict limits on budget deficits for governments participating in EMU. It provides for fines for governments that violate the 3 percent of GDP limit. However, reflecting concerns about growth, flexibility was built into the pact as well. Fines may not be levied for countries in recession, allowing governments to run deficits to encourage growth in such instances. In addition, fines will only be levied after a vote in the European Council; they are not automatic.

French (and others') concerns about growth led to the flexibility built into the pact. Another result of concern about the structure of the ECB as specified in the Maastricht treaty was the creation of the Euro-X group. Euro-X (as it turned out, Euro-XI) is the group of countries participating in EMU. This informal body, created on the insistence of the Jospin government in France, is to serve as a forum for consultation among finance ministers and provide a political counterweight to the ECB. France failed to gain any formal authority for Euro-X, but many expressed concern that it would undermine the independence of the ECB. Although Germany initially proposed that the Stability and Growth Pact take the form of a treaty, fears that it would not be ratified meant that it took a different legal form (Artis and Winkler 1998).

The Stability and Growth Pact, which allowed the EMU process to continue in spite of numerous threats to its success, illustrates the continuing influence of institutional factors. As in the process of bargaining and implementing the Maastricht treaty, the fact that the pact was embedded in the dense institutional structure of the EU was essential. The negotiating forum encouraged Germany and France to make the necessary concessions to make a deal, although at the time many voices were speaking out against pursuing EMU plans at all. The demands of ratification—as discussed in the following section—determined the form of the pact.

Perhaps most importantly, considerations of linkage and reputation allowed members to agree to a pact that could be quite risky in the future. Germany's demands for stringent rules reflected a fear that other countries would fail to enforce fiscal discipline once EMU was in place, spreading problems such as inflation and currency depreciation throughout the euro-zone. In spite of these fears, Germany agreed to the political constraints on rules demanded by France. The fact that the pact was embedded in the EU structure provided assurance that members would live up to their commitments in spite of these political loopholes, and in spite of the fact that governments did not take the step of formally ratifying the pact as a treaty.

Overall, the characteristics of EU bargains, such as those embodied in the Maastricht treaty, are as strongly influenced by the EU's formal structure as by considerations of economic efficiency or state power. Two effects of the institution are evident: the facilitation of stable linkages across issues, and disproportionately large bargaining power of small states. These features resulted in a pattern of concessions and side-payments, allowing us to understand the willingness of government leaders to agree to the Maastricht plan for EMU. They also help us to understand how the plan overcame the challenges that appeared between 1992 and 1997, through the Stability and Growth Pact. However, governmental agreement did not guarantee implementation of EMU; the crucial step of formal ratification of the Maastricht treaty represented another institutional hurdle.

Rules, Weakened Linkages, and Ratification

A focus on institutions helps clarify certain puzzles about the bargains struck at the Maastricht summit, drawing our attention to issue linkages, which are demanded by unanimity rules and facilitated by reputational effects. However, such linkages are no guarantee of success. Implementation of deals struck at Maastricht was difficult, especially following Danish rejection of the treaty in a June 1992 referendum, very narrow French approval, and a commitment by Britain to delay consideration of ratification until a change in the Danish decision. In this section, I consider the effect of domestic ratification requirements on EU bargaining. I focus on Denmark and recent changes in the role of national parliaments to examine both the effect of domestic institutions and the changing context of EU linkage politics.

One threat to cross-issue deals, such as that struck at Maastricht, arises from the differing incentives facing negotiators and domestic interest groups. National representatives in the Council, representing broad constituencies, generally strive to realize aggregate gains arising from cross-issue deals and are thus willing to compromise on some issues. However, those domestic groups whose interests are "traded away" in a grand bargain can be expected to protest, attempting to disaggregate such deals and avoid the compromises to which their national representatives have committed their country, thereby threatening processes of ratification. While national representatives appreciate large-scale bargains, domestic actors with narrower interests may favor a multispeed Europe and/or attempt to disrupt linkages. We find evidence of such a pattern in Germany, where the Bundesbank argued in favor of a flexible approach to EMU that Chancellor Helmut Kohl explicitly rejected, reflecting different valuations of a one-speed, tightly linked EU. Domestic resistance to the Maastricht treaty suggests that we turn our attention to problems of ratification.

The Danish case is illustrative of the impact of institutions on bargaining and ratification. Studies of the EU have noted that Denmark does not behave as do other small member countries. It behaves more as does Britain, being reluctant to surrender decisionmaking authority to supranational bodies, passing amendments to the original Rome treaties by small margins, and accepting EU decisions with reservations (Williams 1991, pp. 159–160). However, until the 1992 referendum, the Danish stance was seen more as a minor irritant than as a major impediment to EU cooperation. From an intergovernmental perspective on cooperation, it would not be possible for such a small country to exercise significant influence over the course of events.

The Danish political system makes it difficult for the government to commit to international agreements without working through stringent ratification procedures in the parliament and/or national referenda. Through these domestic institutional constraints, the Danes have succeeded in maintaining unusually tight control over the scope of EU agreements into which they enter, and over the actions of their representatives once treaties are ratified. Constitutionally, ratification of all treaties in the Folketing (the Danish parliament) requires a five-sixths vote, far exceeding the supermajority requirements of other liberal democracies. If the parliament supports a treaty by only a simple majority, it will be considered ratified only after passing a national referendum with participation of at least 30 percent of the electorate (Petersen and Elklit 1973, p. 198).

In 1972, Denmark held a referendum on the decision to join the EU, which passed with 63.4 percent of the vote (Borre 1986, p. 191; Petersen and Elklit 1973). In 1986, because a parliamentary majority opposed ratification of the SEA, Prime Minister Poul Schlüter called for a "consultative" referendum. A decision to refuse to vote in favor of the SEA was in part a tactical parliamentary move by the opposition Social Democratic party, which wished to force a general election. The prime minister circumvented parliamentary opposition by calling for a referendum, as the Social Democrats would feel bound for electoral reasons to vote according to its results. Thus, when the SEA was approved by 56.2 percent of the voters in February 1986 the Folketing duly ratified the treaty (Worre 1988). Nevertheless, the referendum revealed a significant decline since 1972 in popular support for the terms of European integration. Rural areas voted in favor of the treaty, while opposition came primarily from the region around Copenhagen and other strongholds of left-leaning political parties (Borre 1986, pp. 191–193). In June 1992, support for the Maastricht treaty fell to 49.3 percent (*New York Times*, June 3, 1992, p. A1). This result means that just over 23,000 Danish voters—the difference necessary to have produced a majority yes vote—threw the future of EMU into question.

In addition to rules that give the national parliament and electorate the power to veto treaties, the Folketing attempts tightly to constrain activities of Danish ministers in the European Council. Because Denmark is characterized by frequent minority government, party line voting is not sufficient to guarantee a majority for government legislation and thus ensure implementation of agreements reached in the Council (Auken, Buksti, and Sørensen 1975, p. 16). The Folketing established a Market Relations Committee (MRC) to ensure that Danish ministers would not commit themselves to agreements that would not meet with parliamentary approval (Fitzmaurice 1976). The MRC, on which the parties in parliament are proportionally represented, requires that ministers confer with it regarding proposed negotiating positions prior to discussions in the Council (Møller 1983). If the content of the subject under discussion in the Council changes significantly, ministers are to return for further instructions. Danish implementation of EU directives suggests the effectiveness of consultation and direction. While Danish representatives are obstinate in negotiations, by April 1992 Denmark had implemented nearly 140 of the 158 White Paper measures requiring national approval, the highest approval rate of any EU member (*The Economist,* July 11, 1992, Survey p. 10).

Recognizing the strategic advantages of not fully revealing a negotiating position in advance, instructions for Danish ministers are given orally; thus the MRC acts with significant autonomy from the rest of parliament (Fitzmaurice 1976, p. 283). The short leash on which the MRC keeps ministers creates conditions in which they can credibly threaten "involuntary defection" if EU agreements do not satisfy the demands of domestic politics (Putnam 1988). The pattern of delegation in Denmark enhances its bargaining power beyond what we would predict from a model that did not take institutional constraints into account. For example, Denmark received concessions in the form of addenda to the Maastricht treaty as a condition of reconsidering ratification. In addition, British prime minister John Major postponed parliamentary consideration of the treaty until after Danish ratification, leading to suggestions that British foreign policy was being made in Copenhagen.

Other EU members follow different procedures for domestic control of EU business, and these procedures have effects on the ability of domestic politicians to control the activities of their representatives in the EU. The British House of Commons, like the Folketing, has expressed a great deal of interest in preventing the surrender of sovereign control over policy (Stevens 1976–1977; Kolinsky 1975). It took the unusual step, at the time, of setting up a permanent EU Scrutiny Committee to study issues on the Council's agenda (Miller 1977). However, the Scrutiny Committee has not been as successful in tying the hands of ministers as has the Danish MRC. Because minority government is unusual in Britain, party discipline is a more effective guarantor of commitment than in the Danish system, reducing the demand for prior legislative mandates. The limited powers of the Commons Scrutiny Committee, which can express technical judgments on EU measures but has little power to bind the government, reflect this lower demand.

Denmark and Britain mark one end of a continuum of the extent to which national parliaments attempt to influence EU activities. France and Luxembourg represent the other extreme, with the government rather than parliament implementing the domestic obligations of EU membership (Gregory 1983, p. 80). The French system has been particularly centralized, with authority concentrated in the hands of the president and an executive agency concerned exclusively with European economic cooperation, leaving ministers and the parliament relatively uninvolved (Wallace 1973, pp. 19, 37). Parliaments in the Netherlands, Italy, and Germany fall somewhere between these two extremes (Niblock 1971, p. 33). In Germany, the government appears more constrained by its federal structure and the role of the Länder (regions) than by the national parliament (Bulmer 1983, p. 361).

Since the mid-1990s, spurred by plans for EMU and the admission of new member states with strong traditions of active national parliaments, parliaments have substantially increased their level of oversight activity (Martin 2000, pp. 156–161; Mezey 1995; Bergman 1997). Even the French parliament has created a stronger European Affairs Committee, resulting in a "dramatic" improvement in its powers of scrutiny (Judge 1995, p. 91). Parliamentary activism takes the form of creating European Affairs Committees with more authority and capacity to constrain ministers in EU negotiations.

It also takes the form of more vigorous attempts to gain information in a timely manner about what is going on at the EU level. The Amsterdam treaty of 1997 included a protocol on national parliaments, guaranteeing them a right to information and promising to forward Commission consultation documents to them promptly (De Smijter 1998, pp. 221–222). The European Affairs Committees meet regularly in the Conference of European Affairs Committees (COSAC), hoping to coordinate their activities and gain another channel of information. All of these activities mean that Denmark is no longer unique in the activism of its parliament, although it may still be at the top of the list. The German Bundesrat and Swedish parliament, for example, are approaching the mark set by Denmark. The Danish experience is therefore relevant to further progress on EMU, as well as other EU issues.

Turning to international institutions, we can consider how general EU benefits have contributed to ratification decisions, using the Danish case to further analyze the arguments developed above. The Danish pattern of decisionmaking on EU treaties suggests that discussion of the new concept of a flexible architecture may jeopardize past patterns of cooperation. The initial Danish decision to join the EU was a decision about EU benefits as a whole. In 1985, in the debate over the Single Act, proponents were again able credibly to argue that the referendum was not merely on the specific provisions of the SEA—particularly the acceptance of qualified majority voting on internal market issues—but also a referendum on continued participation in the EU (Borre 1986, p. 190).

The argument that seemed to carry most weight with the electorate in 1985 was that Denmark's reputation within the EU, and thus its ability to secure the diverse benefits of membership, was at stake (Worre 1988, p. 372). The governing Liberal party proclaimed that "a Danish no to the package will be interpreted as a Danish no to further participation in Community co-operation. Thus, a Danish no to the EC package will start a development which will slowly lead to Denmark's withdrawal from the EC" (Worre 1988, pp. 372–373). That this message was accepted by the electorate is illustrated by the high percentage of yes votes coming from rural areas, which benefited from the Common Agricultural Policy (CAP).

However, by the time of the 1992 referendum, the nature of linkage had changed considerably. As the Maastricht treaty pushed the scope of anticipated supranational policymaking well beyond previous bounds, and as members calculated the consequences of enlarging the EU to include European Free Trade Area (EFTA) members and Eastern European countries, the notion that EU obligations must be accepted as a whole by all members lost ground. As the scope (coverage of issues) and breadth (number of members) of the EU increase, so do conflicts of interest. Requiring unanimous approval of all policies under such conditions is a recipe for paralysis. To this extent, the decision to move toward greater use of qualified majority voting goes hand in hand with enlargement of the EU (Keohane and Hoffmann 1991). However, some states—particularly Britain and Denmark—have been reluctant to accept significant expansion of supranational decisionmaking. Confronted with such intransigence and dilemmas created by enlargement, analysts and politicians have begun considering a new, more flexible architecture for the EU.

The new architecture goes by a number of names: Europe à la carte, variable geometry, a multitiered or multispeed Europe, and so on. The core idea is that not all members of the EU would have to sign on to all its obligations, sacrificing the primacy of the *acquis communautaire*. Attention has focused on the benefits of such an architecture, which would allow rapid movement in those areas in which some subsets of members have strong common interests, or on the negative consequences of a multispeed Europe for those who would be "left behind" (Artis 1992, p. 305). Alesina and Grilli (1994) demonstrate another drawback of a multispeed process: its potential for finding an equilibrium that permanently excludes some states. At Maastricht, the multispeed concept was put into practice by allowing Britain to opt out of parts of the treaty (the social protocol and monetary union). Thus, while voters or legislators in eleven member states were asked to ratify the entire Maastricht treaty, the

British government dealt with a smaller set of issues. Other examples of a flexible approach include a subset of eight members, the Schengen Group, which has created a passport-free zone, and the creation of a Franco-German military corps. As the EU contemplates growing to between twenty and twenty-five members by 2010, many of them relatively poor and with diverse foreign-policy interests, discussions of flexibility are more and more pervasive. The Amsterdam treaty formally recognizes substantially greater use of flexible approaches than had previously been considered (Ehlermann 1998).

While flexibility may be unavoidable given the rapid increase of the EU's scope and breadth, if the idea of a flexible architecture supplants the idea of an *acquis communautaire*, the role of the EU in facilitating cross-issue deals will be significantly reduced. Rather than searching for mutually advantageous bargains across issues, members could choose to move forward independently with a few others who share common interests on narrowly defined topics. The threat of excluding members from the accumulated benefits of the EU if they do not sign on to new agreements loses its force under these conditions: the British example demonstrates how a country can retain the benefits it has received in the past without accepting the full range of new obligations.

Acceptance of a flexible architecture rendered those Danish pro-Maastricht claims that the vote on the treaty was indirectly a vote on EU membership less credible than they had been in 1985. The Danish vote on Maastricht became a vote on the specific provisions of the Maastricht treaty, not a sounding of opinion on whether it was better for Denmark to be in the EU than outside of it. Decoupling allowed those who appreciated EU membership but opposed specific elements of the treaty to vote no, creating a severe challenge for proponents of EMU.

Overall, the Danish ratification case illustrates the changing effects of issue linkage as well as a domestic institutional effect, enhanced bargaining power resulting from stringent ratification procedures. These procedures increase Denmark's leverage by raising the probability that EU bargains will be overturned on the domestic level unless they are widely acceptable to the Danish public. National parliaments throughout the EU have become more active since the mid-1990s, suggesting that the Danish experience is now relevant to many more member states. No longer can governments ignore the demands of parliaments, assuming that they are easily circumvented. On the regional level, an additional threat to ratification of agreements has arisen through the likelihood that Denmark and others could choose to sign on to parts of the Maastricht deal while rejecting others, as a result of increasing acceptance of the notion of a multi-speed Europe.

Democratic Accountability

As the analysis of ratification suggests, the process of European union is conditioned by domestic political forces operating through institutionalized procedures. In this section, I consider the apparent upswing in concern about domestic control over EU business and potential solutions to the dilemmas created by lack of accountability. Such concern, argued here to be legitimate, threatened the Maastricht deal and thus EMU. Beyond the threats to ratification, demands for more rigorous procedures for accountability will condition the future of EMU. Formal legislative procedures have created concerns about accountability, and changes in these procedures may increase the control of directly elected representatives over EU business. In addition, concerns about the accountability of the ECB will directly condition the future of EMU.

Most analyses of the EU have found that the effect of domestic politics on past deals has been slight. Some accounts claim that the process leading to the SEA was remarkably free of overt domestic interference, for example (Moravcsik 1991, p. 50). Politicians and academic observers often infer from such a pattern autonomy of the Commission and/or of government leaders. However, consideration of institutional constraints leads us to examine delegation of authority. Attention to delegation in the study of legislative–executive interaction in the United States, for example, shows that the apparent independence of agencies can be misleading (McCubbins, Noll, and Weingast 1989). The European Council and European Commission, like the agencies within the U.S. executive branch, act under delegation of authority from political actors. Analysts often infer from negotiating behavior that principals, such as national parliaments, have abdicated control over policymaking to their agents. One account concludes, for example, that in EU matters "national Parliaments . . . have no obvious part to play except to be compliant in the face of diminishing authority" (Niblock 1971, p. 34). However, because of the costs of exercising tight control over agents, an optimal structure of delegation may be one with little active oversight or overt interference in the negotiating process from principals. Agents rationally anticipate the responses of those they represent. The law of anticipated reactions suggests that we cannot infer a lack of political influence from a lack of observed oversight activity.

In the negotiations over the SEA and the Maastricht treaty, conditions for arm's-length influence of domestic political actors were probably met. Each state had a veto and formal ratification processes. There is little reason to believe that government leaders did not take these constraints into account when negotiating. However, in the day-to-day operations of the EU, the process moves away from such conditions to ones where national publics and legislatures cannot exercise effective constraints on their representatives in the Council. This has led to concern about a "democratic deficit," arising from the fact that the rules for EU legislation create the potential for significant agency slack. In contrast to treaty negotiation, the day-to-day business of the EU often escapes domestic oversight.

The combination of three factors may create a democratic deficit as the EU continues along its present path: the direct effect of EU law in member states, qualified majority voting, and the closed nature of Council and Commission operations. The EU differs from most international organizations in the degree to which its legislation is binding on members. Once the process involving the Commission, Council, and European Parliament has been completed, legislation is immediately applicable in all member states, without explicit acceptance on their part (Garrett 1992, pp. 535–536). Direct effect does not apply to revisions of the Treaty of Rome, and there are some variations in how EU legislation is implemented on the national level. EU regulations are directly applicable without the need for national measures of implementation, while EU directives allow national parliaments to choose the form and method of implementation (Nugent 1991, pp. 168–171). Either method is sufficiently binding on states that it represents a significant surrender of the traditional lawmaking authority of national parliaments to the EU. Because EU legislation automatically comes into effect at the national level, without an opportunity for parliamentary veto or amendment, national-level politicians cannot directly influence its content.[6]

Extralegislative means of parliamentary control over EU legislation may in theory remain, operating through the law of anticipated reactions. In order for parliaments to retain significant control through indirect means, two conditions must be met: parliaments must have reliable information about what their ministers do in the European Council and the ability to reward or punish them on the basis of performance. The move toward qualified majority voting reduces the scope for national parliamentary influence, since ministers, who represent parliaments, can be outvoted in the Council. This creates a reduction in control by national political actors, but one that would exist with any majoritarian method of decisionmaking. A factor that undermines national parliamentary authority to an unusually high degree has been the practice of Council secrecy. Council meetings historically took place in private, with no minutes kept (Nugent 1992, p. 314). No official record of voting patterns existed. Individual state votes on qualified majority voting issues were sometimes leaked, but in a haphazard and often distorted manner.[7]

Thus, national parliaments could not count on having accurate information about the activities of their representatives in the Council. Without such information, and having sacrificed national veto power with the acceptance of qualified majority voting, parliaments cannot bind their representatives. The situation differs from that found on the domestic level in parliamentary systems in that the Council as a whole is not responsible to elected officials as the government is on the domestic level (Bogdanor 1989).[8] While the Luxembourg Compromise held, allowing states to veto policies of "vital national interest," parliaments had some reliable information about ministers' activities, as they knew when ministers had refused to exercise a veto. Thus, the effects of secrecy on accountability were less significant as long as the other two conditions did not hold. But the conjunction of EU legislation, qualified majority voting, and secrecy of Council proceedings severely restricted parliamentary control over the day-to-day proceedings of the EU.

In the aftermath of the Danish and French referenda, attempts to correct this democratic deficit took on new urgency. Jacques Delors, for example, became a convert to the concept of "subsidiarity": the view that the EU should commit itself to deal only with issues on a supranational level that involve significant international externalities. As discussed above, the Council and Commission have committed themselves to making information systematically and quickly available to national parliaments, although dissatisfaction remains with the implementation of these pledges. Most attempts to find an institutional solution to the democratic deficit have concentrated on increasing the powers of the EP. The German and Italian governments have promoted the EP most vigorously, with the British resisting (Laursen 1992, p. 233). Because members of the EP are directly elected, granting legislative powers to it would in part satisfy demands for democratic accountability. The following discussion examines changes in the rules under which the EP has a role in policymaking, in order to determine whether they are likely to have any impact on problems of democratic accountability. Since EMU is linked to other EU issues in the Maastricht treaty, a failure to solve apparently separate accountability problems would have fundamental implications for EMU.

Before 1985, the EP had little role beyond that of consultation in the EU policymaking process. The SEA for the first time gave the EP a formal role in approving legislation, through the "cooperation" procedure (Fitzmaurice 1988). The cooperation procedure applied to the internal market, most significantly, under the terms of the SEA. The Maastricht treaty specifies use of the cooperation procedure in areas such as development cooperation, transportation, and the Social Fund. Under cooperation, the Commission has a potentially powerful role in that it has gatekeeping power. The status quo remains in place unless the Commission decides to introduce a proposal to the Council. The Commission's ability to maintain the status quo allows it significantly to influence outcomes without having its influence perceived as overt bargaining activity. After the

Commission presents a proposal, the Council adopts a position by qualified majority voting. The EP acts on this common position, accepting it, rejecting it, or making amendments. If the EP rejects the Council's position, it can be adopted only by unanimity in the Council. If the EP makes amendments, they are referred back to the Commission. If the Commission accepts the amendments, the Council can adopt them by a qualified majority vote; otherwise, the Council must act unanimously to change the status quo. Thus, if the EP and Commission have similar preferences, they can move outcomes away from the Council's common position. The EP also has veto power unless the Council unanimously prefers its common position to the status quo, that is, unless the Council finds its common position Pareto-superior to the status quo, an outcome not guaranteed under qualified majority voting (see Tsebelis 1994).

Article 189b of the Maastricht treaty enhanced the EP's ability to influence legislation. The Article 189b procedure is commonly referred to as the "codecision" procedure, although British objections kept this terminology out of the treaty. The codecision procedure initially applied to the internal market and free movement of workers; the Amsterdam treaty of 1997 substantially extended its scope (Moravcsik and Nicoläidis 1999).

A straightforward way to understand the implications of codecision is to contrast it to the cooperation procedure. First, a major change is that if the EP rejects the Council's common position, the EP's decision cannot be overridden. Second, any amendments made by the EP go directly back to the Council, without being screened by the Commission. These two changes reduce the number of cases in which the EP can be overridden. The third major innovation is the creation of so-called Conciliation Committees. These committees come into play when the Council rejects EP amendments; they can be understood as analogous to the Conference Committees that resolve differences between Senate and House versions of legislation in the U.S. Congress.

A Conciliation Committee, consisting of twelve representatives from the Council and twelve from the EP and a Commission representative, searches for compromise legislation acceptable to a majority of the EP and a qualified majority of the Council. If such a compromise is found, it goes into effect. If the Conciliation Committee cannot find such a solution, the ball is back in the Council's court. Under the Maastricht rules, the Council could either remain passive, in which case the status quo remained in place, or could reaffirm its original common position. However, this common position could now go into effect only if the EP accepted it on a closed vote, so under codecision, the EP gained effective veto power over qualified majority decisions of the Council. The EP therefore has increased influence over outcomes, but only when it prefers to live with the status quo rather than accept the outcome of qualified majority voting on the Council. The Amsterdam treaty simplified the codecision procedure and changed procedures if the Conciliation Committee fails to come to a decision, removing the Council option of reaffirming its original position. Garrett and Tsebelis (1999) find that the changes to codecision in the Amsterdam treaty increase the power of the EP, as does Dehousse (1998). The Amsterdam treaty further enhanced the powers of the EP by extending the scope of codecision to new issue areas (De Smijter 1998, pp. 189–192).

Although the codecision procedure remedies the democratic deficit to some extent by increasing the influence of directly elected representatives on EU legislation,[9] the scope of the procedure is limited. Moreover, a major impediment remains to relying on the procedure for further satisfying popular demands for accountability: national parliaments. As the scope of EP codecision is extended, national parliaments lose control over issues over which they traditionally have had legislative authority. Since treaty revisions necessary to extend the EP's powers pass through national parliaments, they may block this path toward democratic accountability. The Danish and British parliaments, in particular, demand an alternative mechanism in which national parliaments would have a greater say in day-to-day EU activities. Examination of the institutional constraints on European unification suggests that advocates of EMU would be unwise to believe that they can circumvent the claims of national legislatures. While efficiency may dictate the transfer of powers to organizations that can most effectively exercise them, existing constitutions and procedures create impediments to transfer of authority, leading to a process constrained by existing institutions.

Accountability concerns more directly influence the future and success of EMU when they center on the ECB. The ECB was designed along the lines of the Bundesbank, to assure its independence from political pressures. Steps taken to assure its independence included specifying a primary goal of price stability and mechanisms for appointment of officials that protect them from political pressure (Williams and Reid 1998). Maastricht also included few provisions for transparency of ECB operations. Most analyses of ECB independence assume that demands for greater accountability, for example calls for the ECB to provide fuller justification for its actions and greater transparency, threaten its independence. Accountability and independence are seen as "opposite ends of a continuum"; there is necessarily a trade-off between them, according to this assumption (Lastra 1997).

However, independence and accountability are different concepts. Increasing one does not necessarily mean a decrease of the other; institutions can be accountable yet independent. The Federal Reserve of the United States, for example, is a central bank that exhibits both independence and accountability. All standard measures of central bank independence give the Federal Reserve a high score. Yet it is accountable to a highly politicized institution—the U.S. Congress. Legislation regulating the Federal Reserve could be changed with a simple majority vote in Congress. Thus, the Fed acts independently in a day-to-day manner, yet remains accountable to Congress. If it consistently failed to do its job, legislation putting further constraints on its actions would be highly likely.

Accountability of central banks can be assured through a number of mechanisms. One, as in the United States, is indirect legislative control of the bank. Changing the law regulating the bank is a drastic and risky step, one that legislatures do not take often. Yet the fact that this possibility lurks in the background serves to create accountability. Other central banks, such as New Zealand's, assure more immediate accountability through an explicit contract between the bank and the government, specifying the targets the bank must meet. Transparency provides yet another mechanism of accountability that, if handled properly, does not necessarily compromise independence.

Thus, the correct question is not how much independence to sacrifice for accountability, but how to determine the proper relationship between independence and democratic accountability (de Haan and Gormley 1997, pp. 352–353). Kenen (1999) argues that the ECB has overreacted to calls for greater transparency, confusing "independence with immunity from democratic accountability." Given the importance of accountability, and reasonable concerns about it throughout the EU, Kenen seems correct when he charges the ECB with not recognizing that its legitimacy, and therefore success over the long run, require greater transparency in its operations (see also Dornbusch, Farero, and Giavazzi 1998; von Hagen 1997). "Accountable independence" is not an oxymoron, and efforts to assure it are essential.

Beyond the claims of narrowly defined interests, progress toward EMU is threatened by public concern about accountability. The EMU is tied to other issues on the EU's agenda, since the Maastricht plan for EMU is based on a set of cross-issue deals. For this reason, concern about a democratic deficit has implications for monetary union. Worries about the accountability of the ECB, and misguided analyses that see accountability as necessarily a threat to independence, similarly condition the future success of EMU. Unless solutions are found, the progress of EMU will continue to be plagued by fears of a lack of accountability.

Conclusion

The issue linkages created by existing institutions and the formal procedures they use provide insight into the pattern of deals reached in the

Maastricht treaty as well as dilemmas now confronting EMU. In international politics, one of the primary functions of institutions is to solidify and make credible linkages among issues, allowing states to reach mutually beneficial deals by raising the costs of reneging. Within the EU, linkage among issues has allowed construction of many such deals, which may be threatened in the future by acceptance of the idea of a multispeed Europe. Because EU membership has implied cooperation in many different issue areas, it has decreased incentives for states to renege on particular deals they find distasteful. Such behavior would jeopardize a member's reputation and thus the benefits of EU membership on other issues, those valued highly by an individual state. The EU has thus facilitated mutually beneficial cross-issue deals, such as that on EMU.

Institutions not only provide opportunities; their procedures also impose constraints on decisionmaking and cause outcomes to diverge from predictions based purely on efficiency or national power considerations. The disproportionate influence of smaller actors, such as Spain and Denmark, depends on institutionalized decisionmaking, particularly the rule requiring unanimous approval of changes to the Treaty of Rome. The Maastricht agreement on EMU, and the Stability and Growth Pact, reflect concessions and side-payments that would not have been necessary or credible in an uninstitutionalized environment.

Similarly, domestic ratification requirements allow some national actors to bargain more effectively than state size would lead us to expect. In Denmark, stringent ratification procedures and tight control over EU representatives' activities allow that country to achieve concessions unusual for a small actor in interstate bargaining. As new member states adopt procedures similar to Denmark's, and as other national parliaments also increase the powers of their European Affairs Committees, the experience of Denmark becomes generalizable. Ratification problems also illustrate the changing effects of issue linkage; the anticipated availability of opt-out clauses scuttled the treaty in Denmark's 1992 referendum.

A tie between EMU and other EU issues means that concern about a democratic deficit threatens the performance of EMU, as do concerns about the accountability of the ECB. Analysis of decisionmaking rules in the EU substantiates this concern. While domestic interests have the opportunity to express themselves during treaty ratification, the existing pattern of delegation for daily EU business often allows the Council and Commission to escape accountability to such interests. A protocol in the Amsterdam treaty recognizes the right of national parliaments to timely information. If implemented, this step would mitigate some concerns about accountability. National parliaments exert only indirect control over EU business, but even indirect control can have significant effects.

Attention to institutions leads to several speculations about the future path of monetary union. First, problems with ratification of the Maastricht treaty support the notion that the apparent freedom of the Council from domestic political constraints is an illusion. The Council has been operating under delegated authority and cannot neglect the constraints of domestic politics when attempting to make progress in controversial areas, such as monetary union. Second, the process of European integration is at a key decision point. Up to now, tight linkages among sets of issues have allowed and required mutually beneficial package deals. However, if movement toward a flexible architecture continues to gain momentum in the face of admitting new member states, the pattern of EU cooperation is likely to move closer to a purely intergovernmental one, where cooperation is based on narrowly defined state interests and tends to neglect the interests of less powerful members. A Europe in which cooperation occurred only among those states with an immediate interest in its results would see fewer transfers from rich states to poor, fewer concessions from powerful states on the form of cooperation, and, as a result, perhaps less stability in the face of economic and political shocks.

Notes

1. I gratefully acknowledge the support of the Social Science Research Council's Advanced Foreign Policy Fellowship Program and the Hoover Institution's National Fellows Program. My thanks to Barry Eichengreen, Jeff Frieden, Robert Keohane, Peter Lange, Ron Rogowski, John Woolley, and participants in the workshop on the Political Economy of European Integration for their comments on an earlier version of this paper; and to Mette Rasmussen for research assistance.

2. The term "supranational" is used here to indicate situations in which policymaking authority has been delegated to a body that individual member governments cannot directly control. In practice, within the EU, supranational decisionmaking has consisted of giving up state veto power previously established in the Luxembourg Compromise through acceptance of qualified majority voting.

3. Students of international relations will recognize these two approaches as neofunctionalism (Haas 1958) and intergovernmentalism (Moravcsik 1991; Garrett 1992).

4. While it is conceivable that states could use linkage to block attempts to cooperate, we instead observe frequent linking of issues to expand the set of agreements that are Pareto-superior to the status quo, consistent with the framework of Tollison and Willett (1979); see also Oye (1992, pp. 35–48) and Morrow (1992).

5. For development of a model in which small states acquire disproportionate power in international cooperative agreements, see Casella (1992). Decisionmaking procedures have consequences for the power of differently sized states. A unit-veto system, such as the one in place for treaty ratification, maximizes the power of small states, since they are weighted as heavily as large ones. Supermajority requirements, such as those embodied in the EU's qualified majority vot-

ing, also enhance small states' influence, but to a lesser extent. Some models of intermember bargaining, such as those adopted in intergovernmental studies of the SEA, assert that small states' influence is negligible, with major powers determining outcomes.

6. Enforcement of EU legislation takes place through domestic courts and the European Court of Justice.

7. In response to concerns about secrecy, the Council has drafted a "transparency plan" for making public some debates and the record of formal votes (*Financial Times*, Dec. 5, 1992, 2). The fate and scope of this plan remain in doubt.

8. The distinction between EU and national-level accountability rests on the assumption that national parliaments constrain government activities, a point with which some would disagree. For contrasting views, see Wallace (1975) and Waltz (1967).

9. Successful exercise of the EP's formal powers will require further development of political parties there. Such development, and incentives for ambitious politicians to develop careers in the EP, depend on rules that give the EP a potentially significant role in EU business.

References

Alesina, A., and V. Grilli, 1994, On the feasibility of a one-speed or multispeed European Monetary Union, in: B. Eichengreen and J. Frieden, eds., *The political economy of European monetary unification* (Boulder, Colo.: Westview), 107–127.

Artis, M. J., 1992, The Maastricht road to monetary union. *Journal of Common Market Studies* 30, 299–309.

Artis, M., and B. Winkler, 1998, The stability pact: Safeguarding the credibility of the European Central Bank. *National Institute Economic Review* 163, 87–98.

Auken, S., J. Buksti, and C. L. Sørensen, 1975, Denmark joins Europe: Patterns of adaptation in the Danish political and administrative processes as a result of membership of the European Communities. *Journal of Common Market Studies* 14, 1–36.

Barnard, B., 1997, From Dublin to Amsterdam. *Europe* 363, E1–E2.

Bergman, T., 1997, National parliaments and EU Affairs Committees: Notes on empirical variation and competing explanations. *Journal of European Public Policy* 4, 373–387.

Bogdanor, V., 1989, The June 1989 European elections and the institutions of the Community. *Government and Opposition* 24, 199–214.

Borre, O., 1986, The Danish referendum on the EC Common Act. *Electoral Studies* 5, 189–193.

Bulmer, S., 1983, Domestic politics and European Community policy-making. *Journal of Common Market Studies* 21, 349–363.

Casella, A., 1992, Participation in a currency union. *American Economic Review* 82, 847–863.

Cohen, B. J., 1994, Beyond EMU: The problem of sustainability, in: B. Eichengreen and J. Frieden, eds., *The political economy of European monetary unification* (Boulder, Colo.: Westview), 149–165.

de Haan, J., and L. Gormley, 1997, Independence and accountability of the European Central Bank, in: M. Andenas, et al., eds., *European Economic and Monetary Union: The institutional framework* (London: Kluwer Law International), 333–353.

De Smijter, E., 1998, The constitutional amendments made to the Treaty on European Union by the Treaty of Amsterdam, in: R. Blanpain, ed., *Institutional changes and European social policies after the Treaty of Amsterdam* (The Hague: Kluwer Law International), 183–229.

Dehousse, R., 1998, European institutional architecture after Amsterdam: Parliamentary system of regulatory structure? Working paper RSC 98/11, Florence, Robert Schumman Center.

Dornbusch, R., C. Farero, and F. Giavazzi, 1998, Immediate challenges for the ECB, in: D. Begg, et al., eds., *EMU: Prospects and challenges for the euro* (Oxford: Blackwell Publishers).

Ehlermann, C. D., 1998, Differentiation, flexibility, closer cooperation: The new provisions of the Amsterdam treaty, manuscript, Florence, Robert Schumann Center.

Eichengreen, B., and J. Frieden, 1994, The political economy of European monetary unification: An analytical introduction, in: B. Eichengreen and J. Frieden, eds., *The political economy of European monetary unification* (Boulder, Colo.: Westview), 1–23.

Fitzmaurice, J., 1976, National parliaments and European policy-making: The case of Denmark. *Parliamentary Affairs* 29, 281–292.

_____, 1988, An analysis of the European Community's co-operation procedure. *Journal of Common Market Studies* 26, 389–400.

Garrett, G., 1992, International cooperation and institutional choice: The European Community's internal market. *International Organization* 46, 533–560.

_____, 1994, The politics of Maastricht, in: B. Eichengreen and J. Frieden, eds., *The political economy of European monetary unification* (Boulder, Colo.: Westview), 47–65.

Garrett, G., and G. Tsebelis, 1999, The institutional foundations of supranationalism in the EU, manuscript.

Gregory, F.E.C., 1983, *Dilemmas of government: Britain and the European Community* (Oxford: Martin Robertson).

Haas, E. B., 1958, The uniting of Europe: Political, social and economic forces, 1950–57 (London: Stevens & Sons).

Judge, D., 1995, The failure of national parliaments? *West European Politics* 18, 79–100.

Keohane, R. O., 1984, After hegemony: Cooperation and discord in the world political economy (Princeton: Princeton University Press).

Keohane, R. O., and S. Hoffmann, 1991, Institutional change in Europe in the 1980s, in: R. O. Keohane and S. Hoffmann, eds., *The new European community: Decisionmaking and institutional change* (Boulder, Colo.: Westview), 1–39.

Kenen, P., 1999, The outlook for EMU. *Eastern Economic Journal* 25, 109–115.

Kolinsky, M., 1975, Parliamentary scrutiny of European legislation. *Government and Opposition* 10, 46–69.

Lange, P., 1993, Maastricht and the social protocol: Why did they do it? *Politics and Society* 21, 5–36.

Lastra, R. M., 1997, European Monetary Union and Central Bank independence, in: M. Andenas, et al., eds., *European Economic and Monetary Union: The institutional framework* (London: Kluwer Law International), 291–329.

Laursen, F., 1992, Explaining the intergovernmental conference on political union, in: F. Laursen and S. Vanhoonacker, eds., *The intergovernmental conference on political union: Institutional reforms, new policies and international identity of the European Community* (European Institute of Public Administration, Maastricht), 229–248.

Lipson, C., 1991, Why are some international agreements informal? *International Organization* 45, 495–538.

Marks, G., 1992, Structural policy in the European Community, in: A. M. Sbragia, ed., *Euro-Politics: Institutions and policymaking in the "new" European Community* (Washington, D.C.: Brookings Institution), 191–224.

Martin, L. L., 1992, Institutions and cooperation: Sanctions during the Falkland Islands conflict. *International Security* 16, 143–178.

_____, 2000, *Democratic commitments: Legislatures and international cooperation* (Princeton: Princeton University Press).

McCubbins, M., R. Noll, and B. Weingast, 1989, Structure and process, politics and policy: Administrative arrangements and the political control of agencies. *Virginia Law Review* 75, 431–482.

Mezey, M., 1995, Parliament in the New Europe, in: J. Hayward and E. C. Page, eds., *Governing the new Europe* (Durham, N.C.: Duke University Press).

Miller, H. N., 1977, The influence of British parliamentary committees on European Community legislation. *Legislative Studies Quarterly* 2, 45–75.

Møller, J. O., 1983, Danish EC decision-making: An insider's view. *Journal of Common Market Studies* 21, 245–260.

Moravcsik, A., 1991, Negotiating the Single European Act: National interests and conventional statecraft in the European Community. *International Organization* 45, 19–56.

Moravscik, A., and K. Nicoläidis, 1999, Explaining the Treaty of Amsterdam: Interests, influence, institutions. *Journal of Common Market Studies* 37, 59–85.

Morrow, J. D., 1992, Signaling difficulties with linkage in crisis bargaining. *International Studies Quarterly* 36, 153–172.

Niblock, M., 1971, *The EEC: National parliaments in Community decision-making* (London: Chatham House).

Nugent, N., 1991, *The government and politics of the European Community*, 2d ed. (Durham, N.C.: Duke University Press).

_____, 1992, The deepening and widening of the European Community: Recent evolution, Maastricht, and beyond. *Journal of Common Market Studies* 30, 311–328.

Oye, K. A., 1992, *Economic discrimination and political exchange: World political economy in the 1930s and 1980s* (Princeton: Princeton University Press).

Petersen, N., and J. Elklit, 1973, Denmark enters the European Communities. *Scandinavian Political Studies* 8, 198–213.

Putnam, R. D., 1988, Diplomacy and domestic politics: The logic of two-level games. *International Organization* 42, 427–460.

Sebenius, J. K., 1983, Negotiation arithmetic: Adding and subtracting issues and parties. *International Organization* 37, 281–316.

Stevens, A., 1976–1977, Problems of parliamentary control of European Community policy. *Millennium: Journal of International Studies* 5, 269–281.

Tollison, R. D., and T. D. Willett, 1979, An economic theory of mutually advantageous issue linkage in international negotiations. *International Organization* 33, 425–449.

Tsebelis, G., 1994, The power of the European Parliament as a conditional agenda setter. *American Political Science Review* 88, 128–142.

von Hagen, J., 1997, Monetary policy and institutions in the EMU. *Swedish Economic Policy Review* 4.

Wallace, H., 1973, *National governments and the European Communities* (London: Chatham House).

_____, 1975, *The foreign policy process in Britain* (London: Royal Institute of International Affairs).

Waltz, K., 1967, *Foreign policy and democratic politics: The American and British experience* (Boston: Little, Brown).

Weber, S., and H. Wiesmeth, 1991, Issue linkage in the European Community. *Journal of Common Market Studies* 29, 255–267.

Williams, D., and R. Reid, 1998, A Central Bank for Europe, in: P. Temperton, ed., *The euro*, 2d ed. (Chichester, England: John Wiley & Sons), 123–144.

Williams, S., 1991, Sovereignty and accountability in the European Community, in: R. O. Keohane and S. Hoffmann, eds., *The new European Community. Decisionmaking and institutional change* (Boulder, Colo.: Westview), 155–176.

Worre, T., 1988, Denmark at the crossroads: The Danish referendum of 28 February 1986 on the EC reform package. *Journal of Common Market Studies* 26, 361–388.

7

From EMS to EMU

Are We Better Off?

PAUL DE GRAUWE, HANS DEWACHTER,
AND YUNUS AKSOY[1]

Abstract

In this chapter we compare the stabilizing properties of the European
Monetary Union (EMU) to those of the European Monetary system
(EMS), controlled by Germany. We find that in general the EMU will
provide better stabilization of inflation, output, and the interest rate
than the EMS. However, these results only apply if the European Central Bank (ECB) can effectively control monetary policy. In the case
that the ECB representatives do not coordinate and take a nationalistic
point of view, the EMS regime is preferred by various countries.

At the start of 1999, Europe moved to a drastically new monetary regime.
Eleven countries of the European Union (EU) decided to transfer their
national monetary sovereignty to a new institution, the Eurosystem. This
regime shift has drastically changed the monetary landscape in Europe.
The conduct of monetary policy is now in the hands of the Governing
Council of the Eurosystem, a body where all countries have their representative and where the European Central Bank (ECB) is represented by
its Executive Board.

One may have the impression that the regime change was characterized by a shift from complete decentralization to complete centralization
of national monetary policies. This characterization, however, would not
be correct. Prior to Economic and Monetary Union (EMU), countries had
a monetary arrangement in the context of the European Monetary Sys-

tem (EMS). This regime implied a particular way of coordinating national monetary policies. This coordination was highly asymmetric in that one country, Germany, set its interest rate based on the needs that existed in Germany, while the other countries followed by adjusting their interest rates accordingly, whether or not this corresponded to their national desiderata. Thus, the EMS can be said to have been a monetary regime in which one central bank, the Bundesbank, determined the interest rate for the system as a whole based on the economic conditions that prevailed in just one country, Germany.

Euroland will certainly work very differently. It can be considered as a monetary regime in which the countries participating in EMU use a joint decision process to set the interest rate that will prevail in Euroland. Clearly, national desires about the optimal interest rate will normally be different, because economic conditions will differ, or because of other asymmetries between countries. But whereas in the EMS only the German desires counted, in EMU all national desires matter, and have to be aggregated. The ways this aggregation is done is of great importance for the conduct of monetary policies and for the effectiveness of these monetary policies.

In this chapter we analyze these different ways of aggregating national desires about monetary policies. We first study the EMU and the different ways national views about the optimal interest rates can be aggregated. We then study which countries' desires are best taken care of. Finally, we analyze how well monetary policies under EMU stabilize inflation, output, and the interest rate. We will use the EMS as a benchmark. This will allow us to compare the efficiency of EMU as a stabilization regime to the one that prevailed under the EMS.

The remainder of the chapter is organized as follows: First we set out the optimal monetary policy reaction for a typical central bank and discuss the different types of asymmetries in the model that play a role in this optimal policy. We use the standard framework of Rudebusch and Svensson (1998) to find the optimal linear feedback rules for interest rates. Then we proceed by estimating the optimal interest rate rules and discuss the substantial asymmetry in these policy reactions across countries. In the third section we describe our economic and institutional framework for the simulations in order to analyze the impact of alternative voting schemes and asymmetric economic structures. Then we discuss the implications of majority voting in the Governing Council on the macroeconomic stability under both the EMU scenario and the EMS scenario. Finally, we discuss our conclusions.

The Model for Propagation of Monetary Policy

We use a model that has now become standard in the analysis of optimal monetary policies (see Clarida, Gali, and Gertler 1997, and Rudebusch and Svensson 1998, which we follow closely here). It consists of an aggregate demand and aggregate supply equation. The aggregate demand equation is expressed in terms of the output gap, that is,

(1) $\quad y_t = \sum_{j=1}^{m} \beta_{y,j} y_{t-j} - \beta_i(\bar{i}_t - \bar{\pi}_t) + \eta_t,$

where y_t is the output gap. This is obtained by decomposing output into a permanent and a transitory component. The transitory component then measures the temporary over- or underutilization of the output capacity; $\bar{i}_t$ and $\bar{\pi}_t$ denote the one year moving average of current and past interest and inflation rates; $\bar{i}_t - \bar{\pi}_t$ stands for the real interest rate.

The aggregate supply equation (Phillips Curve) is written as follows:

(2) $\quad \pi_t = E_t\pi_{t+1} + \alpha_y y_{t-1} + \varepsilon_t.$

This is the standard Phillips Curve augmented with an inflation expectation term $E_t\pi_{t+1}$. The actual empirical implementation of this equation will rely on the estimation of an autoregressive inflation variable. The evidence (see Fuhrer 1997) suggests that an autoregressive type of Phillips Curve produces better forecasting results than the theoretically more appealing forward-looking version.

The next step in the analysis is specifying the central bank's loss function. We have:

(3) $\quad \min_{i_t} E[L_t] = Var[(\pi_t - c_1)] + \lambda Var[(y_t - c_2)] + \gamma Var[\Delta i_t].$

where L_t is the expected loss of the central bank; c_1 and c_2 are the target levels of inflation and output gap respectively. We will set these equal to zero. λ expresses the weight the authorities attach to output stabilization; finally the third term reflects the authorities' desire to smooth the interest rate.

Our procedure now will consist in first estimating for each country the model comprised of equations (1) and (2). Using these estimates we then derive an interest rate rule that minimizes the loss function of each central bank as given by equation (3). In other words, we compute how the central bank set their interest rate such as to minimize the variance of inflation, output gap, and interest rate changes (using the weights λ and γ). The technical detail is provided in the Appendix. The next section describes the results.

Estimation Results and Optimal Feedback Rules

In the following we present our results of aggregate demand and supply estimations formalized in equations (1) and (2) over the period 1979.1

and 1994.09. Then, we proceed to derive the optimal interest rate rules in accordance with Rudebusch and Svensson (1998). All output, inflation, and interest rate data are obtained from the International Monetary Fund (IMF) International Financial Statistics. The output gap is generated via (log-)linearly detrended industrial production figures.[2] For monthly inflation we use the first difference of the (log) consumer price indices (CPI). Finally, short-run interest rates are monthly call money and money market rates on an annual basis. (Note the exceptions of STF rate for Ireland, average lending rate for Finland, and lending rate for Portugal.) Since there was already a monetary union between Luxembourg and Belgium before the establishment of the EMU, we assume Belgian short-run interest rates apply in Luxembourg.[3]

In comparison to our previous paper (De Grauwe, Dewachter, and Aksoy 1998), the basic difference in the econometric part of this analysis is that, rather than imposing ad hoc lag lengths for the autoregressive component of aggregate demand and supply equations, we rely on the Akaike Information Criterion to select the most reasonable lag length.[4] Lag lengths differ across countries considerably (see Table 7.8), implying different degrees of size and timing of output and inflation adjustment processes.[5]

Propagation of the monetary policy into inflation and output across countries is presented in Figure 7.1. As is clear from Figure 7.1, countries react differently with respect to changes in the monetary policy (interest rate). Consistent with the empirical literature we find stronger output reactions with respect to policy changes than the inflation reactions. We can subdivide output reactions into three groups. First, monetary policy seems to have significant effect on output in Austria, Belgium, Luxembourg, and Portugal. Second, output gap seems to respond to monetary policy changes in Finland, France, Germany, Ireland, and Italy as well, but to a limited extent. Finally, in the Netherlands and Spain policymakers seem to be absolutely ineffective when they decide to use monetary tools to correct for undesired output fluctuations. Inflation reactions are weak and long-lasting across the board, indicating the price sluggishness in the EMU countries. We find significant price puzzles in Belgium and Luxembourg and to a smaller extent in Ireland.

Then, we derive the optimal interest rate rules for each individual country as described in the previous section. We assume exogenous preferences of the national policymakers. We choose three sets of preference possibilities, representing different preferences regarding stabilization of output (high, medium, and low).[6] We tabulate optimal output, inflation, and interest rate smoothing coefficients under alternative preference specifications throughout Figure 7.2. These numbers express how the authorities adjust the optimal interest rate to present and past output, inflation, and interest rate changes.

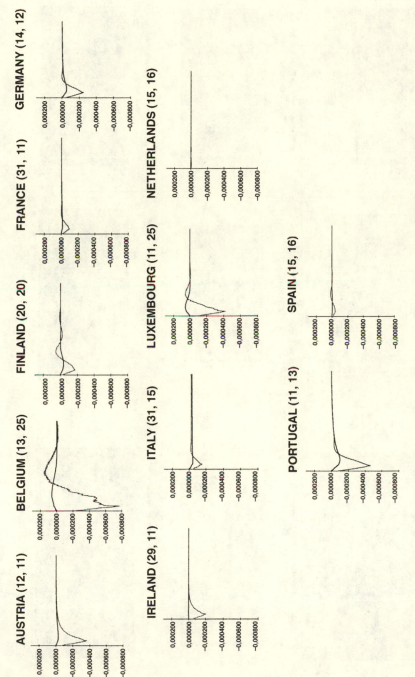

FIGURE 7.1 Output and Inflation Reactions W.R.T. 1 Percent Increase in the Interest Rate (lags of inflation and output are given in brackets)

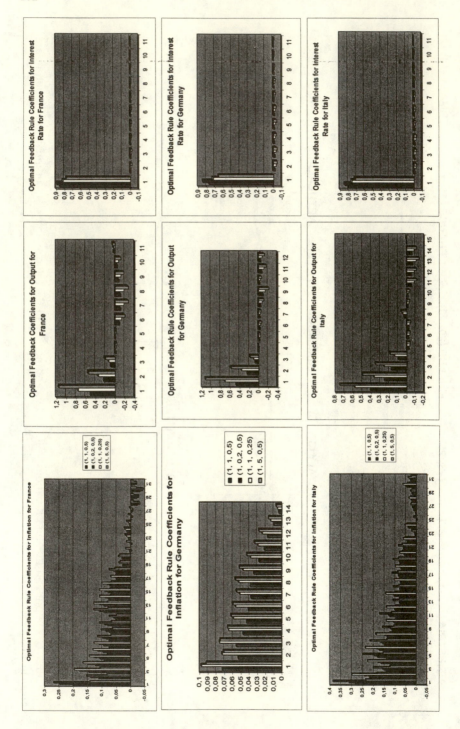

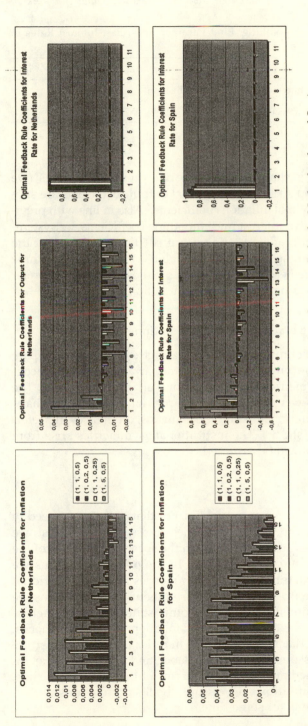

FIGURE 7.2   Optimal Feedback Rule Coefficients for Inflation for France, Germany, Italy, the Netherlands, and Spain

TABLE 7.1   Interest Rate Smoothing: First Parameters on Past Interest Rates in the Optimal Feedback Rules

	Aus.	Bel.	Fin.	Fra.	Ger.	Ire.	Ita.	Lux.	Net.	Por.	Spa.
intermediate output stabilization											
	0.725	0.611	0.790	0.850	0.765	0.796	0.795	0.702	0.997	0.677	0.911

A first observation is that, in line with our previous findings (De Grauwe, Dewachter, and Aksoy 1998) optimal output coefficients are substantially larger than optimal inflation coefficients.[7] Also in line with previous research is the fact that interest rate smoothing coefficients are systematically higher than both inflation and output coefficients. A look at the first interest rate smoothing coefficients in Table 7.1 indicates that three countries, France, the Netherlands, and Spain, are those that heavily prefer to smooth interest rates rather than output or inflation stabilization.

The Framework for Simulations

In this section we will conduct a simulation exercise in order to compare the present EMU regime with the EMS monetary arrangement. We recognize two types of asymmetries, an economic and an institutional one. The economic asymmetries were sketched in the previous sections and have to do with differences in transmission mechanisms, differences in preferences, and asymmetric shocks. The institutional asymmetries arise from the decision modes that will be assumed.

Economic Asymmetries

Let us start with the economic asymmetries. For that purpose we need to take into account three types of asymmetries across countries. First, we will use the asymmetries across countries in the speed and the size of the propagation of monetary policy changes. In the previous sections we have estimated the structure of these asymmetries for each individual country. Second, preferences can differ. Throughout the simulations we will treat them exogenously. Third, economic states can differ across countries as a result of the country-specific inflation and output shocks, which may be correlated across countries.[8] In order to recover the structure of the shocks we assume that product, labor, and financial market institutions will not immediately change in terms of their structure. Thus, the past structure of inflation and output shocks correlations are assumed to remain the same for some time.[9]

Institutional Asymmetries

In order to obtain an insight into the institutional features of the decision-making process of the Eurosystem we show Figure 7.3. The Eurosystem's decisionmaking body consists of seventeen members. Six are members of the executive board of the ECB (ECB board for short). Eleven members are governors of the national central banks (one for each country). Each of the seventeen members has one vote.

We will assume that these representatives can take two different information perspectives. One, called nationalistic, implies that a member computes the interest rate that is optimal from the point of view of its own country. The national desired interest rate policies $(d_{t,j})$ were derived in the previous section and are represented throughout Figure 7.2.

The second is to have a Euro-wide perspective. This consists in taking a weighted average of the nationally desired interest rates,

$$(4) \qquad d_{t,EMU} = \sum_{j=1}^{11} w_j \, d_{t,j},$$

where w_j is the weight attached to country j, which is taken as the normalized share of the capital of the national central bank in the ECB.[10] We will restrict the number of possible scenarios to two:

- ECB rule: The governors of the national central banks (eleven of the members of the Governing Council) take a nationalistic perspective (i.e., use $d_{t,j}$) while the six ECB board members take an EMU-wide perspective (i.e., $d_{t,EMU}$). In this case, the ECB board aggregates individual desired interest rates and proposes this average as the policy to be implemented. Majority voting (median voter) is then applied.[11] In this case the six members of the ECB board always vote the same way.
- Nationalistic rule: All members of the Governing Council (the eleven representatives of the individual central banks and the six members of the ECB board) take a nationalistic perspective. Majority voting is then applied.[12]

These two rules are then compared to the alternative of a fixed exchange rate system with Germany as the anchor country. We label this alternative the EMS rule:

- EMS rule: Germany's desired interest rate becomes the Euro-wide interest rate and is applied to all other countries. Thus, this is equivalent to "dictatorship" where $d_{t,j}$ (with j = Germany) always prevails.

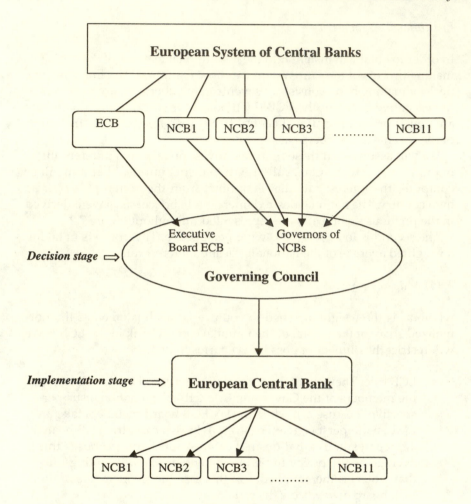

FIGURE 7.3   European System of Central Banks

Simulation Results

In this section we present our simulation results for the ECB rule, nationalistic rule and EMS rule under three different preference schemes: high output stabilization ($\lambda = 5$, $\gamma = 0.5$), low output stabilization ($\lambda = 0.2$, $\gamma = 0.5$), and intermediate output stabilization ($\lambda = 1$, $\gamma = 0.5$). Our procedure is as follows: We start our simulations by assuming that all economies are initially in the steady state. In a first step, shocks in the output gap arrive and have the same correlation structure as the shocks observed over the estimation period. Country-specific output gaps are calculated by using the estimated coefficients of aggregate demand equation and the country-specific output shocks. The obtained output gaps feed into our aggregate supply equations together with autoregressive inflation components and inflation shocks. Here, we use again the estimated coefficients of the aggregate supply equation (2) for each individual country in order to account for country-specific inflation. In a second step, using optimal interest rate rules, the members of the Governing Council determine their own desired interest rates. In the third step, according to each decision rule we designed, the Governing Council decides by majority voting about the unique, Euro-wide interest rate.[13] This interest rate is then used for the calculation of moving averages of real interest rates for each individual country, and so on.

Who Decides About the EMU-wide Interest Rate?

Before doing the welfare comparison between the EMU-type arrangements and the EMS, we use the simulations to shed some light on the behavior of (simulated) interest rates in the two EMU rules (ECB rule and nationalistic rule). Table 7.2 contains the fraction of times that the country's optimal desired interest rate was implemented. As can be seen from this table, in the ECB rule the interest rates are most often (from 81 percent to about 95 percent) determined by the ECB board. So, as long as the ECB board takes an EMU-wide perspective and uses some average of country-specific desired interest rates the ECB board effectively controls monetary policy even if all governors only care about the interests of their own country. This result suggests that the observed asymmetries in the propagation mechanisms across EMU countries are not strong enough to create situations where at least nine countries would oppose the ECB board proposal. Note also that if the ECB board proposal is overruled it is very likely to be replaced by the optimal interest rate of a country with a very high interest rate smoothing coefficient (the Netherlands, Spain, or France).

If the ECB board members also take a nationalistic point of view and thus support the optimal interest rate of their home country this buffer of six ECB board members disintegrates. The consequence of this disintegration is that the median voter must now be a specific country and no longer an average of country-specific demands. As can be seen from the table, the countries that become the median voting country most frequently are those that opt strongly for interest rate inertia: the Netherlands, Spain, France. This result is easily explained. Since countries set the interest rates to stabilize the economy, some countries will be opting for higher interest rates, others will opt for lower interest rates. The countries that will have the stronger preferences for larger interest rate

TABLE 7.2   Voting Power: Fraction of Times That the Country is the Median Voter

	Aus.	Bel.	Fin.	Fra.	Ger.	Ire.	Ita.	Lux.	Net.	Por.	Spa.	ECB
Low output stabilization ($\lambda = .2, \gamma = .5$)												
ECB Rule	0.7	0.6	1.0	1.0	2.0	1.0	0.2	0.8	7.4	0.5	3.7	81.3
Nat. Rule	4.8	3.6	4.4	8.2	9.9	6.1	5.1	4.1	33.2	1.1	19.6	–
Intermediate output stabilization ($\lambda = 1, \gamma = .5$)												
ECB Rule	0.3	0.2	0.4	0.7	0.8	0.5	0.2	0.3	3.4	0.3	1.0	92.0
Nat. Rule	4.4	2.9	5.4	11.8	9.5	4.9	7.7	3.6	34.6	1.0	14.3	–
High output stabilization ($\lambda = 5, \gamma = .5$)												
ECB Rule	0.3	0.0	0.3	1.0	0.3	0.6	0.2	0.2	1.6	0.2	0.2	95.2
Nat. Rule	6.0	3.6	5.7	15.5	7.2	4.0	10.0	2.9	33.6	1.1	10.4	–

changes are those whose economies respond to the changes in interest rates. For countries where the economy does not or only marginally reacts to changes in monetary policy, there is not much scope for macroeconomic stabilization through interest rate policy. These countries can be interpreted to opt for financial stability, which is formalized by the relatively large coefficient on the interest rate smoothing in the optimal feedback rule. These countries are of course the countries that opt for no change in the interest rate and hence tend to be located in the middle of the spectrum of desired interest rate changes.

Table 7.3 then presents the correlations between the desired (country-specific) interest rates and the decided EMU-wide interest rate. In the case of the ECB rule it is not surprising that the correlation between desired and decided interest rate is the highest for the ECB board. Across preference configurations, the correlation is almost perfect, which reflects the fact that in the simulations the ECB board effectively decides about the conduct of monetary policy. For the countries involved, the correlations tend to be highest for the larger countries, France, Germany, Spain, and Italy (because of their large weight in the averaging procedure) and for those countries that opt for strong interest rate inertia (the Netherlands). Thus, although each country representative has only one vote, the ECB rule ensures that the larger countries have a strong impact on the decision process. This feature is due to the fact that with the ECB rule, the ECB board computes a weighted average of the nationally desired interest rate. This weighting procedure benefits the large countries.

This feature is lost when everybody takes a nationalistic perspective. As can be seen from Table 7.3, in the nationalistic scenario, the correlations between desired and decided interest rates tend to decrease substantially for the larger countries and to increase for the smaller ones. The

TABLE 7.3 Correlation Between Desired and Actual Interest Rates

	Aus.	Bel.	Fin.	Fra.	Ger.	Ire.	Ita.	Lux.	Net.	Por.	Spa.	ECB
Low output stabilization ($\lambda = .2, \gamma = .5$)												
ECB Rule	90	42	80	85	94	90	90	82	99	41	99	99.6
Nat. Rule	84	60	73	88	86	91	73	79	99	39	97	–
Intermediate output stabilization ($\lambda = 1, \gamma = .5$)												
ECB Rule	58	2	57	84	82	73	85	42	98	29	92	99.6
Nat. Rule	67	34	72	89	65	75	75	59	95	47	86	–
High output stabilization ($\lambda = 5, \gamma = .5$)												
ECB Rule	31	25	37	64	79	45	72	44	96	.13	75	98.5
Nat. Rule	45	40	51	79	45	56	72	29	96	14	77	–

reason is that in the nationalistic rule there is no ECB board that takes a Euro-wide perspective. The latter tends to give a higher weight to large countries than to smaller ones. Thus, in the nationalistic rule the large countries become smaller (in terms of voting power) while the small countries become larger.

Welfare Analysis: Will EMU Do Better than the EMS?

In this section we compare the EMU regimes with the EMS from a welfare point of view. We obtain this welfare analysis by comparing the losses generated in these different monetary regimes. Since these losses measure the degree to which monetary policies are capable of stabilizing the target variables (output, inflation, and interest rate) they can also be interpreted as measuring the effectiveness of monetary policies. In Figures 7.4 and 7.5 we plot the losses that occur under each of these possible regimes. Throughout Tables 7.4 to 7.7 we translate these figures into relative losses (see Appendix).

A first conclusion that can be drawn from these tables is that in most of the preference constellations, the ECB rule clearly dominates the EMS rule. We observe that all countries, except Germany, prefer the ECB arrangement over the EMS arrangement. Only when the preference for output stabilization is very low are there two small countries (Austria and Belgium) preferring the EMS rule over the ECB rule. Note, however, that the ECB rule assumes that only the national governors take a nationalistic perspective while the six ECB board members, which are almost always the median voter, take an EMU-wide perspective. The economic conditions of all countries are therefore taken into account according to fixed and time-invariant weights. Thus, one can conclude that EMU (provided it follows the ECB rule) allows for more efficient monetary policies than the EMS regime for ten of the eleven countries. Put differently, in EMU ten of eleven member countries experience a better stabilization of their national inflation and output variables and of the interest rate than in the EMS regime. This welfare improvement provided by EMU increases the more the countries desire to stabilize output. For obvious reasons the only loser is Germany.

The assumption of all six ECB board members taking an EMU-wide perspective is not innocuous. It basically determines the superiority of the ECB rule over the EMS rule. When all the members of the Governing Council take a nationalistic view, the median voter's desired interest rate is no longer some average of country-specific desires but the desired interest rate of some (different across time) country. When monetary policy would be conducted under this scenario, the EMS type of arrangement starts to dominate for several countries. Except for an extremely high weight on output variability the EMS would be clearly preferred by Germany, France, Spain, and some other smaller core countries such as the Netherlands. This observation is fairly robust across preference configurations. Apparently, decision procedures seem to matter a great deal for the success of the EMU.

Conclusions

In this chapter we analyzed alternative ways to coordinate monetary policy in Europe. We compared the present EMU regime with the EMS regime in which one country, Germany, dictated the monetary policies for the other EMS countries. In order to do so we constructed simple models of the eleven countries in EMU and derived the optimally desired monetary policies. We took into account asymmetries in shocks, in the transmission of shocks, and in preferences.

Our main results can be summarized as follows. First, except for Germany, all EMU countries profit from the entry into Euroland in the sense that they come closer to their optimally desired monetary policies (interest rates) than under the preceding EMS regime. This welfare gain increases with the desire of the EMU countries to stabilize output.

Second, the welfare gain of EMU only holds if the ECB board takes a Euro-wide perspective, that is, if the ECB board targets a Euro-wide average of inflation and output. If all the members of the Governing Council (including the ECB board) were to take a nationalistic perspective (a quite unrealistic assumption) some countries may actually prefer the previous EMS regime rather than the present EMU.

Third, large countries have the greatest impact on the monetary policy of the ESCB (which is not really surprising). However, smaller countries (e.g., the Netherlands) turn out to have a surprisingly large influence in that on average they come very close to the actually implemented policies. The rea-

TABLE 7.4 Relative Losses in Percentage (intermediate output stabilization)

	Aus.	Bel.	Fin.	Fra.	Ger.	Ire.	Ita.	Lux.	Net.	Por.	Spa.
EMS/ECB	114	113	113	120	82	108	127	121	108	114	107
EMS/NAT	105	133	104	92	65	93	106	117	77	130	84
ECB/NAT	92	117	93	77	79	86	84	97	72	114	78

Preference specifications are $\lambda = 1$, $\gamma = 0.5$.

TABLE 7.5 Relative Losses in Percentage (low output stabilization)

	Aus.	Bel.	Fin.	Fra.	Ger.	Ire.	Ita.	Lux.	Net.	Por.	Spa.
EMS/ECB	90	86	104	116	77	100	151	113	106	114	106
EMS/NAT	78	121	95	80	66	77	142	107	63	170	72
ECB/NAT	86	140	91	69	85	77	94	94	59	149	68

Preference specifications are $\lambda = 0.2$, $\gamma = 0.5$.

TABLE 7.6 Relative Losses in Percentage (high output stabilization)

	Aus.	Bel.	Fin.	Fra.	Ger.	Ire.	Ita.	Lux.	Net.	Por.	Spa.
EMS/ECB	141	243	112	130	83	108	119	137	108	113	114
EMS/NAT	159	261	106	109	65	99	108	135	90	128	96
ECB/NAT	113	107	95	84	78	91	89	98	83	114	86

Preference specifications are $\lambda = 5$, $\gamma = 0.5$.

TABLE 7.7 Relative Losses in Percentage (low interest rate smoothing)

	Aus.	Bel.	Fin.	Fra.	Ger.	Ire.	Ita.	Lux.	Net.	Por.	Spa.
EMS/ECB	113	126	109	122	83	108	125	131	108	114	108
EMS/NAT	109	141	103	95	64	94	105	126	81	132	88
ECB/NAT	96	112	94	78	78	88	84	97	75	116	81

Preference specifications are $\lambda = 1$, $\gamma = 0.25$.

TABLE 7.8   Lag Lengths of Autoregressive Representation for Each Country

	Aus.	Bel.	Fin.	Fra.	Ger.	Ire.	Ita.	Lux.	Net.	Por.	Spa.
AS equation	12*	13*	20*	31*	14*	29*	31*	11	15*	11	15*
AD equation	11	25*	20	11*	12*	11*	15	25*	16	13*	16

* denotes that the best lag structure applied as suggested by AIC

TABLE 7.9   Maximum and Minimum Eigenvalues of Matrices A and M

	Aus.	Bel.	Fin.	Fra.	Ger.	Ire.	Ita.	Lux.	Net.	Por.	Spa.
MaxA	.97	.97	.98	.98	.97	.96	.999	.95	.96	.98	.99
MinA	−.84	−.93	−.93	−.91	−.79	−.95	−.95	−.94	−.95	−.97	−.88
Low output stabilization											
MaxM	.96	.98	.94	.94	.94	.96	.91	.95	.999	.94	.98
MinM	−.84	−.93	−.94	−.91	−.79	−.95	−.95	−.94	−.95	−.97	−.88
Intermediate output stabilization											
MaxM	.96	.98	.97	.96	.95	.96	.95	.95	.997	.97	.99
MinM	−.84	−.93	−.93	−.91	−.79	−.95	−.95	−.94	−.95	−.97	−.88
High output stabilization											
MaxM	.96	.98	.97	.97	.95	.96	.98	.97	.99	.99	.99
MinM	−.84	−.93	−.94	−.91	−.79	−.95	−.95	−.94	−.95	−.97	−.88

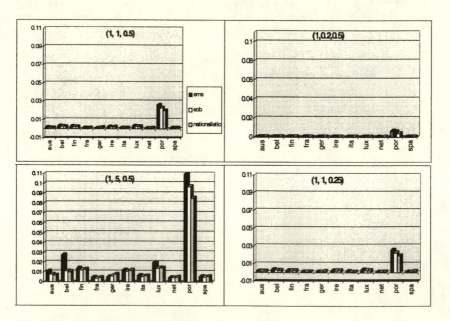

FIGURE 7.4   Welfare Losses Under Different Preferences

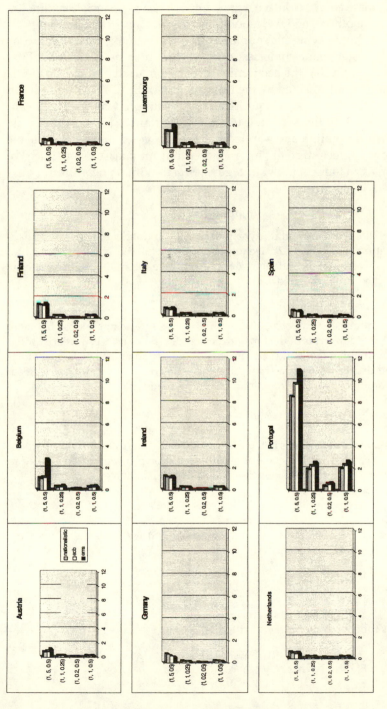

FIGURE 7.5   Welfare Losses Under Different Preferences for Each Country

son is that these countries attach a great importance to financial stability (interest rate smoothing) and correspondingly less to output stabilization.

It goes without saying that our analysis must be interpreted with some caution. We have made some assumptions that may be questioned. First is the assumption that the economic structures in each of the countries is not fundamentally affected by the introduction of EMU. This assumption exposes us to the Lucas critique. There is no simple way to circumvent this critique. Only time will tell us how important it is. Second, we assumed majority voting and applied the median voter theorem. Thus, we completely neglect strategic interactions that may arise over time. We plan to analyze the scope for strategic interaction in the near future.

Appendix

The state of the economy and its dynamics can be summarized by the state space representation of (1) and (2). Denoting the state of the economy by X_t an $(n+m+11) \times 1$ vector of the inflation rates, the output gaps and the interest rate, its dynamics can be reformulated as: [14]

(5) $X_{t+1} = AX_t + Bi_t + v_{t+1}$

The central bank has an objective to minimize its intertemporal loss function, which is defined in terms of the time t expected difference between (yearly) inflation, the output gap $(-y)$ and their targeted values, c_1 and c_2, respectively. Moreover, some degree of interest smoothing is assumed for the central bank. Formally, we assume the following minimization problem:

(6) $\min_{i_t} \sum_{j=0}^{+\infty} \delta^j E_t[(\pi_{t+j} - c_1)^2 + \lambda(y_{t+j} - c_2)^2 - \gamma(i_{t+j} - i_{t+j-1})^2]$.

If the frequency of meetings in the ECB is sufficiently high such that the discount rate $\delta \to 1$, it can be shown that the above minimization problem can be restated in terms of an unconditional loss function (see Rudebusch and Svensson, 1998):

(7) $\min_{i_t} E[Lt] = Var[(\pi_t - c_1)] + \lambda Var[(y_t - c_2)] - \gamma Var[\Delta i_t]$.

Again, following Rudebusch and Svensson (1998) we write the target variables, π_t, y_t and $i_t - i_{t-1}$ in function of the state variable X_t:

(8) $Y_t = \begin{bmatrix} \pi_t \\ y_t \\ i_t - i_{t-1} \end{bmatrix} = C_x X_t + C_i i_t$.

The loss function can now be rewritten as:

(9) $L_t = E[Y_t' K Y_t]$, where $K = \begin{bmatrix} 1 & 0 & 0 \\ 0 & \lambda & 0 \\ 0 & 0 & \gamma \end{bmatrix}$.

Given the empirical evidence that central banks base their interest rate policy on current (and previous) values of output and inflation, we consider the class of linear feedback rules, that is, linear rules based on the current economic states:

(10) $i_t = fX_t$.

where f denotes a 1x $(n + m + 11)$ vector. Using the above relations and substituting the linear feedback rule we obtain the dynamics of the state variable, taking into account the actions of the central bank (on interest rates), as:

(11) $X_{t+1} = MX_t + v_{t+1}, M = A + Bf$

and for the goal variables:

(12) $Y_t = CX_t, C = C_x + C_i f$.

Note that according to equation (10) the central bank can change the dynamics of the economic state by conditioning its interest rate policy on the current state of the economy. The optimal linear feedback rule is then defined as that interest rate rule that generates a state-space dynamics that minimizes the loss function (7). Under the assumptions made so far, Rudebusch and Svensson (1998) show that the optimal (linear) policy rule is given by:

(13) $i_t = -(R + B'VB)^{-1} (U' + B'VA) X_t$.

where the matrix V is defined by:

(14) $V = Q + Uf + f'U' + f'Rf + M'VM$

$Q = C_x'KC_x, U = C_x'KC_i$ and $R = C_i'KC_i$.

Inspection of the optimal linear feedback rule f shows that the optimal feedback rules (interest rate policies) can diverge across countries for three reasons. First, the economic conditions, as summarized by the state variable, X, can differ and hence require different policy actions. Second, the impact differential of interest changes, B, and different transmission speeds across countries, incorporated in A, can demand different policy reactions. Third, country-specific preferences over inflation, output, and interest rate smoothness (entering through K) may vary across countries.

Notes

1. We are grateful to Filipa Correia for excellent research assistance and to A. Van Poeck and R. Dumke for their suggestions. This paper benefited from comments of participants of the University of Munich/ IFO Institute joint seminar.

2. More precisely, we apply the Hodrick Prescott filter with a very high $\lambda = 500{,}000$, which is basically equivalent to linear detrending.

3. Estimated coefficients are not presented but available upon request.

4. By choosing the lag lengths we took care of the stability properties of the A and M matrices in order to generate the optimal feedback rules. Hence, with some AIC-suggested lag structures we observed unstable state space representation. In that case, we opted for the closest alternative suggestion. Chosen lag structures are tabulated in Table 7.8.

5. We check the stability of the system (eigenvalues). For a description of how this is done, see De Grauwe, Dewachter, and Aksoy (1998).

6. High desire to stabilize output ($\lambda = 5$, $\gamma = 0.5$), medium desire to stabilize output ($\lambda = 1$, $\gamma = 0.5$), and low desire to stabilize output ($\lambda = 0.2$, $\gamma = 0.5$).

7. This is essentially a feature of the monthly data. Inflation responses after one month are much smaller than one would observe in the quarterly data. Recent empirical literature vastly focused on the monetary transmission across European countries. For evidence on the transmission of monetary shocks in Europe see, among others, Dornbusch, Favero and Giavazzi (1998), Giovannetti and Marimon (1998), Kieler and Saarenheimo (1998), and Ramaswamy and Sloek (1998). For G7 evidence, see Clarida, Gali, and Gertler (1997), Peersman and Smets (1998), and Kim (1999).

8. For recent evidence on the macroeconomic fluctuations in different European economies see Bayoumi and Prasad (1995) and Ballabriga, Sebastian and Vallés (1999). For evidence in the G7 countries, see example Kwark (1999).

9. Residuals of estimations (1) and (2) will serve for our purpose. Let S_1 denote the variance-covariance matrix of residuals of the aggregate demand estimation (2). Then, Cholesky decomposition of the variance-covariance matrix is $S_1 = L_1 L_1'$ being the lower triangular of S_1. Thus, in line with De Grauwe, Dewachter, and Aksoy (1998) we can recover the covariance structure by the vector of shocks $\varepsilon = [\varepsilon_1 t_1, \ldots \ldots \varepsilon_{11,t}] = L\xi_t$ where ξ-(0,1). For the inflation shocks we apply the same procedure. Hence, our statistical framework is complete.

10. These weights are a function of the country's population and GDP in EMU-wide population and GDP. As such they can be taken as relevant proxies for the weight each country gets in the decision taken by a representative with an EMU-wide perspective. The weights are for Austria 0.0299, Belgium 0.0366, Finland 0.0177, France 0.2138, Germany 0.3093, Ireland 0.0106, Italy 0.1896, Luxembourg 0.0019, The Netherlands 0.0542, Portugal 0.0244, and Spain 0.1119.

11. Median voter models have also been considered by others as a likely outcome of the voting procedure; see, for instance, von Hagen (1998).

12. Note that the current ECB board will consist of Dutch, French, Finnish, German, Italian, and Spanish central bankers.

13. Obviously, with the Benchmark Rule each member country can keep their desired interest rate. Thus, here we have eleven interest rates.

14. See Rudebush and Svensson (1998) or De Grauwe, Dewachter, and Aksoy (1998) for a more elaborated formulation of the state-space representation.

References

Ballabriga, F., Sebastian, M., and Vallés, J., 1999, European asymmetries. *Journal of International Economics* 48, 233–253.

Bayoumi, T., and Prasad, E., 1995, Currency unions, economic fluctuations and adjustment: Some empirical evidence. CEPR Discussion Paper, no. 1172, May.

Clarida, R., Gali, J., and Gertler, M., 1997, Monetary policy rules in practice: Some international evidence, CEPR Discussion Paper, no. 1750.

De Grauwe, P., 1997, Economics of monetary integration, 3rd ed. (New York: Oxford University Press).

De Grauwe, P., Dewachter, H., and Aksoy, Y., 1998, The European Central Bank: Decision rules and macroeconomic performance. CEPR Discussion Paper, no. 2067.

Dornbusch, R., Favero, C., and Giavazzi, F., 1998, Immediate challenges for the European Central Bank. *Economic Policy* 26 (April), 15–52.

Fuhrer, J. C., 1997, The (Un)Importance of forward-looking behavior of price specifications. *Journal of Money, Credit and Banking* 29:3, 338–350.

Giovannetti, G., and Marimon, R., 1998, An EMU with different transmission mechanisms. CEPR Discussion Paper, no. 2016, November.

Kieler, M., and Saarenheimo, T., 1998, Differences in monetary policy transmission? A case not closed. Economic Papers, no. 132, European Commission.

Kim, S., 1999, Do monetary policy shocks matter in the G–7 countries? Using common identifying assumptions about monetary policy across countries. *Journal of International Economics* 48, pp. 387–412.

Kwark, N. S., 1999, Sources of international business fluctuations: Country-specific shocks or worldwide shocks? *Journal of International Economics* 48, 367–385.

Peersman G., and Smets, F., 1998, The Taylor rule: A useful monetary policy guide for the ECB. Mimeo, University of Gent.

Ramaswamy, R., and Sloek, T., 1998, The real effects of monetary policy in the European Union: What are the differences? *IMF Staff Papers*, forthcoming.

Rudebusch, G. D., and Svensson, L.E.O., 1998, Policy rules for inflation targeting. Paper prepared for NBER Conference on Monetary Policy Rules.

Taylor, J., 1993, Discretion versus policy rules in practice. *Carnegie Rochester Conference on Public Policy* 39, pp. 195–214.

von Hagen, J., 1998, The composition of bank councils for monetary unions. Mimeo, ZEI, University of Bonn.

8

Beyond EMU

The Problem of Sustainability

BENJAMIN J. COHEN

Abstract

A common currency, as envisioned in the Maastricht Treaty, is thought to be the surest way to "lock in" commitments to monetary cooperation among sovereign states. But historical evidence suggests otherwise. Comparative analysis of seven currency unions demonstrates that while economic and organizational factors are influential in determining the sustainability of monetary cooperation, interstate politics matters most. Compliance with commitments is greatest in the presence of either a locally dominant state, willing and able to use its influence to sustain monetary cooperation, or a broad network of institutional linkages sufficient to make the loss of monetary autonomy tolerable to each partner.

Students of international monetary relations have long understood that in a world of high capital mobility and separate national currencies, governments are perennially confronted with a problematic trade-off between the goal of exchange-rate stability and a desire for monetary-policy autonomy. For both economic and political reasons, stability of exchange rates is frequently sacrificed for the presumed benefits of policy autonomy. Even among countries formally committed to monetary cooperation, joint interests are often compromised by the pursuit of independent national objectives. Can otherwise unreliable commitments to international monetary cooperation be reliably "locked in" in some way?

Logically, the surest solution would seem to be a common currency (or its equivalent, a formally irrevocable freezing of exchange rates), where individual monetary sovereignty is—in principle—permanently surrendered by each partner government. The hallmark of a currency union is the supposed irreversibility of the commitment, not unlike a marriage. In the words of Michael Mussa: "For a monetary union, 'What the Lord hath joined together, let no man put asunder'" (Mussa 1997, p. 218). For the members of the European Union (EU), the equivalent of marriage is the strategy laid out in the Maastricht treaty for Economic and Monetary Union (EMU). At the start of Stage III, which began January 1, 1999, exchange rates among participating countries' currencies were fixed, ostensibly forever, thus formally abrogating monetary-policy autonomy at the national level.

In a world of sovereign states, however, nothing can be regarded as truly irreversible. Governments may always change their minds. Just as a wedding ring is no guarantee of an everlasting marriage, divorce remains a practical option for currency partners. Conditions must be right for states to voluntarily share—and then stick to their commitment to share—something as highly prized as national monetary sovereignty. Getting to Stage III, therefore, was really only half the battle. Europeans still cannot breathe easily. Even beyond Stage III, care will have to be taken to ensure that joint interests are not once again jeopardized by unilateralist impulses. The possibility of a breakup has been acknowledged by no less an authority than Alan Greenspan, who is quoted as once saying "The Euro will come but it will not be sustainable" (Eltis 1997, p. 2). So long as member states retain political independence, the risk remains that one or another government might eventually choose to reassert its monetary autonomy.

How serious is that risk? Circumstances that might provoke a collapse of EMU are beginning to be explored systematically by economists, including notable contributions by Walter Eltis (1997) and Peter Garber (1997, 1998).[1] Few of these efforts, however, look to history for useful insight or instruction. EMU is by no means the first attempt to lock in the gains of monetary cooperation through a marriage of national currencies. In fact, the nineteenth and twentieth centuries have seen a number of such unions among nominally sovereign states Some still exist. Others have ultimately proved unsustainable in practice. Much can be learned from an analysis of these past experiences.

The purpose of this chapter, which updates an earlier study (Cohen 1993), is to use historical analysis to identify some of the key conditions that may be influential in determining the sustainability of interstate commitments to monetary union.[2] The discussion is based on a comparative analysis of seven past examples of formal currency union among sovereign governments.[3] These seven include three unions still in existence (the East Caribbean Currency Area, the CFA Franc Zone, and the Common Monetary Area), as well as three that eventually failed (the East African Community, the Latin Monetary Union, and the Scandinavian Monetary Union), and one that was voluntarily folded into the broader EMU (the Belgium-Luxembourg Economic Union).[4] The circumstances of the seven cases provide considerable insight into the challenges facing EU members in their efforts to avoid rupture or divorce. Three separate sets of variables are considered: economic, organizational, and political. Systematic evaluation of the seven cases demonstrates the disproportionate importance of key political factors in determining the durability of commitments to currency unification. Economic and organizational factors matter, but interstate politics appears to matter most of all.

The chapter begins with a brief outline of the analytical approach to be used and a short factual description of each of the seven historical cases. Comparative analysis of the seven cases follows, with the principal implications of the discussion summarized in the concluding section.

The Analytical Approach

The central analytical issue, the problem of sustainability, stems directly from the persistent risk of time-inconsistency inherent in the familiar trade-off between exchange-rate stability and monetary-policy autonomy: the possibility that so long as governments attach importance to monetary independence, they may be tempted to renege on prior commitments to policy cooperation. Such risks are omnipresent, of course, in relations between sovereign states, where compliance mechanisms are by definition normally weak or nonexistent. The challenge is to find some compliance mechanism that will actually work—some institutional arrangement that will truly deter governments from breaking bargains that turn out to be inconvenient. Logically, the surest solution would seem to be a common currency or its equivalent, since in principle such policy commitments are supposed to be permanent and irrevocable. Yet, as indicated, not even the most formal currency union may prove to be sustainable in practice. The question thus is: What are the key conditions that determine the sustainability of commitments to monetary union among sovereign national governments?

Prior to my earlier study, neither economists nor political scientists had addressed much attention directly to this question.[5] The voluminous literature by economists on the theory of "optimum currency areas" (OCAs) clearly does involve issues of international monetary union. Most of the work in this area, however, has tended to focus on factors thought to be decisive in a government's selection of an exchange-rate policy at a particular point of time—ordinarily posed as a binary choice between the two extremes of independent floating or unconditional pegging—rather than on conditions that might ensure the durability of exchange-rate commitments, once made, over time. The voluminous literature by political scientists on "international regimes"—more or less formally institutionalized agreements to promote cooperation between nations—might also be thought to have applications to the question at hand. But in fact relatively little has been written specifically about the particular type of regime represented by a monetary or currency union.

For the purposes of this chapter, therefore, an alternative, more historical approach is taken, drawing in part on the separate literatures on optimum currency areas and international regimes, but relying mainly on a methodology of comparative case-study analysis. My discussion focuses on seven relatively recent examples of formal currency unions among sovereign governments: the Belgium-Luxembourg Economic Union (BLEU), the CFA Franc Zone (CFA), the Common Monetary Area (CMA), the East African Community (EAC), the East Caribbean Currency Area (ECCA), the Latin Monetary Union (LMU), and the Scandinavian Monetary Union (SMU). Excluded from this sample are currency unions that were created as a direct counterpart of political unification, as in Germany and Italy in the nineteenth century.[6] Also excluded from formal consideration are currency unions based on political federations, such as Czechoslovakia, Yugoslavia, and the former Soviet Union, that were dissolved as soon as their constituent states gained independence.[7]

Though this sample is by no means exhaustive,[8] it does illustrate a wide range of relevant experience, including three unions that have been successfully sustained, as well as three that ultimately were not and one that was blended into EMU; three unions among industrial nations as well as four among less developed economies; three unions that have featured a common currency, at least for a time, as well as four that have relied exclusively on formally linked national or regional currencies; and two unions from the nineteenth century as well as five from the twentieth. None of the seven cases replicates EMU's circumstances precisely, of course. But collectively the sample does provide instructive lessons for the EU as it tries to maintain the momentum of monetary unification.

The discussion is structured in terms of three sets of possible explanatory variables: economic, organizational, and political. The economic factors considered are drawn directly from OCA theory and include such characteristics as wage and price flexibility, factor mobility, geographic trade patterns, the openness of economies, and the nature and source of potential payments disturbances. Organizational factors include legal provisions concerning currency issue and monetary management: Are national currencies replaced by a single common currency? Are national central banks replaced by a single monetary authority? Political factors, which for purposes of brevity are limited here only to considerations of interstate politics, include the presence or absence of either a locally dominant state (a "hegemon") or a sufficiently dense network of institutional linkages to successfully preserve a currency union over time. Although in a short chapter analysis can be impressionistic at best, the evidence does seem clearly to suggest that political conditions are most instrumental in determining the sustainability of monetary union among sovereign governments.

The Sample

The basic facts of the seven cases are summarized in the Table 8.1.[9] The two nineteenth-century examples, the Latin Monetary Union and Scandinavian Monetary Union, both originated at a time when national currencies were still largely based on metallic monetary standards; their subsequent histories were largely conditioned by the broader evolution of money systems at the time, from bimetallism to the gold standard and from full-bodied metal coinage to various forms of paper currency. Each was built on a standardized monetary unit (respectively, the franc and krone) issued by nominally autonomous central banks; and each was successfully sustained as a distinct currency area, despite recurrent difficulties in the case of the LMU, until effectively terminated with the outbreak of World War I.

The immediate purpose of the Latin Monetary Union, formed by Belgium, France, Italy, and Switzerland in 1865, was to standardize the existing gold and silver coinages of all four countries.[10] In practical terms, a regional monetary bloc had already begun earlier as a result of independent decisions by Belgium, Italy, and Switzerland to adopt currency systems modeled on that of France, with the franc (equivalently, the lire in Italy) as their basic monetary unit. Starting in the 1850s, however, serious Gresham's Law–type problems had developed as a result of differences in the weight and fineness of silver coins circulating in each country. The LMU established uniform standards for national coinages and, by making each member's money legal tender throughout the Union, created a wider area for the circulation of a harmonized supply of specie coins. In substance, a formal exchange-rate union was created; responsibility for the management of participating currencies remained with each separate government. Group members were distinguished from other countries by the reciprocal obligation of their central banks to accept one another's currencies at par and without limit. Although subsequently subjected to considerable strain by a global depreciation of silver beginning in the late 1860s, which led eventually to suspension of silver coinage by all the

TABLE 8.1   Comparison of Seven Formal Currency Unions

	Belgium-Luxembourg Economic Union (BLEU)	CFA Franc Zone (CFA)	Common Monetary Area (CMA)
Date of Origin	1922	1959	1986
Membership	Belgium, Luxembourg	Benin, Burkina Faso, Cameroon, Central African Republic, Chad, Congo, Côte d'Ivoire, Equatorial Guinea (from 1985), Gabon, Guinea-Bissau (from 1997), Mali (withdrew in 1962, rejoined in 1984), Niger, Senegal, Togo	Lesotho, Namibia, South Africa, Swaziland
Precursors	None	French franc zone (le franc des Colonies Françaises d'Afrique, 1945)	Rand Monetary Area (from 1920s, formalized in 1974)
Currencies	Separate national currencies: Belgian franc, Luxembourg franc	Two regional currencies: franc de la Communauté Financière de l'Afrique and franc de la Coopération Financière Africaine (both called CFA francs)	Separate national currencies
Legal Provisions	Belgian franc legal tender in both nations; Luxembourg franc legal tender in Luxembourg only	Each regional currency legal tender only in its own region	South African rand legal tender in all members except Swaziland
Monetary Institutions	Central bank (National Bank of Belgium) in Belgium; bank of issue (Luxembourg Monetary Institute) in Luxembourg	Two regional central banks: Central Bank of West African States and Bank of Central African States	National central banks
Related Agreements	Benelux, European Community	West African Monetary Union and Central African Monetary Area	None
Dissolution	1999 (absorbed into EMU)	Still in operation	Still in operation

East African Community (EAC)	East Caribbean Currency Area (ECCA)	Latin Monetary Union (LMU)	Scandinavian Monetary Union (SMU)
1967	1965	1865	1873
Kenya, Tanzania, Uganda	Antigua and Barbuda, Dominica, Grenada (from 1967) Montserrat, St. Kitts and Nevis, St. Lucia, St. Vincent and the Grenadines	Belgium, France, Greece (from 1868), Italy, Switzerland	Denmark, Norway (from 1875), Sweden
East African Currency Board (1919)	British Caribbean Currency Board (1950)	None	None
Common currency (East African shilling) until 1965; then separate national currencies (shillings)	Common currency: East Caribbean dollar	Separate national currencies: francs (lire in Italy) (drachma in Greece)	Separate national currencies: kroner (crowns)
East African shilling legal tender throughout until 1965; thereafter, national shillings exchanged at par	Legal tender throughout	Legal tender throughout	Legal tender throughout
National central banks	Single central bank: East Caribbean Central Bank (established 1983; formerly the East Caribbean Currency Authority, established in 1965)	National central banks	National central banks
None	East Caribbean Common Market (1968); Organization of East Caribbean States (1981)	None	None
1977	Still in operation	1914–1927	1914–1931

partners (effectively transforming the LMU from a bimetallic standard into what came to be called a "limping gold standard"), the Union managed to hold together until the generalized breakdown of monetary relations during World War I. Following Switzerland's decision to withdraw in 1926, the LMU was formally dissolved in 1927.[11]

The Scandinavian Monetary Union, too, was designed to standardize existing coinages, although, unlike the LMU, the SMU was based from the start on a monometallic gold standard. Formed in 1873 by Sweden and Denmark, and joined by Norway two years later, the Union established the krone (crown) as a uniform unit of account, with national currencies permitted full legal circulation in all three countries. As in the LMU, members as a group were distinguished from outsiders by a reciprocal obligation to accept one another's currencies without limit; likewise, mutual acceptability was initially limited to coins only. In 1885, however, the three members went further, agreeing to accept one another's bank notes and drafts as well, thus facilitating free intercirculation of all paper currency and resulting eventually in the total disappearance of exchange-rate quotations among the three moneys. By the turn of the century the SMU had come to function as a single region for all payments purposes, and it continued to do so until relations were disrupted by the suspension of convertibility and floating of individual currencies at the start of World War I. Despite subsequent efforts during and after the war to restore at least some elements of the union, particularly after the members' return to the gold standard in the mid-1920s, the agreement was finally abandoned following the global financial crisis of 1931.[12]

The third European case is the Belgium-Luxembourg Economic Union, which remained in force for more than seven decades after its inception in 1922 until blended into EMU in 1999. Following severance of its traditional ties with the German Zollverein after World War I, Luxembourg elected to link itself commercially and financially with Belgium, agreeing to a comprehensive economic union including a merger of their separate money systems. Reflecting the partners' considerable disparity of size (Belgium's population is roughly thirty times Luxembourg's), Belgian francs under BLEU formed the largest part of the money stock of Luxembourg as well as Belgium, and alone enjoyed full status as legal tender in both countries. Only Belgium, moreover, had a full-scale central bank. The Luxembourg franc was issued by a more modest institution, the Luxembourg Monetary Institute; was limited in supply under a currency-board arrangement; and served as legal tender just within Luxembourg itself. Despite the existence of formal joint decisionmaking bodies, Luxembourg in effect existed largely as an appendage of the Belgian monetary system.

The four remaining examples all involve developing countries, and all had their origins in earlier colonial arrangements. In the case of Francophone Africa, the roots of today's CFA Franc Zone go back to 1945, when the French government decided to consolidate the diverse currencies of its various African dependencies into one money, "le franc des Colonies Françaises d'Afrique (CFA francs)." Subsequently, in the early 1960s, as independence came to France's African empire, the old colonial franc was replaced by two new regional currencies, each cleverly named to preserve the CFA franc appellation: for the eight present members of the West African Monetary Union,[13] "le franc de la Communauté Financière de l'Afrique," issued by the Central Bank of West African States; and for the six members of the Central African Monetary Area, "le franc de la Coopération Financière Africaine," issued by the Bank of Central African States.[14] Together the two groups comprise the Communauté Financière Africaine (African Financial Community). Though each of the two currencies is legal tender only within its own region, the two are equivalently defined and have always been jointly managed under the aegis of the French Ministry of Finance as integral parts of a single monetary union.

The roots of two other examples, both involving former British dependencies, go back to Britain's use of currency boards to manage its colonial financial affairs. In the Caribbean, Britain's monetary legacy has proved remarkably successful. The British Caribbean Currency Board, first created in 1950, has evolved first into the East Caribbean Currency Authority, in 1965, and then into the East Caribbean Central Bank, in 1983, issuing one currency, the East Caribbean dollar, to serve as legal tender for all seven participating states.[15] Embedded in a broadening network of other related agreements among the same governments, such as the East Caribbean Common Market and the Organization of Eastern Caribbean States, the East Caribbean Currency Area has functioned as a true monetary union without serious difficulty since its establishment in 1965.

In East Africa, on the other hand, Britain's colonial legacy ultimately failed, despite creation of an East African Currency Board as early as 1919 to administer a single money, the East African shilling, for the territories of Kenya, Tanganyika (later part of Tanzania), and Uganda. The three colonies also had a customs union dating from 1923 as well as a variety of other common services for railways, harbors, air transport, and the like. Yet once independence arrived in the region (for Tanganyika in 1961, for Uganda in 1962, and for Kenya in 1963), joint institutions, including the common currency, quickly began to break apart; and by the middle of the decade, all three countries had decided to install central banks and national currencies of their own to replace the East African shilling. In 1967 a fresh attempt was made to preserve some semblance of the former currency union in the context of the newly established East African Community and Common Market, which specifically provided for free exchange between the separate national currencies at par. Although the EAC for the first time provided a formal legal basis for the integration of the three economies, regional cooperation continued to disintegrate; and by the mid-1970s, all vestiges of the economic community had completely disappeared. The final nail in the coffin was hammered home in 1977, when all three governments extended existing exchange controls to each other's currencies.

The last example is the so-called Common Monetary Area combining the Republic of South Africa—a sovereign state for decades—with two former British colonies, Lesotho and Swaziland, and South Africa's own former dependency, Namibia (formerly the UN trust territory of South West Africa). The origins of the CMA go back to the 1920s when South Africa's currency, now known as the rand,[16] became the sole legal tender in three of Britain's nearby possessions, Bechuanaland (later Botswana), British Basutoland (later Lesotho), and Swaziland, as well as in South West Africa, previously a German colony. Since decolonization came to the region in the late 1960s the arrangement has been progressively formalized, first in 1974 as the Rand Monetary Area, later in 1986 as the CMA (though, significantly, without the participation of diamond-rich Botswana, which has preferred to promote its own national money, the pula). The CMA has always been distinctly hierarchical, given South Africa's economic dominance of the southern African region. With the passage of time, however, the degree of hierarchy has diminished considerably, as the three remaining junior partners have asserted their growing sense of national identity. What began as a monetary union based on the rand has gradually, since the 1970s, been transformed into a looser exchange-rate union as each of South Africa's partners has introduced its own distinct national currency; one of them, Swaziland, has even gone so far as to withdraw the rand's legal-tender status within its own borders. Moreover, though all three continue to peg their moneys to the rand at par, they are no longer bound by currency board–like provisions on money creation and may now in principle vary their exchange rates at will. The CMA may still be a far cry from a true union of equals, but it is no longer as asymmetrical as, say, the BLEU used to be.

Economic Factors

Manifestly, the historical record is varied. Only four past unions (BLEU, CFA, CMA, and ECCA) may fairly be described as successful, having been sustained for decades. Others, including EAC as well as the Soviet Union's ruble zone and other former federations such as Czechoslovakia and Yugoslavia, have disintegrated almost as soon as their members gained political independence and can only be judged failures. And the nineteenth century's two major examples, the LMU and SMU, elicit a mixed verdict. Each functioned more or less effectively up to World War I (a not inconsiderable achievement) yet ultimately proved unsustainable. What explains these striking contrasts in experience?

To begin, we may consider some of the factors that have come to figure centrally in the optimum-currency-areas literature.[17] The standard approach of OCA theory is to identify criteria that seem most likely to influence a government's choice of a currency regime, emphasizing in particular conditions affecting the costs of balance-of-payments adjustment with either a pegged or floating exchange rate. Most prominently, these variables are thought to include wage and price flexibility, factor mobility, geographic trade patterns, the openness of economies, and the nature and source of potential payments disturbances. Countries are expected to prefer mutually fixed exchange rates to the extent that prices and wages are flexible, factors of production are mobile, trade interdependence is high, economies are open, and shocks tend to be synchronized rather than asymmetric. Might these characteristics be key in determining the *sustainability* of mutually fixed rates as well?

A firm answer to this question is precluded by inadequate statistics and knotty measurement problems. Little evidence appears to exist in our seven cases, however, to suggest a decisive role for any of the economic factors cited, either singly or in combination. Wage and price flexibility, for instance, might help to explain why the Latin and Scandinavian Unions were able to last as long as they did, before being effectively dismantled at the start of World War I. Certainly we know that costs and prices were far less "sticky" in the nineteenth century than they have tended to become in the twentieth. But nothing in the available data indicates that wages or prices are any less flexible in East Africa, where currency integration failed, than in Francophone or southern Africa or in the East Caribbean, where it has so far succeeded. Likewise, factors of production, particularly capital, were undoubtedly fairly mobile in the two nineteenth-century unions, as well as in BLEU during its decades of existence; but there seems no reason to suppose that resource mobility was any less in East Africa before the breakup of the EAC than in the CFA Franc Zone, CMA, or ECCA.

Trade patterns are particularly unhelpful, indicating no systematic relationship at all with the outcomes of our seven cases. Only in three of the seven—LMU, BLEU, and CMA—has trade interdependence been comparatively high. In all three cases, however, the pattern has been distinctly asymmetrical, reflecting primarily the economic importance of the dominant member (respectively France, Belgium, and South Africa).[18] In SMU, the volume of reciprocal trade was not particularly small but was greatly overshadowed by relations with two outside powers, Britain and Germany.[19] And in the three remaining cases, all involving developing countries, intragroup trade has barely existed at all. In typical postcolonial fashion, most of the African and Caribbean states do far more business with industrial countries than they do with each other (Masson and Taylor 1993, p. 13).

Nor are the remaining variables any more helpful. Members of the CFA Franc Zone, CMA, and ECCA, for instance, have relatively open economies, a characteristic that is supposed to favor exchange-rate pegging rather than floating; and the same may also be said of the two members of the old BLEU as compared with their immediate trading partners. Among these four successful unions, however, only in the East Caribbean do balance-of-payments disturbances tend, for the most part, to be synchronous (owing to the members' common reliance on the same narrow range of exports, mainly sugar and bananas). In Francophone and southern Africa and in Belgium and Luxembourg production structures are rather more diverse, causing external shocks to affect regional partners in quite different ways, a characteristic that is supposed to favor floating rather than pegging. The three former members of the East African Community had open economies and a history of relatively symmetrical payments shocks, yet ultimately chose to go their separate ways. This stands in sharp contrast to the Latin and Scandinavian Unions, which for several decades managed effectively to stay together despite the fact that by the standards of the nineteenth century, most of their members had relatively diversified economies and were subject to rather more differentiated external disturbances.

In short, for every one of the characteristics conventionally stressed in the OCA literature, contradictory examples exist—some cases conform to the expectations of theory, and others do not.[20] No factor seems sufficient to explain the outcomes in our sample. This is not to suggest that economic factors are therefore unimportant. Clearly they do matter insofar as they tend, through their impact on adjustment costs and speculative incentives, to ease or exacerbate the challenge of monetary cooperation. But, equally clearly, more was going on in each of our seven cases than can be accounted for by such variables alone. Other things matter too.

Organizational Factors

Some of those other things might have been organizational in nature. It is evident that formal legal provisions concerning currency issue and monetary management have differed sharply in the seven cases. Only in three cases have members ever relied exclusively on a common currency—in the East Caribbean and, more briefly, in East and southern Africa. In all the others, including EAC after 1967 and CMA after 1974, arrangements have featured national or regional currencies that were officially linked to a greater or less extent. And in parallel fashion monetary institutions have also varied greatly, ranging from a single central authority in three cases (ECCA, EAC before the mid-1960s, and CMA before 1974) to two regional authorities in one case (CFA) and to separate national agencies in all the others (BLEU, EAC after 1967, CMA after 1974, LMU, and SMU). Might these organizational differences explain the contrasting experiences in our sample?

In principle, such differences might be thought to matter insofar as they affect the net costs of compliance or defection by individual states. The recent theoretical literature on transactions costs emphasizes the key role that organizational design can play in promoting credible commitments, by structuring arrangements to match anticipated incentive problems (North 1990). From this perspective, creation of a single currency would appear to be superior to a formal linking of national currencies because of the higher barriers to exit: reintroducing an independent money and monetary authority would be much more costly.[21]

This was also the conclusion of early policy discussions of alternative strategies for EMU, following the signing of the Maastricht Treaty, which directly addressed the relative merits of full monetary union versus simple exchange-rate union (Gros and Thygesen 1992, p. 230–233; von Hagen and Fratianni 1993). Most analysts expressed doubt that a system retaining existing moneys and central banks, no matter how solemn the political commitments involved, would be as credible as a genuine joint currency, precisely because the risk of reversibility would presumably be greater. Compliance mechanisms are likely to be weaker to the extent that governments continue to exercise any control over either the price or the quantity of their currency. Thus one might expect to find a direct historical correlation between the degree of centralization of a monetary union and its practical sustainability over time.

Indeed, one economic historian, Mark Griffiths (1992), suggests that that is precisely the reason why the Latin Monetary Union ultimately collapsed. Much of the strain experienced by the LMU in the decades before World War I was directly attributable to its decentralized structure, which permitted each national central bank to pursue its own domestic policy objectives. Once global depreciation of silver began in the late 1860s, several members (in particular, Italy) succumbed to the temptation to increase the amount and circulation of their silver coinage, in effect seeking to extract additional seigniorage gains at the expense of their partners (especially France, where many of the silver coins ended up). To hold the union together, members first restricted and finally, in 1878, suspended all silver coinage other than token money (the limping gold standard); and subsequently, from 1885, added a liquidation clause at the behest of France requiring any state wishing to leave the group to redeem its silver held by other member governments in gold or convertible paper. Even before the financial disruptions of World War I, the only sense of common interest remaining among union members was a mutual desire to avoid a potentially costly dissolution. In Griffiths's words: "This demonstrates the rather obvious point that a monetary union based on independent central banks is potentially unstable" (1992, p. 88).[22]

But what then of the Scandinavian Monetary Union, which was also based on independent central banks yet managed to function far more smoothly than the LMU in the decades before World War I? Or the CFA Franc Zone and Common Monetary Area, both of which are still sustained successfully even though they lack either a joint currency or a single central institution? Or the East African Community, where neither a common currency nor a central authority in the end could stop disintegration? Once again, contradictory examples abound. And while, once again, this is not to suggest that such factors are therefore unimportant—clearly, the degree of organizational centralization does matter insofar as it influences the potential cost of exit—it is equally clear that there is still something else at work here. That something, of course, is politics.

Political Factors

From the perspective of interstate politics, two characteristics seem to stand out as crucial to the outcomes in our sample. One, suggested by traditional "realist" approaches to the analysis of international relations, is the presence or absence of a dominant state willing to use its influence to keep such an arrangement functioning effectively on terms agreeable to all. The other, suggested by an "institutional" approach of the sort stressed by Lisa Martin (see Chapter 6, this volume), is the presence or absence of a broader constellation of related ties and commitments sufficient to make the loss of monetary autonomy, whatever the magnitude of prospective adjustment costs, basically acceptable to each partner. The first calls for a local hegemon and is a direct reflection of the distribution of interstate power.[23] The second calls for a well-developed set of institutional linkages and reflects, more amorphously, the extent to which a genuine sense of solidarity, of *community*, exists among the countries involved—what Keohane and Hoffmann (1991, p. 13) call a "network" form of organization, in which individual units are defined not by themselves but in relation to each other. Judging from our seven cases, it seems clear that one or the other of these two factors is necessary for the sustainability of monetary union among sovereign states. Where both are present, they are a sufficient condition for success. Where neither is present, unions erode or fail.

Consider, for example, the Belgium-Luxembourg Economic Union, by far the most durable among our seven cases until absorbed into EMU.

Both of these necessary political characteristics were long evident in BLEU. As indicated earlier, Belgium from the beginning was the acknowledged dominant partner, in effect making all important monetary decisions for both countries. While institutionally the two states retained separate national agencies for currency issue, de facto there was just one central authority. In the words of Donald Hodgman, writing a quarter of a century ago: "Luxembourg . . . has no capacity for an independent monetary policy . . . Through mutual agreement these powers are exercised by the Belgian authorities" (1974, p. 23).[24] In part, the success of the arrangement reflected Belgium's willingness as well as ability to shoulder the responsibility of managing the partners' joint affairs. And in part it reflected the broader constellation of reciprocal ties shared by the two countries, in BLEU itself as well as in related regional groupings like Benelux and the European Community. Between these states there clearly was a network of institutional linkages and sense of common interest sufficient to make a sustained commitment to monetary cooperation attractive, or at least not intolerable, to both sides.

At the opposite extreme is the East African Community, the least durable among our seven cases. Here neither of the necessary political characteristics was to be found. Certainly there seems to have been little feeling of solidarity among the three countries, despite their legacy of common colonial services and institutions. Much more influential was a pervasive sensitivity to any threat of encroachment on freshly won national sovereignty. Once independent, each of the three new governments eagerly concentrated on building state identity rather than on preserving regional unity. A hardening of national priorities and interests, compounded by sharp divergences of ideology and political style, quickly eroded any commitment to continued economic cooperation (Rothchild 1974; Ravenhill 1979).

Nor was any locally dominant power in the EAC willing and able to use its influence to counteract these disintegrative forces. Kenya was the most advanced in terms of industrial development but was still too poor to act the role of hegemon. Instead of using its leading position in intraregional trade to promote community ties, Kenya was understandably tempted to exploit its position for its own ends, thus aggravating rather than moderating strains and tensions among the members (Mugomba 1978; Mbogoro 1985). Beyond the EAC, Britain as former colonial master might have continued support for regional institutions but, burdened by its own economic difficulties, chose instead to distance itself from its former dependencies. Once the sterling area was dismantled in the early 1970s, the last barrier was removed to pursuit of independent monetary policies by each government. These inauspicious political circumstances made it hardly surprising that the EAC failed totally.

The importance of a local hegemon is also demonstrated by the two successful African cases, both of which are clearly dominated by a single core country (Honohan 1992). In the Common Monetary Area, South Africa is the leader. It not only stands as lender of last resort for its junior partners but even compensates two of them, Lesotho and Namibia, for the seigniorage they forego in using the rand as legal tender. (Compensation is based on an estimate of the income that would accrue to them if they had reserves of equivalent amount invested in rand-denominated assets). In the CFA Franc Zone leadership is provided by France, the former colonial power. The durability of the CFA, most sources agree, is directly attributable to the pivotal role played by the French Ministry of Finance in underwriting—in effect, subsidizing—Francophone Africa's joint currency arrangements.

Although never formally a member of the CFA Zone, France has always exercised a decisive influence through the so-called operations accounts maintained by the group's two regional central banks at the French Treasury, into which each is obliged to deposit the bulk of its foreign-exchange reserves. In return, France has enhanced the credibility of the CFA franc by guaranteeing its convertibility at a fixed price. Monetary discipline has been implemented through rules affecting access to credit from the Treasury as well as through the firm peg of the CFA franc to the French franc, which remained at a ratio of 50:1 for nearly half a century before a 50 percent devaluation (to 100:1) in 1994. CFA countries also share some sense of community, of course: a common language and colonial experience and a constellation of related regional agreements. But for better or worse,[25] the role of France has been and remains paramount, even after the start of EMU. On January 1, 1999, the CFA peg was seamlessly shifted from the French franc to the new euro. But in all other respects operating features of the zone remained unchanged, with France's Ministry of Finance still playing the role of local hegemon.[26]

French hegemony was decisive as well in the Latin Monetary Union, albeit in rather less benign form. In this case, the dominant state used its power in a much more narrowly self-interested fashion, first to promote France's monetary leadership and later to prevent a costly dissolution. As Griffiths (1992) has written: "Throughout its evolution the influence of France remained ever-present, extracting concessions from its fellow members. Although only one country out of four, France remained dominant, reflecting the realities of its economic and political power."

Even before the LMU was formally established, France's influence, mainly based on its dominating position in regional trade, was evident in the willing adaptation to its currency system by its smaller trading partners. French hegemony was further evident in the bloc's initial decision to base the LMU on a bimetallic standard even though France's partners would all have preferred a monometallic gold standard (Bartel 1974, pp.

695–696). And it was certainly evident after the LMU was transformed into a limping gold standard, when France resorted to a threat of penalties—formalized in the liquidation clause added at its behest in 1885—to discourage member withdrawals that would have left the French with large holdings of unredeemable silver coins. But for this pressure from France, the LMU might have broken up even well before the financial disruptions of World War I.

The importance of an institutionalized sense of community was amply demonstrated, in a negative way, by the speed with which the old Soviet ruble zone and similar failed monetary federations (e.g., the Austro-Hungarian Empire, Czechoslovakia, Yugoslavia) fell apart once competing nationalisms gained political ascendancy. Disintegration of the ruble zone, in particular, was hastened by an unwillingness on the part of successor states to place group cohesion above their separate desires for seigniorage revenue. After 1991, as Patrick Conway has written, the zone "became a battleground for securing seigniorage resources" (1995, p. 40). Breakup became unavoidable after Russia, the acknowledged senior partner, made clear in 1993 that it was prepared to bear the responsibilities of leadership only on its own terms (Cohen 1998, pp. 78–80).

In a more positive manner, the importance of community is demonstrated by two long-lived alliances, the East Caribbean Currency Area and Scandinavian Monetary Union, neither of which could in any way be described as hegemonic systems. In the ECCA the partners are all island microstates, comparably small and poor, and have been left more or less on their own by their former colonial master. In the SMU Sweden may have been first among equals, but it exercised nothing like the power that France enjoyed in the LMU. Yet both unions functioned reasonably well for decades—the SMU until World War I, the ECCA to the present day. The explanation for their longevity seems directly related to the genuine feeling of solidarity that has existed among their members.

In the East Caribbean, unlike in East Africa, there has never been much value placed on separate sovereignties: identities have always been defined more in regional than in national terms, institutionalized in a dense web of related economic and political agreements. The ECCA, as one observer has noted, is just one part of a much broader effort by which these seven governments "have pooled their resources in a symbolic, symbiotic and substantive way with the aim of furthering their development" (Jones-Hendrickson 1989, p. 71). Likewise, the Scandinavian nations, unlike the members of the LMU, had long shared a tradition of cooperation based on a common cultural and political background. As one source puts it: "Language, social life, administration, legislation, judiciary, poetry and literature, science, and many other aspects of life created bonds between these peoples who had been intimately linked for such a long and important period" (Wendt 1981, p. 17). Given the density of existing ties, a common currency system seemed not only natural but almost inevitable until it was fatally disrupted by World War I.

Implications

What are the implications of all this for the sustainability of EMU? My analysis suggests that studies of monetary union that principally emphasize either economic variables or organizational characteristics miss the main point. The issue is only secondarily whether the members meet the traditional criteria identified in OCA theory or whether monetary management and the issuing of currency happen to be centralized or decentralized. The primary question is whether a local hegemon or a fabric of related ties exists to neutralize the risks of free-riding or exit. Sovereign governments require incentives to stick to bargains that turn out to be inconvenient. The evidence from history suggests that these incentives may derive either from side-payments or sanctions supplied by a single powerful state or from the constraints and opportunities posed by a broad network of institutional linkages. One or the other of these political factors must be present to serve as an effective compliance mechanism.[27]

In this respect Europeans have reason to be hopeful, since both factors would appear to be present in the context of EMU. There clearly is a large and monetarily dominant state, Germany, which at least until now has shown every indication of willingness to use its influence to promote development of the euro. Even more clearly, after half a century of construction, there is also now a well-established sense of solidarity and commitment to a common project in the European Community. Though the possibility of divorce will always lurk in the background, the chances for a successful union seem better than for many new marriages these days.

Nearly three decades ago, economist Norman Mintz wrote:

> It has often been argued that the conditions under which monetary integration might reasonably be expected to succeed are very restrictive. In fact, these conditions appear no more restrictive than the conditions for the establishment of a successful common market. The major, and perhaps only, real condition for the institution of either is the *political will* to integrate on the part of prospective members. (1970, p. 33. Emphasis added)

At one level, this conclusion may appear naive—yet another example of the economist's propensity to compress all the complexities of political process into the simple notion "political will." But at another level Mintz shows profound insight if we understand "political will" to refer either to the motivations of a local hegemon or to the value attached to a common endeavor. In fact, these *are* the main conditions necessary for success.

Notes

1. Other examples include Berthold, Fehn and Thode (1999) and Calomiris (1999).

2. As in my earlier study, sustainability—the dependent variable in my analysis—is defined strictly in terms of longevity. Other possible criteria by which to judge the "success" or "failure" of commitments to monetary union (e.g., impacts on price stability, employment, or economic growth) are not directly considered.

3. The terms "currency union" and "monetary union," as in my earlier study, will be used here interchangeably and are defined to encompass both forms of currency integration—common currencies as well as their equivalent, formal exchange-rate unions.

4. Only six cases were included in my earlier study. The Common Monetary Area, comprising the Republic of South Africa and several of its neighbors, has been added to this updated analysis.

5. For a rare exception, see Graboyes (1990). More informal comments could also be found in Hamada (1985: 34–39) and Hamada and Porteous (1992). Several additional comparative analyses have appeared since my earlier study, including Bordo and Jonung (1997, 1999), Capie (1999), and Hamada (1999).

6. Bordo and Jonung (1997, 1999) label such examples "national" monetary unions in contradistinction to "multinational" monetary unions among two or more sovereign states like those included in my sample. For other discussions of nineteenth-century "national" monetary unions, see Vanthoor (1996), Capie (1999).

7. For more on these recent instances of monetary disintegration accompanying political dissolution, see Cohen (1998, ch. 4). Another celebrated example that has received much attention in the formal literature occurred after World War I, when the Austro-Hungarian Empire was dismembered by the Treaty of Versailles. Almost immediately, in an abrupt and quite chaotic manner, new currencies were introduced by each successor state—including Czechoslovakia, Hungary, Yugoslavia, and ultimately even shrunken Austria itself—to replace the old imperial Austrian crown (Dornbusch 1992, 1994; Garber and Spencer 1994).

8. Other examples could be cited, including a number of smaller states that have long relied on a foreign government's money for domestic legal tender, such as Liberia and Panama (which use the U.S. dollar) and a scattering of microstates in Europe (e.g., Andorra, Liechtenstein, Monaco, and San Marino) and the Pacific (e.g., Kiribati, Marshall Islands, and Micronesia). There were also additional examples in the nineteenth century, e.g., the Austro-German Monetary Union established in 1857 by Austria and the members of the German Zollverein, which lasted only nine years until the Austrian-Prussian War of 1866. None of these cases, however, may be considered as relevant to the case of EMU as the seven selected for the purpose of this chapter.

9. Comprehensive sources on these cases are not easy to come by. The best available introductions are as follows: for the Latin and Scandinavian Monetary Unions, Krämer (1971), Bartel (1974), De Cecco (1992), Perlman (1993), Vanthoor (1996); for the Belgium-Luxembourg Economic Union, Meade (1956), van Meerhaeghe (1987);

for the CFA Franc Zone, Boughton (1993a, 1993b); for the East African Community, Letiche (1974); for the East Caribbean Currency Area, McClean (1975), Nascimento (1994); and for the Common Monetary Area, Honohan (1992).

10. Greece subsequently adhered to the terms of the LMU in 1868, though it did not become a formal member until 1876. In addition, several other states—including Austria, Romania, and Spain—also associated themselves with the Latin Monetary Union in one manner or another, though never becoming formal members. By 1880 some eighteen states used the franc, the basic monetary unit of the LMU, as the basis for their own currency systems (Bartel 1974, p. 697).

11. Useful recent analytical discussions of the LMU include Griffiths (1992), Flandreau (1993, 1995), Redish (1994).

12. The SMU experience has been evaluated most recently by Jonung (1987) and Bergman, Gerlach, and Jonung (1993).

13. Benin, Burkina Faso, Côte d'Ivoire, Guinea-Bissau (a former Portuguese colony, which joined in 1997), Mali, Niger, Senegal, and Togo. The West African Monetary Union (WAMU) was formally established in 1962.

14. The six members of the Central African Monetary Area (CAMA) are Cameroon, Central African Republic, Chad, Republic of Congo, Equatorial Guinea (a former Spanish colony, which joined in 1985), and Gabon. Although the Bank of Central African States was not formally established until 1964, the West African Central Bank had already been created earlier, in 1959. In the Central African group, the bank issues an identifiable currency for each member, although each country's currency is similar in appearance, carries the same name (franc de la Coopération Financière Africaine), and is legal tender throughout the region. This is in contrast to the West African group, where the central bank issues a single currency that circulates freely in all eight states.

15. Antigua and Barbuda, Dominica, Grenada, Montserrat, St. Kitts-Nevis, St. Lucia, and St. Vincent and the Grenadines.

16. Prior to 1960, the Republic's currency was the South African pound.

17. This is the approach taken by Garber (1997, 1998) and others in the developing literature on a possible EMU breakup, focusing in particular on the risk of a crisis provoked by asymmetric business cycles or other economic shocks. For recent surveys of OCA theory, see Kawai (1992); Masson and Taylor (1993); Tavlas (1993, 1994).

18. In the case of the Latin Monetary Union, according to early estimates by Mulhall (1899), France accounted for 34 percent of the aggregate foreign trade of Italy during the 1880s; 25 percent of Belgium's; and 22 percent of Switzerland's. France's biggest trading partners, on the other hand, were Great Britain and Germany rather than the other LMU members. (See also Flandreau 1995.) Similarly, while Belgium and South Africa each account for as much as a third of the foreign trade of their monetary partners, their partners are too small to provide important reciprocal markets or sources of supply.

19. While reciprocal trade within SMU, according to Mulhall's (1899) estimates for the 1880s, amounted on average to less than 15 percent of members' aggregate foreign trade, Britain and Germany each accounted for as much as one-third of the total.

20. Not that these results should come as any surprise, since it is well known that the country characteristics themselves are often inherently contradictory.

(For example, should a small open economy subject to severe external shocks prefer a fixed exchange rate because of its openness or a flexible rate to insulate itself from outside disturbance?) As one source puts it, quite bluntly, "theoretical ambiguities abound" (Argy and De Grauwe 1990, p. 2). Moreover, empirical tests of the determinants of exchange-rate choices by individual governments persistently find that, in most instances, variables that are supposed to matter in theory fail to do so in practice. Concludes one recent study: "Overall the country characteristics do not help very much to explain the countries' choice of exchange rate regime. It might be that the choices are based on some other factors, economical or political" (Honkapohja and Pikkarainen 1994, pp. 47–48). For further critical discussion, see Goodhart (1998).

21. The same point is also suggested by a companion theoretical literature on the economics of investment under uncertainty, which stresses the importance of "sunk costs" as a barrier to exit: the greater the cost of starting up again in the future, the lower is the incentive to abandon an unprofitable investment in the present. See e.g., Dixit (1992).

22. Graboyes (1990, p. 9) concurs, arguing that the fatal flaw of LMU was that it "decreed a common monetary policy but left each central bank to police its own compliance." But for an alternative point of view, see Flandreau (1993).

23. On a broader global scale, the role of a hegemonic power in promoting and enforcing monetary cooperation has of course been frequently explored. Notable recent contributions include Eichengreen (1990, ch. 11); Walter (1991); Frieden (1992).

24. Only once did the Luxembourg government attempt to assert its own will, in 1935, following a 28 percent devaluation of the Belgian franc: Luxembourg also devalued, but by only 10 percent, unilaterally changing the partners' bilateral exchange rate from par to a ratio of 1.25 Belgian francs per Luxembourg franc (Meade 1956, pp. 14–16). Over the long haul, however, that solitary episode proved to be the exception rather than the rule. From the time parity was restored during World War II, Luxembourg willingly followed Belgium's lead on most monetary matters (though reportedly it did not hesitate to make its views forcefully known in private).

25. While for some authors (e.g., Guillaumont, Guillaumont, and Plane 1988; Boughton 1993a, 1993b) the impact of France's role is on balance positive, promoting monetary discipline and stability, for others the effect is clearly for the worse insofar as it perpetuates dependency, retards economic development, and reinforces income inequality. See e.g., Martin (1986); van de Walle (1991), Devarajan and Rodrik (1992).

26. EMU does not cause any substantive change in CFA zone arrangements, except for the substitution of the euro as anchor for the CFA franc. Since support for the convertibility of the CFA franc is provided by the French Treasury under a specific budget line, rather than by the Bank of France, the arrangement can be regarded as budgetary rather than monetary in nature. See e.g., Berrigan and Carré (1997); Hadjimichael and Galy (1997).

27. This conclusion, first articulated in my earlier study, has been endorsed by most subsequent discussions. See e.g., Goodhart (1998); Bordo and Jonung (1999). The dominance of politics in this context, though not spelled out in detail, is also

stressed by Hamada and Porteous (1992); Capie (1999); Hamada (1999). Objections to my conclusion have been raised by only one source, Andrews and Willett (1997), who contend that a combination of economic and organizational factors perform as well as the political considerations I identify in explaining outcomes—despite the fact that, as Andrews and Willett themselves admit, three of the six cases included in my earlier study fail to confirm their alternative view. Nor is their view confirmed by the CMA, the seventh case added in this present updated analysis.

References

Andrews, David M., and Thomas D. Willett, 1997, Financial interdependence and the state: International monetary relations at Century's End. *International Organization* 51:3 (Summer), 479–511.

Argy, Victor, and Paul De Grauwe, eds., 1990, *Choosing an exchange rate regime: The challenge for smaller industrial countries* (Washington, D.C.: International Monetary Fund).

Bartel, Robert J., 1974, International monetary unions: The XIXth century experience. *Journal of European Economic History* 3:3 (Winter), 689–704.

Bergman, Michael, Stefan Gerlach, and Lars Jonung, 1993, The rise and fall of the Scandinavian Currency Union 1873–1920. *European Economic Review* 37:2/3 (April), 507–517.

Berrigan, John, and Hervé Carré, 1997, Exchange arrangements between the EU and countries in Eastern Europe, the Mediterranean, and the CFA Zone, in: Paul R. Masson, Thomas H. Krueger, and Bart G. Turtelboom, eds., *EMU and the international monetary system* (Washington: International Monetary Fund), ch. 5.

Berthold, Norbert, Rainer Fehn, and Eric Thode, 1999, Real wage rigidities, fiscal policy, and the stability of EMU in the transition phase. Working Paper WP/99/83 (Washington, D.C.: International Monetary Fund).

Bordo, Michael D., and Lars Jonung, 1997, The history of monetary regimes—some lessons for Sweden and the EMU. *Swedish Economic Policy Review* 4, 285–358.

_____, 1999, The future of EMU: What does the history of monetary unions tell us? Paper prepared for a Conference on Monetary Unions, City University Business School, London (May, unpublished).

Boughton, James M., 1993a, The CFA Franc Zone: Currency union and monetary standard, *Greek Economic Review* 15:1 (Autumn), 267–312.

_____, 1993b, The economics of the CFA Franc Zone, in: Paul R. Masson and Mark P. Taylor, eds., *Policy issues in the operation of currency unions* (New York: Cambridge University Press), ch. 4.

Calomiris, Charles W., 1999, The impending collapse of the European Monetary Union. *Cato Journal* 18:3 (Winter), 445–452.

Capie, Forrest, 1999, Monetary unions in historical perspective: What future for the euro in the international financial system, in: Michele Fratianni, Dominick Salvatore, and Paolo Savona, eds., *Ideas for the future of the international monetary system* (Boston: Kluwer Academic Publishers), 77–95.

Cohen, Benjamin J., 1993, Beyond EMU: The problem of sustainability. *Economics and Politics* 5:2 (July), 187–203.

_____, 1998, *The geography of money* (Ithaca: Cornell University Press).

Conway, Patrick, 1995, *Currency proliferation: The monetary legacy of the Soviet Union.* Essays in International Finance 197 (Princeton: International Finance Section).

De Cecco, Marcello, 1992, European monetary and financial cooperation before the First World War. *Rivista di Storia Economica* 9, 55–76.

Devarajan, Shantayanan, and Dani Rodrik, 1992, Do the benefits of fixed exchange rates outweigh their costs? The CFA Zone in Africa, in: I. Goldin and A. L. Winters, eds., *Open economies: Structural adjustment and agriculture* (Cambridge: Cambridge University Press), ch. 4.

Dixit, Avinash, 1992, Investment and hysteresis. *Journal of Economic Perspectives* 6, 107–132.

Dornbusch, Rudiger, 1992, Monetary problems of Post-Communism: Lessons from the end of the Austro-Hungarian Empire. *Weltwirtschaftliches Archiv* 128:3, 391–424.

_____, 1994, *Post-Communist monetary problems: Lessons from the end of the Austro-Hungarian Empire* (San Francisco: International Center for Economic Growth).

Eichengreen, Barry, 1990, *Elusive stability: Essays in the history of international finance, 1919–1939* (New York: Cambridge University Press).

Eltis, Walter, 1997, *The creation and destruction of the euro,* Policy Study 155 (London: Centre for Policy Studies).

Flandreau, Marc, 1993, On the inflationary bias of common currencies: The Latin Union puzzle. *European Economic Review* 37:2/3 (April), 501–506.

_____, 1995, Was the Latin Monetary Union a Franc Zone? in: Jaime Reis, ed., *International monetary systems in historical perspective* (London: Macmillan).

Frieden, Jeffry A., 1992, The dynamics of international monetary systems: International and domestic factors in the rise, reign, and demise of the classical gold standard, in: Robert Jervis and Jack Snyder, eds., *Coping with Complexity in the international system* (Boulder, Colo.: Westview), ch. 6.

Garber, Peter M., 1997, Is Stage III attackable? *Euromoney* (August), 58–59.

_____, 1998, The TARGET mechanism: Will it propagate or stifle a Stage III crisis? (Brown University, unpublished).

Garber, Peter M., and Michael G. Spencer, 1994, *The dissolution of the Austro-Hungarian Empire: Lessons for currency reform.* Essays in International Finance 191 (Princeton: International Finance Section).

Goodhart, Charles A. E., 1998, The two concepts of money: Implications for the analysis of optimal currency areas. *European Journal of Political Economy* 14, 407–432.

Graboyes, Robert F., 1990, The EMU: Forerunners and durability. *Federal Reserve Bank of Richmond Economic Review* 76:4 (July/August), 8–17.

Griffiths, Mark, 1992, Monetary union in Europe: Lessons from the nineteenth century—an assessment of the Latin Monetary Union (Virginia Polytechnic Institute, unpublished).

Gros, Daniel, and Niels Thygesen, 1992, European monetary integration: From the European Monetary System to European Monetary Union (New York: St. Martin's Press).

Guillaumont, P., S. Guillaumont, and P. Plane, 1988, Participating in African monetary unions: An alternative evaluation. World Development 16:5 (May), 569–576.

Hadjimichael, Michael T., and Michel Galy, 1997, The CFA Franc Zone and the EMU. Working Paper WP/97/156 (Washington, D.C.: International Monetary Fund).

Hamada, Koichi, 1985, The political economy of international monetary interdependence (Cambridge, Mass.: MIT Press).

_____, 1999, The choice of international monetary regimes in a context of repeated games, in: Michele Fratianni, Dominick Salvatore, and Paolo Savona, eds., Ideas for the future of the international monetary system (Boston: Kluwer Academic Publishers), 47–75.

Hamada, Koichi, and David Porteous, 1992, L'Intégration monétaire dans une perspective historique. Revue d'Économie Financière 22 (Autumn), 77–92.

Hodgman, Donald R., 1974, National monetary policies and international monetary cooperation (Boston: Little, Brown).

Honkapohja, Seppo, and Pentti Pikkarainen, 1994, Country characteristics and the choice of the exchange rate regime: Are mini-skirts followed by maxis? in: Johnny Akerholm and Alberto Giovannini, eds., Exchange rate policies in the Nordic countries (London: Centre for Economic Policy Research), ch. 3.

Honohan, Patrick, 1992, Price and monetary convergence in currency unions: The Franc and Rand zones. Journal of International Money and Finance 11:4 (August), 397–410.

Jones-Hendrickson, S. B., 1989, Financial structures and economic development in the organisation of Eastern Caribbean states. Social and Economic Studies 38:4, 71–93.

Jonung, Lars, 1987, Swedish experience under the classical gold standard, 1873–1914, in: Michael D. Bordo and Anna J. Schwartz, eds., A retrospective on the classical gold standard, 1821–1931 (Chicago: University of Chicago Press).

Kawai, Masahiro, 1992, Optimum Currency Areas, in: Peter Newman, Murray Milgate, and John Eatwell, eds., The new Palgrave dictionary of money and finance 3 (New York: Macmillan), 78–81.

Keohane, Robert O., and Stanley Hoffmann, 1991, Institutional change in Europe in the 1980s, in: Robert O. Keohane and Stanley Hoffmann, eds., The new European Community: Decisionmaking and institutional change (Boulder, Colo.: Westview).

Krämer, Hans R., 1971, Experience with historical monetary unions, in: Otmar Emminger et al., Integration through monetary union? (Tubingen: J.C.B. Mohr), 106–118.

Letiche, John M., 1974, Dependent monetary systems and economic development: The case of sterling East Africa, in: Willy Sellekaerts, ed., Economic development and planning: Essays in honor of Jan Tinbergen (White Plains, N.Y.: International Arts and Sciences Press), ch. 9.

Martin, Guy, 1986, The Franc Zone, underdevelopment and dependency in Francophone Africa. *Third World Quarterly* 8:1 (January), 205–235.

Masson, Paul R., and Mark P. Taylor, 1993, Currency union: A survey of the issues, in: Paul R. Masson and Mark P. Taylor, eds., *Policy issues in the operation of currency unions* (New York: Cambridge University Press), ch. 1.

Mbogoro, D.A.K., 1985, Regional grouping and economic development: Some lessons from the East African integration scheme, in: W. A. Ndongko, ed., *Economic cooperation and integration in Africa* (Dakar, Senegal: CODESRIA), ch. 8.

McClean, A. Wendell A., 1975, *Money and banking in the East Caribbean currency area* (Kingston, Jamaica: Institute of Social and Economic Research, University of the West Indies).

Meade, James E., 1956, *The Belgium-Luxembourg economic union, 1921–1939: Lessons from an early experiment*. Essays in International Finance 25 (Princeton: International Finance Section).

Mintz, Norman N., 1970, *Monetary union and economic integration* (New York: New York University Graduate School of Business Administration).

Mugomba, Agrippah T., 1978, Regional organisations and African underdevelopment: The collapse of the East African community. *Journal of Modern African Studies* 16:2, 261–272.

Mulhall, Michael G., 1899, *The dictionary of statistics*, 4th ed. (London: George Routledge and Sons).

Mussa, Michael, 1997, Political and institutional commitment to a common currency. *American Economic Review* 87:2 (May), 217–220.

Nascimento, Jean-Claude, 1994, Monetary policy in unified currency areas: The cases of the CAMA and ECCA during 1976–1990. Working Paper WP/94/11 (Washington, D.C.: International Monetary Fund).

North, Douglass C., 1990, Institutions and a transaction-cost theory of exchange, in: James E. Alt and Kenneth A. Shepsle, eds., *Perspectives on positive political economy* (New York: Cambridge University Press).

Perlman, M., 1993, In search of monetary union. *Journal of European Economic History* 22:2 (Fall), 313–332.

Ravenhill, John, 1979, Regional integration and development in Africa: Lessons from the East African community. *Journal of Commonwealth and Comparative Politics* 17:3 (November), 227–246.

Redish, Angela, 1994, The Latin Monetary Union and the emergence of the international gold standard, in: Michael D. Bordo and Forrest Capie, eds., *Monetary regimes in transition* (New York: Cambridge University Press), ch. 3.

Rothchild, Donald, 1974, From hegemony to bargaining in East African relations. *Journal of African Studies* 1:4 (Winter), 390–416.

Tavlas, George S., 1993, The 'new' theory of optimum currency areas, *The World Economy* 16:6 (November), 663–685.

_____, 1994, The theory of monetary integration. *Open Economies Review* 5, 211–230.

van de Walle, Nicolas, 1991, The decline of the Franc Zone: Monetary politics in Francophone Africa. *African Affairs* 90 (July), 383–405.

Van Meerhaeghe, M.A.G., 1987, *The Belgium-Luxembourg economic union* (Tilburg, Netherlands: Société Universitaire Européenne de Recherches Financières).

Vanthoor, Wim F. V., 1996, *European monetary union since 1848: A political and historical analysis* (Brookfield, Vt.: Edward Elgar).

von Hagen, Jurgen, and Michele Fratianni, 1993, The transition to European Monetary Union and the European Monetary Institute. *Economics and Politics* 5:2 (July), 167–186.

Walter, Andrew, 1991, *World power and world money* (New York: St. Martin's Press).

Wendt, Frantz, 1981, *Cooperation in the Nordic countries: Achievements and obstacles* (Stockholm, Sweden: Almqvist and Wiksell).

Contributors

Yunus Aksoy is Research Scholar at the Catholic University of Leuven. Among his publications are "Exchange Rate Pass-Through in Vertically Related Markets," *Review of International Economics* 8 (2000) (coauthor with Yohanes E. Riyanto).

Benjamin J. Cohen is Louis G. Lancaster Professor of International Political Economy at the University of California, Santa Barbara. He is the author of nine books, including *In Whose Interest? International Banking and American Foreign Policy* (1986) and *The Geography of Money* (1998).

Paul De Grauwe is Professor of International Economics at the Catholic University of Leuven. His publications include *The Economics of Monetary Integration* (1997) and *International Money: Postwar Trends and Theories* (1996).

Hans Dewachter is Professor of International Economics at the Catholic University of Leuven. Among his publications are (with Paul De Grauwe and Mark Embrechts) *Exchange Rate Theory: Chaotic Models of Foreign Exchange Markets* (1993), and (with Paul De Grauwe and Dirk Veestraeten) "Price Dynamics under Stochastic Process Switching: Some Extensions and an Application to EMU," *Journal of International Money and Finance*, 18 (1999).

Barry Eichengreen is the George C. Pardee and Helen N. Pardee Professor of Economics and Professor of Political Science at the University of California, Berkeley; Research Associate of the National Bureau of Economic Research; and Research Fellow of the Centre for Economic Policy Research. His books include *Toward a New International Financial Architecture* (1999), *Globalizing Capital: A History of the International Monetary System* (1997), and *European Monetary Unification* (1997).

Charles Engel is Professor of Economics and Public Affairs at the University of Wisconsin. His research is in open economy macroeconomics and international finance. Some of his recent work on the global integration of markets has appeared in such journals as the *American Economic Review*, *Journal of Political Economy*, *Journal of Monetary Economics*, and *Journal of International Economics*.

Jeffry Frieden is Professor of Government at Harvard University. He specializes in the politics of international monetary and financial relations, and is the author of *Banking on the World: The Politics of American International Finance* (1987) and of

Debt, Development, and Democracy: Modern Political Economy and Latin America, 1965–1985 (1991).

Matthew Gabel is Associate Professor of Political Science at the University of Kentucky. His research focuses on mass politics and democratic processes in the European Union. He is the author of *Interests and Integration: Market Liberalization, Public Opinion, and European Union* (1998).

Geoffrey Garrett is Professor of Political Science at Yale University. He is author of *Partisan Politics in the Global Economy* (1998). His current research focuses on the institutional structure of the European Union and on the politics of globalization.

Lisa L. Martin is Professor of Government at Harvard University. She is the author of *Coercive Cooperation: Explaining Multilateral Economic Sanctions* (1992) and *Democratic Commitments: Legislatures and International Cooperation* (2000).

Index